Recreating the Historic House Interior

Bedroom, White Face Camp, U Lazy S Ranch, Lubbock, Texas, 1978.—*Ranching Museum, Texas Tech University*

Recreating the Historic House Interior

William Seale

American Association for State and Local History

Nashville

Publication of this book was made possible in part by funds from the sale of the Bicentennial State Histories, which were supported by the National Endowment for the Humanities.

Library of Congress Cataloguing-in-Publication Data

Seale, William.
  Recreating the historic house interior.

  Bibliography: p.
  Includes index.
  1. Historic buildings—United States—Conservation and restoration—Handbooks, manuals, etc.
2. United States—History, local.   3. Interior decoration—United States.   I. Title.
EL159.S49   069.53   78–14361
ISBN 0–910050–32–5

To
Edward P. Alexander

Contents

Preface

WHILE this book was being prepared for publication I asked the various people who had read the manuscript to help me arrive at a title. I wanted something that incorporated the word *restore*, but we finally agreed that the word was not suited to my subject. William T. Alderson, at that time director of the American Association for State and Local History, offered *recreate* as a substitute. Though *recreating* is not so familiar in this context as *restoring*, it is, by definition, more appropriate.

What happens when one attempts to take an interior back to its lived-in appearance in the past is nearly always less restoring than it is recreating. In the strict sense, to restore a historical interior is to return it to its exact appearance at a specific time in its past. That is seldom possible because of the lack of comprehensive documentation. To *recreate* is to *approximate*. An interior is recreated in much the same way that a history book is written. Both are based upon historical investigation, analysis, and synthesis. Yet research for recreating an interior setting is likely to involve even more of a mixture of types of facts than is brought to bear in restoration, or, for that matter, than is admissible to most orthodox historical research. There will be facts related to or parallel to the central subject, others that are "universals," and still others that are particular facts of place.

Many books have already been published on period interiors. In nearly all instances, however, their emphasis is really on antiques in modern design. Such an approach to the furnishing of interiors should not be confused with the historical point of view presented in this book. Nor is the usual methodology taken in architectural restoration of great relevance to our purpose here. Architectural restoration splits off from our subject at an early stage. For the structure itself, the word *restore* will frequently ring true on down the line, for there are often conclusive clues in the surviving building. For the recreating of an interior, however, only a small part of the information needed is likely to be found in the building. It can be scattered very far afield.

This book does not presume to replace detailed monographs on specific subjects; indeed, I hope it suggests areas where such works are sorely needed. My ambition in writing the book has been to serve the ideal of well-finished historical interiors in two ways: to provide a framework for thinking; and to provide signals in the form of various basic facts, to help keep one alert for what may appear along the way. Although I have written to the general reader, there should be much here to interest the specialist—or specialists, for many disciplines combine in recreating interiors. The words *rooms* and *interiors* in this book refer to entire settings, from the architecture that encloses the space to the most seemingly remote object within it.

By and large, various historical interiors are recreated for educational purposes and are connected with museum operations. The book is written with museum houses in mind. Recreating interiors has, in recent years, become of increasing interest to private individuals, who restore old houses to live in. The barren "architect-white" interiors imposed upon old houses in the 1960s are giving way in the late 1970s to rooms refurbished to reflect, if they do not attempt sometimes actually to duplicate, the past of the house. This book can also be of use to people in decorating their private habitations. I confess to having enjoyed the recreating pastime, myself.

Illustrations are vital to a book of this kind. I have been careful in selecting these. Historical

x room settings do not always photograph well, and many museums are hesitant to rearrange their interiors to provide better camera angles. The illustrations are divided fairly evenly between "historical" or documentary views and present-day views taken inside museum houses; the first half of the black-and-white picture section consists largely of the former, while the balance includes the latter. I have partially indexed the illustrations so that they will provide ready visual references to subjects that come up in the text. Each illustration is dated according to the year in which it was made, and the captions comment on what the room is supposed to represent. The great bulk of the rooms are from the nineteenth century. While there are, even so, many illustrations representing the eighteenth and twentieth centuries, I have placed a certain emphasis upon the nineteenth century because within it were periods of remarkable change in the way people lived in houses. Understanding the changes is vital to understanding how life was before and after they took place. I cannot guarantee the total excellence of every interior illustrated. Where flaws exist, they will be evident to the careful reader.

I extend heartfelt thanks to the following people who helped, many of them, in countless ways: William T. Alderson, Robert Beardsley, Ellen Beasley, Marylou Birchmore, Haworth P. Bromley, Jane Brown, Joseph T. Butler, Patrick Butler III, Sally S. Cahlan, Margaret S. Cheney, E. Blaine Cliver, A. Robert Cole, John J. Cooney, Jr., Philip H. Curtis, Gail Dennis, Roberta Deveno, Charles Dorman, Alison Eckard, Anne Farnam, Wilson H. Faude, William Barrow Floyd, Christopher Forbes, Marjorie C. Freytag, Mr. and Mrs. James Giraytys, James M. Goode, Ruth K. Hagy, Mr. and Mrs. Robert Harper III, Constance Hershey, William D. Hershey,Graham Hood, Carroll J. Hopf, Richard Kearns, Allan Kemper, Nina Fletcher Little, Christopher Lloyd, Mrs. William G. Lockwood, Richard McCrensky, Patricia G. Maccubbin, Jill McDougal, Cathryn McElroy, Milly McGhee, Samuel E. McIntosh, Bruce D. MacPhail, Christine Meadows, Nancy Melin, William R. Mitchell, Roger W. Moss, Denys Peter Myers, Richard S. Myrick, Carol Nelson, Jane C. Nylander, Richard C. Nylander, Janis Obst, Arthur Olivas, Ann B. Parks, Mrs. Walter Charles Parlange, Mrs. Leonard J. Panaggio, Rodris Roth, Paul Sampson, Frank Sommers, Roger Stroup, John A. H. Sweeney, Lonn Taylor, David Underwood, Mrs. Carroll E. Ward, Rodd L. Wheaton, Kenneth M. Wilson, Ronald G. Wilson, and Joseph B. Zywicki.

And those who designed, edited, and helped to send the book on its way: Gary Gore, Director of Publications for the Association; Deborah F. Cooney, Martha I. Strayhorn, and Joan Cash.

1

In Beginning

RECREATING the historic house interior begins with research. This research is orderly and thorough. It is developed into usable conclusions before the house itself is touched. The house as it stands is already a period piece; the delicatessen in the hall and the walk-up rooming house that seem to deface it are, after all, valid expressions of human living, and they will always have that advantage over your attempted restoration. So do not rush in with change. If you have good reason to peel away traces of the years and journey into the past, first determine through research where you are going.

Nothing is easy or quick about doing research. For all its rewards, it is hard and, by nature, slow work for which you train in harness. Until all possible sources have been investigated, and you have a sound historical analysis in hand, your decisions about the house are irrelevant and usually destructive. This country is filled with house museums and period museum rooms that are the results of sloppy, if any, historical research. Think of the future when impatient people try to hurry you along: what you discover in research and the point of view you help establish will make the difference between a project of substance and one for which you may have to make apologies later.

The vital preliminary step involves preservation more than research. You must see immediately to the safety of the sources at hand. The house itself, certainly a principal source, must be protected from vandalism and the weather. Box up any papers and store any objects that may have been left there; while they may now appear to be junk, they could prove extremely important. Interview, preferably using a tape recorder, as many former occupants of the house as you can locate. They will not be accessible forever, and when they are gone, what they know about the house and life in the house goes with them. Perhaps they own papers and furnishings that have bearing on the house. At least obtain photographs of these things. Learn the recent legal history of the house: was it tied up in an estate, maybe administered by a bank that will be legally free to destroy the records after so many years? You want those papers. Such preliminary efforts are likely to produce a mass of odds and ends. Set them safely aside, awaiting the time—which, rest assured, will come—when they fall into place in the more orderly process of formal research.

Research in Written Records

In beginning the formal research program, think in the broadest possible terms. Do not separate research for the interior from the research program for the rest of the house; do not begin with architecture and the decorative arts. Let your first energies go toward reading general histories for a historical context. Under advice perhaps from a member of a history faculty, develop a small, workable bibliography. If you are not accustomed to reading and retaining in-depth historical studies, cultivate your taste for them with "readable" openers. Biographies will often serve this purpose best.

The beginning bibliography should cover all the years the house has stood. As limited research time is sometimes a problem, you may have to abandon this ideal for a more practical spot-survey in which you concentrate only upon the historical milestones. As an example, a house built in 1840 might be approached through a study of the following events: the Panic of 1837, the war with Mexico, the Civil War, the Panic of 1873, the Panic of 1893, the Spanish-American War, World War I, the Great Depression, and World War II. Once you

2 are familiar with the national and international character of these events, you have at least a working familiarity with what was going on in the world in the important periods during which your house has stood. The value of this becomes more evident as your research becomes increasingly detailed later on.

Next, turn to the state histories. You may already feel that you have a useful acquaintance with your state's story; since history is more than a story, however, you should read the best interpretive works available. A general textbook may suggest numerous areas of special relevance—Indian wars, political upheavals, migrations, periods of prosperity. These events and trends may be further detailed only in special monographs, articles in state historical publications, and masters' and doctoral theses in college libraries. Some of these readings will be more directly important to your house than others. But do not hurry to the cream and bypass the rest. It is well enough to learn about the local volunteer company's organization in 1846; but know first what the Mexican War and your state's involvement was all about. You will find that the specifics of local history have more meaning for you when you are able to place them in context.

Your initial reading will result in a bibliography, as well as copious notes. The bibliography will include perhaps four surveys, one or two world histories, and several United States histories. There will be perhaps ten or twelve monographs, books, and articles covering certain events. If you are fortunate there will be as many published travel accounts and diaries. The state histories might be many or few, depending upon the state, but the scholarly articles are probably numerous and are likely to exist on practically every subject, some dealing with the state, others the region, and still others the locality. These will give you grassroots politics, biography, some social life and customs, the analyzed contents of personal letters and diaries, and now and then a taste of local architecture and decorative arts. These are the building stones of a firm historical foundation.

From that point on, you are your own historian. You will be combing through large quantities of primary material for information that will be useful in practically every aspect of your project. The overview you have gained in your reading of secondary sources prepares you for the evaluation and analysis of isolated documentary information. To approach the primary material without that overview is to approach it blind.

You must establish names, ages, and dates of occupation for the inhabitants of the house, then fit the information chronologically into the historical framework. All the usual research tools of the genealogist apply here, and there is a fair chance in most areas of the United States that some of this work has already been done, particularly where prominent individuals are concerned. But never limit your research to the one or several famous people who might have lived in your house. Everyone who lived there is important in your thinking about the proposed restoration; likewise try to find out about outsiders who knew the house and family intimately. In the latter instance you may have only clues, but even fragments help round out the picture. For the nineteenth century the various United States Census returns, decade by decade, 1790 to 1900 (except for most of 1890, which burned), will prove to be rich sources, not only by giving certain specifics about the family who lived in your house, but in providing an overview of the community—the butchers, the bakers, who and how numerous they were.

Make sure what you examine is the full census return, and not a printed summary; microfilm copies of the actual paper the census-taker carried around are available from the National Archives, if your state or local library does not already have a print. There are, in addition, many different sorts of census returns—free population, slave population, agricultural, manufactures, and social statistics. All must be considered as possibilities in your work.

The economic status of the particular household in question must be investigated to a greater degree than the simple designation "farmer" or "lawyer," which is about the most you will get from the earlier census returns and city directories. City and county tax records can often be a great help here, when they list acreage, livestock, tools and machinery, and personal property. How much of the land was productive? What, so far as you can tell, was the relative value of the family's income from year to year? The fluctuation of income and holdings is usually a mirror of the broader scene and is no small issue in the decoration of houses.

The county clerk can be the project's most valuable ally, for in the exercise of his responsibilities he gains familiarity with the courthouse records, as well as the irregularities that seem always to exist in filing public papers. Go to the courthouse with written chronological guidelines: names of the members of the family, with birth and death dates. Soundly documented dates will keep you from going astray into records from irrelevant periods of time. Also begin to keep on hand a catalogue of secondary names and dates, such as those of the friends, relatives, and business associates of the particular characters in question. This catalogue will constantly grow as new names appear in connection with your house or the people who lived there.

At the courthouse you will seek documents connected with these names. Here, if you are lucky, will be the complete deed records, wills, contracts, land plats, civil and criminal proceedings, tax and license records, commission minutes, and inventories accumulated over the life-span of your county. Few people who pass through a county's history escape having their names entered in some way into the ponder-

ous volumes and packed document drawers of the county courthouse. This can sometimes require real detective work, for early records especially may have been dispatched to the basement or attic or even to some other public building and forgotten. If these are unknown to the clerk, they may have to be sought out by you. Perhaps records long gone from the courthouse survive in copies at an abstract and title company. Fire and thoughtless destruction have taken and continue to take a toll of county records, but it is always amazing what persistent searching can turn up.

Like any archival collection, the courthouse papers must be used with imagination. You are ill-advised to restrict yourself only to your particular house and family, for while that may be your main concern, there must be a basis for comparison. A household inventory, for example, will be far more revealing when contrasted to all the other inventories of the same period in the same area. This analysis can be seen against similar analyses of previous and subsequent local inventories to clarify further the one that interests you most. It is always an asset to the restorer of interiors to have an original inventory of the building. The absence of an inventory sometimes leads people far astray into academic prototypes, when a careful evaluation of the local inventories that do survive would give more certain directives toward refurnishing. Inventories will be dealt with in some length later on, but the same principle applies to wills, deeds, and any other documents that are likely to bear reference to houses or their contents.

While you will never really finish with the courthouse as a source, there will be a point at which you feel that your characters and your house have an official sort of substance; in other words, you can at last understand them as local figures in the broader context of history. Then turn to the newspapers. These special sources deserve the most meticulous attention, for they illuminate nearly every aspect of

4 a community's life and expand your knowledge of the area as your characters knew it. Should the runs of newspapers you need—one or several—be in a distant location, you would be wise to purchase microfilm, so that you can keep the sources on hand. The material should be excerpted and filed according to categories. Political opinion and personal anecdotes will be useful in the interpretation of the house, so be very liberal in transcribing what you find. Newspaper advertisements will abound in material relating to house interiors. You can also expect a reference now and then to a house as it appeared for a wedding or a party, or passing mention of it in a builder's obituary or in the announcement of an auction or the report on a fire. Still, it is the advertisements that always seem the most useful indicators of what was current in household furnishings: in 1790 a Massachusetts merchant advertises a large supply of patent lamps; in 1844 a cabinetmaker in Savannah advertises his own "Grecian" sideboards, in addition to fine furniture "imported from the North"; in 1876 a Texas river captain schedules for dockside auction a shipment of "First Class Furniture From Indiana"; and in 1924 the papers everywhere are uniform in running advertisements for local furniture establishments that carry the mass-produced products of midwestern and eastern manufacturers.

In the eighteenth century and for about two-thirds of the nineteenth, stores might list in newspaper advertisements precisely what they had on hand. Tradesmen frequently placed "cards" in the press, advising the public of their skills, from painting floorcloths to hanging household bells. Your previous census work will have turned up the names of cabinetmakers, builders, storekeepers, and tradesmen, some of whom are never mentioned in the newspapers. On the other hand, unexpected names in the newspaper advertisements may well mean that the particular tradesman or cabinetmaker was from a city

nearby, or a town considered the regional center at the time. It was very common in the nineteenth century for Boston tradesmen to advertise in various papers throughout New England. San Francisco tradesmen and storekeepers placed notices in papers elsewhere in California, and in Nevada and Utah. Besides indicating the availability of goods and services in certain places at given times, advertisements also give clues that may help identify old furnishings that survive.

Public building records are great sources of detail and should always be examined. Because public buildings were built before the public's eye and rose under the direction of committees and commissions, their records were sometimes meticulously kept and can be treasure-troves. Town halls, courthouses, office buildings, hospitals, state capitols, and governors' mansions built or remodeled about the time of your house are usually documented to a greater or lesser degree in the appropriate public depository. Though not exactly "public," church records should be considered in this category.

In using these sources never feel confined to your own immediate locality, especially on a building begun after about 1840. Regional structures and those of the then-recognized centers are quite as useful. Also remember that while your present city hall was built, say, in 1932, there was doubtless an earlier structure, and maybe several before that. Some—even most—records are likely to remain intact in the city hall, and of course the same follows with courthouses and state structures, the records of which are in the state archives or historical society. Records of past and present federal buildings are on deposit in the National Archives, and consist of the title papers and, most important, the letters of 1840 to 1939, including numerous broadsides, brochures, and advertisements of all kinds collected in the course of bidding and construction. Sometimes included with these papers are sketches for lighting devices, bathroom fixtures, and so on. The nine regional depositories of the National Archives, outside the main facilities in Washington, D.C., are in Boston, New York, Atlanta, Chicago, Kansas City, Fort Worth, Denver, San Francisco, and Auburn, Washington. These various arms of the federal archives house some of the materials pertaining to the regions in which they stand. The papers and the proceedings for building-related federal lawsuits are sometimes mines of information on architecture and the decorative arts.

Last, or concurrently with the investigation of public building records, examine any relevant private collections, which are likely to include nearly anything from old letters to furniture to early drawings and photographs. By this time your research will have given you a good idea of the period or periods, as well as those personalities most worthy of interpretation in your restoration. You will then probably curb your research in other areas.

Before going thoroughly into private collections of papers and objects, you might plan to make preliminary inventories, to gain an idea of what the collections contain. This can often be done quickly, in bulk, to save time. For much of what we know about local history we are indebted to string-savers; what they have cannot rightly be called a "collection," but rather an accumulation. A cursory examination of a trunkful of letters might involve writing down the dates most of the papers seem to cover. After that, move on to the next body of materials and make similar notations. This superficial glimpse must not be mistaken for real research. It merely provides you with the opportunity to establish priorities by which you can return to the promising collections first. All the different collections will have to be read carefully before your research program can be considered comprehensive.

Now and then you might have to cast aside this quick inventory plan for even faster action. You may, for example, have reason to be-

lieve that the one time will be your only access to the material. The least desirable thing to do is to excerpt from the letters; they should be copied in full. At most times, the owners of manuscripts, when assured of your scholarly purposes, will permit copying of one kind or another. Do not even ask to go away with trophies. It is usually wrong to break up a collection of papers in that way. Leave the originals where they are, unless you are offered the lot, in which case, lacking proper facilities, you are obliged to see that the papers are sent to a suitable library or archive. In your zeal for information, never forget the importance of preserving the originals.

Research in Objects

Objects are documents of another sort. They convey information in ways both subtle and bold. A written letter is an object, too, in that it has material substance—the paper, the ink or pencil marks—as well as its literary content. Being better accustomed to communicating in words, we tend to make only superficial use of objects as documents and thus fail to allow the past to speak to us in as many ways as it can. In the historic house museum, objects will carry a greater part of the burden of interpretation than words. They will reveal the relative degree of comfort and convenience in which the inhabitants lived. In their materials and means of construction, objects will speak of the technological capabilities of those who made them, whether the user himself, a local craftsman, or a distant manufacturer; their presence will explain what was available to people in a given time and place. The form of the object will express ideas of appropriateness and beauty held by people long dead. An object, the symbol of its own function, thus symbolizes aspects of living, and many objects, brought together in a room with historical sensitivity, combine with the room itself—the warmth of its hearth, the light from its

6 windows—to create for alien eyes and senses an essay on how life was lived there.

Yet it is true that most of the object-secrets of the vacant house are never found out. Household things are transient, moved from room to room and house to house. They scatter easily, and we must count ourselves blessed to recover as much as 15 percent of what was in a room at a given time, once the contents of the house have been dispersed.

The collection of objects eventually assembled for the historic house should develop from sound research. A product of this is the objects catalogue, which will become more valuable as it grows. The objects catalogue is quite simply a list of objects that you come across, through reading or first-hand knowledge, which have some historical or traditional connection with your locality. Ideally, each entry should be accompanied by a photograph and any documentation that is available. While this list will soon become rather confined to the several periods you determine are the most important to your house museum, it should not in any sense be limited to furniture or the obvious decorative accessories. Pots and pans convey more of a feeling about daily living than the parlor's fancy chair. You will have no difficulty in deciding what to place in this catalogue if you remain free-handed and include the homely with the grand.

Where the difficulty usually comes in the collection list is with fragments or materials that are barely recognizable. These are things you might normally overlook, tucked away in a drawer or trunk. Fabric bits, for example, are among the most common attic finds. A bundle of letters or, say, several fine old handkerchiefs, might be wrapped in a piece of old chintz or cotton domestic. Wallpaper occasionally turns up, the classic example being the little box Dolly Madison lined with remnants of White House wallpaper and borders for her friend Mrs. Benjamin Henry Latrobe. Little girls sometimes pasted fabrics and wallpaper

Vignette from a little girl's scrapbook of the 1880s, composed of clippings from magazines and catalogues. —*Haworth P. Bromley Photo, Allan Kemper Associates*

in their scrapbooks. However it is found and whatever it is, a good color slide and careful measurements should be made of each specimen. If the specimen is given to you, it must be stored in an acid-free envelope. The tiniest sliver may become one of your most revealing documents.

By now your research collection should be rather full. Your house stands exactly as you found it, but intellectually you have put it through a real investigation. It must seem a very different place to you now than when you began! You know who lived there and when; you are aware of the issues of the day that would have interested them; you know about their work and their finances, and from an abundance of detail you sense their day-to-day anticipations, even though you know how it all came out in the end. They have expressed themselves to you in letters, or maybe you learned about them through the letters of their friends. Even lacking diaries and letters, you see them in the context of their community, as imprecise images, perhaps, but suggesting the lives of many or a few or no others within a locality and the wider spectrum of human life. Your on-going-objects catalogue has given you a taste of the household possessions they lived with or may have lived with, or knew, whether they owned them or not.

Researching the House

You are not, however, ready to restore. The research program now turns to the house itself, and you will need professional assistance.

An archaeological investigation of the immediate grounds will be essential, if your research is to be of top quality. This can be very expensive, although in recent years state historical programs have begun to provide archaeological services, under various circumstances, that are somewhat less costly. In your later work on the interiors, archaeology will provide exacting details that you could not get by any other means. This work can never be piecemeal. Your restored interiors, yet to come, will only suffer if the sole objective of the archaeological program is to poke about for foundations of vanished buildings, walks, and such. That practice is about dead, fortunately. It dates from a time when architecture was the principal concern in a restoration. Through historical archaeology you can learn amazing things about life in your house. Pieces of plates and bowls, the leg of an iron stove, the arm from a tiny china doll, the knob from a doorbell, a hammer-head—all these things are the footnotes archaeology can turn up for your interiors, if given the chance. Your richest documentation for furnishings may lie beneath the ground.

The archaeologist, in preparing for the dig, will want to study all the historical materials you have gathered. He will not allow a spade in the ground before he has a historical frame of reference. Rooms in a house may be

emptied every generation, and all record of them lost, but each generation leaves traces of itself in the earth, and those remain, their longevity less threatened than that of the piece of chintz mentioned earlier that was wrapped around the letters. Bear in mind, however, that through quick action the chintz can be recovered from the garbage can and one may at leisure return to the archive to re-examine the collection of manuscripts. There is no such second chance on a site when the earth has been disturbed: once the fragment of china, or the encrusted coffee pot, or the curtain ornament is lifted from the ground, it is removed from its chronological context and its location in relation to other buried artifacts. Unless proper record is kept, most of the documentary value vanishes. You should be no more willing to undertake a haphazard program in archaeology than you would be to burn a collection of intimate manuscript letters regarding your house, or indeed, to tear into a building without first exhausting the written sources.

Assuming that your house is "tight" and needs no emergency stabilization, the first work on the structure is to record it as it stands. It must be fully photographed, inside and out. Scaled elevations should be made of each wall in each room. The same is also desirable for floors and ceilings. Such drawings are usually done by the architect in the course of his work, but in your study of the interiors you will need more detailed information than his drawings are likely to provide. If the architect does scaled room-elevations, take these as your work-sheets; otherwise either make simple elevations of your own on graph paper, or score good, clear photographs, taken straight-on, for purposes of scale. Each wall of each room should be thoroughly checked for hooks, nails, or screws, or the holes left by them, and the locations of these accordingly noted on the appropriate work sheet. Where there is wallpaper, this examination should be made before and after the paper is removed, using

8 separate sheets for each stage in the stripping of the wall. Check very carefully for plugged holes (a diagonal beam of light is helpful) along the walls and around the windows. These holes usually indicate picture arrangements and designate the location of fixtures for curtains. Their message is much clearer on the diagram than in the room. On the floor, the layout of tack holes will suggest the sort of floorcovering, be it a carpet, tacked down wall to wall in strips, or a rug centered in the room and tacked down around the edges. Pale spots left by pictures are noted to scale, though they may seem to be of recent date.

Removing wallpaper, when you have to study and preserve it in the process, is complicated. If you have the slightest suspicion that the paper will be of use now or later on, let it alone, for surely it will be ruined in the removal process. On an average, one finds in an old house layer upon layer of wallpaper which, because of poor walling behind it, or because of its incompatibility with the historical objectives of the project, needs to be taken down. It should be peeled off very carefully by layer, if possible, in strategic spots on each wall.

Begin with an area about two feet across, near the baseboard. If all else fails and you can find no place where the paper has become disengaged, slice the surface at a place where the paper appears to be loose. Fold the paper back at that point, and dissolve the clinging paste bit by bit with a stream of steam from a hand steamer or warm water from a spraying device. As the various layers are revealed, make a well-lighted photograph in color, placing a measuring stick in the frame to indicate the scale of the pattern. Often the paper will not be exposed layer by layer on the wall, but a whole section will have to be removed and soaked in water to separate it. In this case, as soon as the water begins to dissolve the paste that binds the layers together, remove the paper layers and allow them to dry separately.

To avoid running of the colors, submerge the paper as briefly as possible.

Take samples similarly in other areas of the room. Several layers beneath the surface, you might come upon a paper that appears to be of historical interest because it relates to something you found in your research. Stop and either call in an expert or send a sample away for evaluation by a professional who knows wallpaper. It could well be that the paper is original to a particularly well-documented period in the history of the house and worthy of the tedious process of exposing it again. When the walls are in such bad condition that they will have to be replaced, your sample may serve as the model for a reproduction.

Once your peeling has taken you down to the bare walls, inspect the remote places against the architectural elements. Cornices, mantels, doors, and windows sometimes conceal odd fragments that may have remained when in the past the wallpaper was stripped away. At Mount Vernon, during restoration of the Banqueting Room, the woodwork was removed and in several places revealed vestiges of the original green wallpaper and wallpaper border, sufficiently complete to serve as patterns for reproducing the entire wallcovering of the room.

Your diagrams must record everything that seems to have been added to the room after the house was finished. On the risers of the stairs, are there fixtures that once held carpet-rods? Are there capped nubs of pipes on the walls where gas brackets were attached? Are there certain floors that have a border of stained and varnished natural wood, with a rug-sized bare or painted area in the center? What are the patterns of wear on the floors? If a great deal of stripping of plaster and partitions becomes necessary in the architectural restoration, you will find still other traces of human habitation. Rat nests, unoccupied for a century within the walls, have been known to yield shreds of fabric, straw matting, buttons, and the like. While these discoveries make for triumphant moments in research, you are, however, better off letting the walls alone if the building is structurally sound. Even if you might find something among the bones of the house, it makes little sense to tear out original walls trying to find wallpaper and fabric documents, when you will only end up with modern reproductions and modern walls.

Paint analysis, of the greatest interest to the restorer of interiors, has become very sophisticated, and with constant improvement, serves an important truth-finding role on the interior, as archaeology does outside. Unless the woodwork has been previously stripped—and paint analysis can determine that—there is, in the succession of layers of paint and varnish, a chronicle of the entire color history of the house. Under the microscope, tiny chips will tell the story of the specific spot they came from; color-corrected by the expert, to account for natural aging, these documents can fairly well be depended upon for accuracy. It is best for the color expert to take the samples himself, for there is more to that task than merely taking a chip here and there. If, however, having him on the scene is not possible, a package of chips can be sent to him, each one in its own envelope, and specifically labeled as to where it came from. He then examines these chips under the microscope and can make color slides of the microscopic views. The ultraviolet bleaching of each layer determines the original color; and when the circumstances are particularly difficult, there is spectrophotometric analysis, a more thorough scientific technique.

In an archaeological sense the importance of identifying the original location of every chip cannot be overemphasized. A chip is not from "the bedroom," for example; it is from the "right upper corner of the northwest doorframe, southeast bedroom," or from the "lower portion of the east wall, exactly between the two windows and two feet above the baseboard."

A comprehensive group of paint chips may bring surprises in analysis. There may be, for example, thirteen coats of paint on the window facings, the sixth of which is blue, while across the room several chips taken on the large double doors may show only eight layers, the first color of which, directly on the wood or over a primer, is blue. Thus you can deduce that the sliding doors were added, and at the same time the woodwork in the room was painted blue. Written evidence you already have may date the sliding doors. Together with the paint analysis, this fixes the approximate date the room was painted blue. Otherwise the doors and architrave may suggest a period because of their design.

Sensitive paint analysis can determine if surfaces were marbled or grained or simply varnished; it can tell you if your walls were first whitewashed, or in detecting wallpaper paste, whether they were papered. Splinters of flooring can document varnish, paint, or that the floors were for many years waxed, scrubbed with lye, or left raw. The science of paint analysis can produce revealing information on surfaces apparently free of any alien coatings at all.

The value of paint analysis and archaeology to the historical interior is very great. Both are expensive to undertake. If you cannot afford this highly specialized work, leave your "archives"—the site, the woodwork, floors, and walls—undisturbed. You can usually plant the grounds as you wish without harming the documents below, and you can paint the interior on top of what is there.

When you have amassed most of the other research, an architectural investigation of the building can take place. Too often this is a destructive process, revealing little information that truly justifies the damage. If the structure

10 must be cut into, insist that an expert do it. Seek one who, though experienced, never forgets that he is confronting a document of history. It is questionable how often complete or drastic stripping is actually necessary, even from the structural aspect. The placement of a buttress might in the long run be a happier solution than the reconstruction of a wall. Advances in the *science* of restoration research are bringing us methods that, properly applied, result in new dimensions of accuracy, with no damage to the structure. Traditional stylistic analysis can now be supplemented by structural and constructional information gained through X-ray. Progress in the study of nail, screw, and hardware chronology assists in dating various parts of a building; in the science of dendrochronology, certain types of wood samples are used to determine the year in which the tree was cut down and thus establish at least a possibility for when the wood was incorporated into the house.

Architectural investigation, in any case, should be done slowly, disturbing the building as little as possible. Discovering the location of what was once a window does not necessarily mean that the window should be reopened. To the contrary, your interpretation of the building may center in the later period, and the closing of the window represents the wishes of someone who lived in the house. In seeking the "original," never lose sight of your principal focus, human life. The house is more important to you as your historical characters lived in it over the years than it was before they moved in. Do not remove traces of them without the most careful consideration.

Your architect's search will establish both the original and subsequent changes in the structural progression of the house. It is very likely that you will be able to date his progression through written documents. The two types of information should be co-ordinated into a detailed chronology, accompanied by drawings, and placed with the rest of your research as historical evidence.

Research in Decorative Arts

Last in your research program, make a general study of decorative arts, to familiarize yourself with the period or periods important to the restoration. Begin with the literature. As you proceed, visit as many relevant museum collections as you can, looking up whatever catalogues these institutions have published about their collections.

The "house books" are myriad. Few will be much help, for by and large the rooms they feature are decorated less for historicity than for modern living. What you need is a good general understanding of furniture styles and household objects that apply to your house. While the field of published scholarship is still surprisingly small, you will find a sufficient number of monographs and exhibit catalogues to give you a general impression of styles through the years. It is well to remember that most of what you will find in print shows the exceptional—the finest furniture, the best porcelain, the richest fabrics. No matter how little these exceptional objects may seem to relate to your project, it will be useful to gain your first impressions of style from them. It is in the best specimens that style trends are usually the most clearly articulated. What you will have to learn from sources other than books is the quality of contrast among objects that characterizes most houses. Until very recently, decorative arts scholarship has nearly always assumed the special point of view of the art historian. The tendency is naturally to feature objects that kindle strong aesthetic responses in us today. Take special note that such books are by their nature highly selective in what they present; the standard of this selection is as "modern" as the publication date of the volume and is usually irrelevant, in any comprehensive sense, to recreating the historical interior. Do not treat these works as "wish books," basing your objectives in furnishing the house solely on the objects that appear in their pages. They were never intended to be used in that way. The final decisions on how to furnish your house must come from the analysis of your research in local and regional sources.

The research effort has been in three directions: literary, statistical, and material. While further information will continue to turn up, in the main you have arrived at a time to decide the form in which the information will be organized. This is done by two means, the historical file and the written report, which will be described in the following chapter.

The historical file is the simplest organized form for the mass of material you have brought together. It will become an institution within your project, and with care it will perpetually expand and serve an increasingly important function. The file must be established at the outset in a basic, logical way, by subject. An over-all perspective is maintained on this bulky file by a parallel chronological card file in which the information is entered on separate cards and filed in order according to date. The text of the cards is really only notes: for example, "January 15, 1800, inventory taken by Willie Jones, Notary." The inventory is, of course, copied in full and placed with any related material under its proper heading in the subject file.

The card file is broken into major chronological divisions based upon historical events, according to how these events might have affected your household. Thus a group of cards might be divided, for example, by such a series of headings as The Great Depression, The Local Oil Workers' Strike, World War II, with each of the sections devoted to the documentation that falls between those spans of time. The events are considered turning points and are the natural breaks in your chronology. Undated material in the subject file appears in the card file in a special section at the end of the major division in which it seems to belong. It is helpful to use a different color of card for undated entries.

There are many more complex ways to set up a historical file. But the object of the file is to provide a ready reference from its establishment onward. It must not be encumbered in that purpose by the elaborateness of its design.

With the file established, the process of analysis and synthesis begins that will lead to the final decisions regarding the future of the house.

2

The Report

*T*HE historic house report is a synthesis of the research. It contains an explanation of what you have found and analyzed, and, based upon that, your proposals for the way the house and its interiors will be interpreted.

Make the report clear and to the point, beginning in general terms and moving to specifics. Open with an introduction that describes those historical periods your house most fully reflects. If the house was built in 1761, but the earliest information you have found dates from the decade 1809 to 1819 or 1896 to 1917 or even now, then say so: the direction your restoration takes should be determined by those periods for which the material is the richest.

History and People

Briefly cover the national and international scene as it might have affected life in your house. Had recent world or national events brought changes to the community and altered the circumstances of life in the house? What was the state like during those periods? If it was a colony or a wilderness territory, by what means and how far did one have to journey to reach a population center? What were the sources of trade? What was the state of mobility of most of the inhabitants and particularly those who occupied your house? Was the community self-contained? What was its character? What was the role of your personalities in the community? How did they make a living; how did their source of income vary with time, and what external forces—panics, droughts, gold strikes—created these changes? Did your people, or others in the community, remember life in a previous place,

now almost inaccessible to them, and was there the powerful urge to recreate that life in the new surroundings? How well did it work?

If your people were city dwellers, what about the city as they knew it? Why were they there? Were they well known about town, or was their daily life generally restricted to the area of the city in which they lived? Where were they likely to have obtained food, being removed from agricultural surroundings? Where did they go, about the city—shops, parks, streetcars, offices, saloons, the homes of friends? Did they belong to and attend a church? Were they country folk moved to the city? Had their economic situation changed since they moved to town? Had they adapted well to city life? Did they live in the city all year long, or did they leave town and return to a farm, or remove to the seashore from June until September? Or was that a sort of leisure unknown to them?

What within the community was the median of good living, and where did the conduct of life in your house stand in relation to it? Did the family live a frugal life? Did they live lavishly? How would their manner of living have ranked in other areas of the state and, in very general terms, to the nation? What were the decidedly regional traits of life in this house?

When you have answered such basic questions as these, then direct your report toward specifics about individuals. Famous family members should be described as their careers justify it, but you must not let them dominate to the exclusion of everyone else, even though the main interest of the house may be its association with them. The most important member of the family, as far as the household was concerned, may have been the spinster aunt who lived there, giving stability to a half-dozen lives, while her famous brother-in-law was a senator in Washington. In that case the house might have represented the aunt's ideas in its interiors instead of those of the senator and his wife. Give a broad sampling of the personalities that lived in or were intimate with your house; although some of those people will remain forever off-stage, it is the object of the well-conceived historical room to make it seem that at any moment they could return and not be astonished at what they saw. The degree to which you deceive yourself on this depends upon the quality of your research and analysis.

The Historical Treatment

Thus far your report has concentrated upon history and people. Now you will recount in as much detail as you can what the interiors looked like through the years. Understandably the greatest emphasis should be placed upon the periods for which the information is most complete. The reader will have the historical context sufficiently in mind for minutiae in this section to be important, so do not hold back. Here you call forth all the applicable documentation and begin a simple synthesis. For example: there was no inventory, but the owner's will dated 1805 listed a mantel clock, a featherbed, and a rifle, bequeathed to two daughters and an infant son. The will further listed the total "household effects and kitchen furniture" at a value of $75; compared to inventories of households elsewhere in the county, this one was very humble, and the fact is underlined by the owner's documented wish that his prized possessions be carefully distributed among his children.

Do not digress with "what ifs," even when the information is sparse. You will need to make some general observations as to the uses of the rooms, but stick otherwise to the facts and the conclusions to which you have come because of them. For some rooms, the most you may know is the colors, and from firsthand knowledge, the sort of natural light, the sense of space, and the probable view they offered from the windows. Other rooms will

keep fewer secrets. Their floors may bear the marks of matting tacks, their walls the stumps of broken-off picture pins; there may be a full inventory, of which nearly everything survives in several local attics, and there may even be an old drawing or photograph of the room made many years ago. In any case, it is hard to think that a thorough research program on most houses would not yield something, though you may ultimately have to establish typicals by synthesizing evidence from other houses in the region.

What we have heretofore called the *proposals* for your interiors can be comfortably replaced by the term *treatment,* which belongs to the jargon of screen-writing. The treatment for a film is a preliminary sketch in words, in more or less detail, of what the finished product should look like. This is what the final part of your report should be. A treatment for the historical interior is inspired and shaped by historical documentation of every kind. It will establish the intellectual form your historic house will take as a museum. In the treatment you will designate the historical period or periods your house will cover, you will point out the personalities whose prominence or obscurity makes them worthy of emphasis, and you will analyze the interiors room by room, in historical terms.

Making a room a historical essay is not a simple matter. Even the best-intentioned restorers usually stumble into the mire of superficialities, and occupy themselves with the trees, forgetting the forest. You must first of all establish what the house, once restored, will try to show—or better, what in history does it most effectively illustrate *already*? Unless there is some momentous event that overshadows all else, you are wisest, and most economical, to concentrate upon the period from which there are the most physical remains, rather than to embark upon an arbitrary "restoration." But even with that well established, there are still questions about what the house will show. Is

14 it to give an impression of a moment in time? A period in history? A sense of the continuity of several generations' habitation? How can it become a true mirror of another time, so that by contrast it will fill a useful educational function today? It is this last question that is the most difficult to answer, and yet the most important. The historic house museum, after all, represents the adaptive use of a structure and its interiors to a purpose other than that for which it was built. It is made into a museum instead of a house or boutique because people believe it has something to say; the house must sing for its supper. Only when its historical *raison d'etre* is clearly articulated, and its means of expression carefully planned, can it perform satisfactorily.

Like a book, a play, or a lecture, a historical exhibit needs a theme. With houses, the root of this theme is likely to be private lives. That is both because private lives are what houses represent best, and because personal history is always the strongest point of identity and understanding to the visiting public. The theme need not be profound. "Life as it was lived by the Murphy family in Tallahassee during the Seminole War" is an example of a perfectly valid theme; it presents the opportunity to deal with the war itself through the ambience of one family. "George Washington in retirement" might be Mount Vernon's theme, for the house and immediate farm are preserved and restored to be as they were during the last years of Washington's life. An old family home showing the accumulations and changes of many generations—whether original or to be recreated—might be a composite comfortably contained in the theme "Five generations of the Mitchell family in Providence, from the American Revolution until World War II."

Within the general theme are individual theses, which are dealt with in various spaces in the house. Consider the rooms chapters in a history book. Directives in the treatment regarding rooms should begin with a historical or an anthropological thesis. This thesis may be conjectural, but you will attempt to support it through subthemes.

Many relevant theses will have surfaced in your research. One can imagine a family sitting-dining room in a millworker's house of 1875 being viewed from the thesis that in an industrial society the family unit occupied a more powerful place in human life than ever before. That thesis need not be restricted to so obvious a place. Being universal, it would, for example, apply only less dramatically to a Brooklyn brownstone dwelling of the 1850s. A modern kitchen of 1921 suggests the thesis that the role of women in society had changed since World War I, that a symbol of this is in the transformation of her kitchen from a place of drudgery into a sort of domestic laboratory. Common to most bedrooms of the late eighteenth century would be the thesis that the concept of privacy, not a major issue in early colonial times, had begun to make its mark on family life.

Subthemes are plentiful in the historical room. They are varied and require more specific material illustration than either the theme of the house or the theses in the rooms. The millworker's sitting-dining room mentioned above might contain, besides the table and chairs, a lounge, emphasizing the room's dual function; the family Bible, indicating the family's religious inclination. It might contain tableware, to demonstrate the manner in which meals were eaten, and printed cotton curtains, with matching pillows on the lounge, cloth on the table, and scarf on the sideboard, itself ornamented by a large model in walnut hulls of the ship on which the man of the house served in the Civil War. All these objects proclaim the family's idea of beauty, and at a certain level, the taste of the era. Subthemes are carried out with such details of furnishing.

Enumerate as many subthemes in the treatment as your research tells you are needed to fill out the picture, assigning the themes to the appropriate rooms. Generally it might be said that parlors, halls, bedrooms, and porches lend themselves best to themes based upon the family, while in kitchens, storage-rooms, out-buildings, and even attics, themes can be developed that shed light on the age.

Research will have yielded some specifics about objects that were in your house. You may have some or many of the actual materials, or you may have only an inventory. Whatever the case, these things fall in the treatment where they seem best to illustrate subthemes. Remember that your subthemes are, first of all, historical—whether religious customs, habits of dress, war, education, personal history. Do not be bewitched at this stage by pretty things. The decorative arts are not an issue here in the traditional museum sense, unless that aspect supports a historical idea or is in itself historical.

The report, when completed properly, will represent both concentrated thought and common sense. To bypass this step in any restoration or preservation is unthinkable. No matter how much good information you have collected, it is still raw material without analysis and synthesis. In short, it is not history. In preparing the report and treatment, you subject yourself and your facts to intellectual discipline. Ideas that might otherwise rattle about aimlessly in your head are refined and polished. You make your mistakes on paper, not on the physical house. The entire project is dignified and enlightened by a point of view.

3

Developing the
Collections List

ALMOST every restored interior represents a combination of fact and supposition.
The latter is sometimes better described as fic-
tion. The restorer is very vulnerable in the area
of supposition; presented with several alternatives, he is inclined to respond according to
his personal preferences, which are generically
"modern." What may seem to him perfectly
natural solutions in furnishing a house nine
times out of ten is historically incorrect. The
best way to avoid subtle pitfalls is to delay
final decisions on furnishings as long as you
can, allowing them to grow from a vigorous
historical questioning of your sources. The collections list facilitates this process.

The collections list is just what the name
implies: a list of furnishings. Each entry is justified by documentation of one kind or
another. In its early stages the collections list is
expansive; analyzed and synthesized, it is
gradually trimmed and reshaped until it becomes the precise basis for a furnishings plan.
It remains flexible to the last, where supposition is concerned. But one hopes that the research program has already turned up enough
particulars about the house to give your collections list a firm foundation to start with.

Begin the list with your "givens," those objects you know for sure were in the house.
These may not be specific enough to stand on
their own, so you strengthen them. For example, if you know from an old letter that the parlor had a center table, a lamp, and a sofa, but
no description of the three survives, concentrate upon learning the most you can about
what these objects could have been like.

You may come up with several alternatives.
The objects catalogue should by this stage
yield local examples of tables, lamps, and sofas
contemporary with your reference. If such objects do not appear in your catalogue, seek
sources progressively more distant. Persistent
detective work will usually make it unnecessary for you to go beyond your region.

The inventories, travel accounts, diaries, advertisements, and so on that you have collected have been excerpted by object, including any descriptive material that may accom-
pany their mention. Try to reconcile your givens with what you find in these sources. An
entry for a "hair sofa" in a local inventory says
nothing about style, but it does indicate that
hair cloth was used for sofa upholstery in your
area. So the style and type of sofa may come
from one source, while documentation for the
upholstery and use come from another. You
will find some of your strongest validation that
way, in bits and pieces, which you evaluate
and combine to make a single entry in the collections list.

Bankruptcy and estate sale records aside, inventories are the documents most typically
concerned with household effects. By and
large, inventories are taken to list the effects of
one who has died. While the historian hopes
the house remained at that time exactly as the
owner had left it, that is not always the case.
Sometimes changes will be obvious, as when
the contents of the house are listed by category, "7 bedsteads, 61 chairs," which, if not a
regional custom (as it was often in the
eighteenth century along Chesapeake Bay) implies that the furnishings were probably
massed together in one place for purposes of
division or sale. The inventory applies only to
objects owned by the deceased, not the possessions of his children, who may have lived
with him, or property he and his wife did not
own jointly. Furthermore, the age of the deceased is important, for you can usually assume that an old person long in residence in

one house would not have owned only the latest modes of furnishings.

Any documented object, whether original to your house or merely to the area, will speak to you more vividly after being understood in the context of a variety of inventories. You will learn where these objects fit into the general picture of the locality, how typical or how exceptional they were, and where they were used in houses of the day. The collections list will also contain objects that do not still exist but which, because of documentary references, you know once existed. List these materials in abundance, with the idea of thinning them later. Subdivide your list according to the rooms in your house; objects will usually be categorized similarly in the inventories. Sometimes they are not, but even then the sequence of objects should make the divisions fairly evident. When you cannot tell from the inventory what object went where, lay that particular document aside until last. It may seem clearer after you have studied all the rest.

In examining inventories, pay special attention to the manner in which objects are listed, for this may tell you something about the class and quality of the particular entry. "1 lott dishes" is likely to mean material of a lesser sort than when the various pieces are enumerated. Objects described as "fancy" are not necessarily fine, but may be cheap and store-bought, as a showy chalk image or an oilcloth table cover. The designation of an object as "old" can either mean out-of-date or worn out, rather than "antique." Whoever took the inventory may have been confused in his terminology, may have known nothing about furnishings, or may have been given to using archaic terms. His shortcomings or abilities should be defined as accurately as possible and accounted for in his listing.

There are geographical areas in which no inventories exist. Inventories do become sparse in the late nineteenth and twentieth centuries, especially west of the Mississippi River. But

even much earlier there were places where inventories either were not taken at all or were not very detailed. There is also the unfortunate problem of records that are lost. In such situations the object references you turn up will be from diverse sources such as advertisements, which may not designate where in a house an object was to be used. It will be necessary, for the sake of clarity, to develop a hypothetical inventory for your house, modeled on a series of inventories that come from outside your locality. This will be a useful tool for comparison when you hone the collections list to its final form.

The prime alternative to the inventory for the later nineteenth and twentieth centuries is the documentary photograph, showing a room or a part of a room. The photographic record in all the states becomes rather full after the late 1880s, with the appearance of the Kodak. It is always desirable to have old photographs of your interiors; when interior photographs of your house do not exist, those of other houses of the same period will be useful. Like a variety of inventories, collections of photographs can provide an overview. Date old photographs as carefully as possible. Always question and attempt to verify any date that might be inscribed on them. You may never know the day, month, and year the photograph was taken, but such details as lighting devices can help you establish at least the decade, if not only the earliest possible date it could be. Analyze the photograph object by object, just as you would an inventory; the result will be richer, for you have an image.

Photographs sometimes prove valuable sources even for interiors that predate the widespread use of the camera for inside shots (ca. 1870), recording objects that have remained in use in a house from generation to generation. A word of caution, in this regard: the 1870s saw the beginning of the collection of antiques, and by the twentieth century antiques had become plentiful in houses of the

18 upper middle class and above, especially along the eastern seaboard, making it difficult to discern in photographs of that time the relevance of what you see to earlier local history. Whatever the hazards, photographs are excellent tools for the restorationist. Good collections presently in public depositories, such as the Montana Historical Society and the Society for the Preservation of New England Antiquities, hint that still greater reserves lie as yet unknown in private hands.

Choosing Specific Objects

As it develops, the collections list goes through various drafts. It comprises the vocabulary for your room. You have already established on paper in your report what each room will say about the past; still, you have only a general, rather literary idea of what the final results will be. Specifics will come from the collections list. Narrowing down the alternatives requires a special sort of thinking about the documentary materials, a process of evaluation and comparison.

Let us experience this thinking through an example. Suppose you are restoring a house built between 1735 and 1743. Your only source on particular furniture is the builder's will, one typical of a farmer of that time, and dated 1751. The will states that a "featherbed and furniture" is left to an unmarried daughter, and otherwise only lists land and farm implements. For convenience we will place this house in Chester County, Pennsylvania, to make use of Margaret B. Schiffer's model study *Chester County, Pennsylvania, Inventories, 1684–1850*. This work, a quantitative analysis of the inventories of one county, represents a scholarly ideal desirable for any locality; but since, in practical terms, yours may be no more than a file of inventories contemporary with your house, we will use only the documents in Mrs. Schiffer's book.

From monographs on eighteenth-century

American decorative arts, you already know that a "featherbed and furniture" may mean bedstead, mattress, sheets, pillows, and bedcurtains, or it can simply refer to the mattress and textiles associated with the bed. Assuming that the mattress and equipment would have been used in conjunction with a bedstead of some kind, you can suppose that the house contained such an item, which may or may not have been one of fine quality, by local standards. The reason the owner singled out his daughter as heiress of the bed will likely never be known for certain, although the custom was so common for a century at least that it should not be construed to suggest that the bed was at issue because it was elegant. In any event, you will eventually acquire a bed dating from the first half of the eighteenth century. Without the original, and with only circumstantial evidence that it existed, the best you can do is to secure another local example known to have been used in the county; the bed "furniture"

Wainscot armchair, walnut, Chester County, Pennsylvania, second half of the eighteenth century.—*Chester County Historical Society and the William Penn Museum*

you are likely to have to reproduce, using as a model some document from far beyond your county's boundaries.

Thus you have illuminated and built upon the stark reference in the will, and have, if not the original, an approximation of something that was actually in the house. What of the rest of the furnishings, which you know absolutely nothing about? You must go to the closest sources you can find: among the inventories listed in Mrs. Schiffer's study are six that you decide are relevant to your house, spanning the years 1731 to 1760. Four and possibly five of these list beds in the parlor or best rooms of the house. Your will and legal documents of the fifteen years before it place the financial status of your farmer closest to that of one William Lewis, whose home at Haverford was inventoried in 1754. Going on the inventory, his house may be bigger or smaller than yours in the number of rooms; nevertheless, the difference is not striking, so his inventory will serve as a place to begin the development of your collection list.

Certain that you are safe in designating the parlor as the place for your one given, the bed, you note the contents of William Lewis's parlor, which was apart from his "Hall" or more common gathering room:

In the Parlour

To 1 Feather Bed and furniture	£11	0	0.
To 1 Desk		7 15 0
To 1 Walnutt Oval Table and 2 Tea Tables		4 10 0
To 1 Couch and Couch Bed		2 0 0
To 1 Looking Glass		1 10 0
To 1 Arm'd Chair and Cussion and 5 others		1 1 0
To Fire doggs shovel Tongs and Fender		1 0 0
To 2 Peuter Tea Potts with China and delph Ware		1 15 0
To 6 Large Silver Spoons 8 Tea ditto and Tongs		6 1 0

			19
To 1 Counterpain and Window Curtains & c		1 0 0	
To 7 Table Cloths and 19 Napkins		4 18 6	
To other Table linnen & c		1 10 0.	

It seems characteristic of inventories—and not surprising—that the conspicuous pieces in a room are listed first. Thus, beginning with the dominant bed, desk, and walnut table, this parlor contains thirteen items of furniture, a mirror, probably on the wall, fireplace equipment, and a small number of pewter, china, and silver objects of the table, some of which may have been kept in a built-in cupboard or the desk, along with the tablecloths and linens.

Whether or not the Lewis house survives for a close spatial comparison, the parlor inventory may imply a bigger room given to more formal uses than your house could have had. The size of a room and arbitrary ideas about how it might have functioned are dangerous grounds for making judgments about eighteenth-century interiors. Yet even if in most respects the Lewis inventory seems appropriate, you should not consider making the inventory of one house the sole source for fur-

Louis XVI revival parlor table, ca. 1872, White's Furniture Manufactory, Philadelphia.—*Peter Strickland*

20 nishing another verbatim. What you must do is to compare the Lewis parlor inventory, which in most respects seems appropriate, to others of as close proximity as possible. A 1742–1743 inventory of a similar but apparently smaller house also in Chester County lists the contents of the "Lower Room," clearly the principal room, serving as both hall and parlor:

In the Brick House lower room			
One Bed and Furniture	£12	0	0
One eight Day Clock	14	0	0
One walnut Oval Table	2	0	0
Six black Chairs			
one of them armed	15		
Two poplar chests	12		
Eight Table Cloths and			
Five Napkins	2		
Eleven pair of Sheets	5		
Four loaves of sugar	1		
A Quantity of Butter			
1:10 do of Cheese	4		
Three pair of old Cards and			
an Old Hackle	7		
Two Bibles	1	10	
Pooles Annotations to the			
End of Jeromy's Lamontations	15		
A case of Bottles	12		
A Quantity of Flax and Cotton	6.		

The similarities between this and the Lewis parlor are seen at once. There is the predominating bed, the oval walnut table, the armchair, and five other chairs without arms, listed as though they must match or be similar in character. The more varied use of the second room is evident in the presence of four times as many chairs, perishable foods, tools for working with textile fibers, flax and cotton, and three books. Is your parlor to represent a special sort of place or one for the conduct of everyday life?

Your collection begins to expand beyond the bed. John Lea's inventory, 1759, also lists "1 walnut oval table" in his parlor; John Hannum's inventory in 1730–31 begins in an unnamed but seemingly important room with "1 Oval Table"; Grace Lloyd's "back room," apparently a parlor, contained in 1760 "A Walnut Oval Table." Thus is established what might be called a secondary given for your Chester County house, an oval table of walnut.

Elsewhere you will not find evidence so conclusive. For example, in these same inventories several parlors have clocks, others have mirrors, but none have both. For your parlor, decide that you will have either a clock or a mirror; both will be entered in the collections list, and the acquisition of one automatically removes the other from the list. Elsewhere the number of chairs you acquire might be based upon how many people lived in your house, rather than the inventories. It is well rooted in fact that there was but one armchair, so list accordingly.

Slowly and with certainty the collection list for your parlor takes form on paper, through the careful comparison of various historical sources, and wherever possible, a close scrutiny of surviving examples. Early houses' inventories are the best sources you can have for the total room. But they are by no means infallible and can be deceptive, even when they seem obvious in what they say. A classic example is in the inventory of Mrs. Wade Hampton of Columbia, South Carolina, whose household furniture was appraised soon after her death in 1863.

When Mary Hampton's house was being researched for restoration in 1969 and 1970, the 1863 appraiser's inventory turned up in due course. While the number and distribution of the rooms as listed was confusing, their contents seemed clear. The following were listed as the furnishings of the drawing room:

1 Marble top pier table and French
   Clock $500
2 large mirrors @ $500, $1,000

Two large velvet chairs $100
8 rosewood chairs covered with
   damask $40
3 rosewood arm chairs $30
2 sofas $150
4 small corner tables $100
1 small center table $50

Mirrors, marble, rosewood, and damask all conjured up an image of the sort of mid-nineteenth-century drawing room one would expect General Hampton's widow to have. Her husband, a Revolutionary War hero, had left her an immense fortune in the early 1830s, and most of her life since had been spent in company—or at least frequent association—with her wealthy and fashionable daughter and son-in-law, Caroline and John Smith Preston, seasoned world-travelers and well-known collectors of sculpture.

The inventory valued Mary Hampton's silver at $20,000 (presumably in Confederate money), her household slaves at $33,000. Her magnificent ornamental garden, sketched and photographed during the Civil War, had survived well into recent memory, and even in 1969 a walk through the derelict mansion was enough to convince anyone that the inventory could only have meant stylishness and grandeur. One of two superb, nearly cubical rooms off the street entrance contained a finely carved mantel in statuary marble; it was only too obvious that this chamber had been the drawing room listed in the inventory.

The interest of the restorers centered in the oldest (ca. 1820) section of the house, a lofty, stuccoed block with striking lines. The house had been doubled in size at one time or another, no one knew when, by a very large addition to the rear. Though scarcely visible on the street-elevation, the appendage was an encumbrance to the classical purity of the original structure, and this, rightly or wrongly, sealed the wing's fate. While very little other research was brought to bear, the

inventory—which was ambiguous—did seem to indicate that the unhappy wing might have been there in the days of the Hamptons, but if so it had been purely utilitarian, containing bedrooms. In any case, the mysterious wing fell before the bulldozers in the summer of 1969.

Once the structural work on the remaining building was finished, the drawing room, with its white marble mantel, was completed more or less in the French Antique mode of the 1850s. The great fascination of the room was that it was furnished almost entirely with objects of family provenance donated or loaned by Hampton and Preston descendants. While none of these furnishings had probably ever been in the house before, they had a sort of validity because they had been known to the family in its other houses during antebellum days. There was to the finished drawing room a theatrical tone of realism, from the tattered crimson curtains to the family portraits, that invited lively historical interpretation.

But historical it proved not to be. In the steady stream of family memorabilia that flowed to the Hampton-Preston house after its opening in April 1970, photographs finally appeared taken inside the house sometime between 1859 and 1863. One was a close-up view of the sideboard in the dining room, showing some of the silver, which was recognizable because it had been listed in a subsequent family will, and the other two were of Mary Hampton and a step-granddaughter seated in the corner of another room in the house. A comparison among all three photographs, the inventory, and the house revealed that the two women were posed in the drawing room.

The photographs were a cold and telling glance into the past. This room had not been decorated with an up-to-date French Antique ensemble from New York, Philadelphia, or Baltimore, as the inventory and the family's tastes and circumstances had suggested. It had been a mixture of many things of many differ-

22 ent qualities. Mary Hampton's "small center table" was not ornate and marble-topped, but was an earlier, plainer table, contemporary with a sofa and armchair, also in the pictures. These were the sorts of pieces of furniture she might well have brought to the house when she moved there in the 1820s. The chair in which she was seated—probably one of the "Two Large Velvet Chairs"—was a fine one of the 1850s, in the style originally believed to have been common to all the furniture in the room. The "4 corner tables," going on one in the pictures, were merely shelves for heavy sculpture which, it is well established, belonged to the Prestons. Nothing in the inventory tells us about the little decorative trifles that were scattered about, the bouquets in vases, the odd books, the deer antlers, all determining factors in the drawing room's general character, which was more homey than formal.

For the Hampton-Preston house the document was a lucky find, if late. With this source, and an excellent collection of family furnishings, the restorers could labor to produce a historical setting very close to the truth. Yet with the joy of discovery came hopeless pain. Further comparison of the photographs with the actual house and written sources unlocked the once-obscure inventory's most alarming secret: the Hamptons had indeed added the rear wing, and reoriented the house to face the garden instead of the street. Mary Hampton's well-documented drawing room had been in the wing. The room with the beautiful marble mantel had been a bedroom!

Ambiguous documents cannot bear the entire burden of blame for errors in authenticity. Tax records, wills, inventories, and the like were not written to serve restorationists. Information must be squeezed from them. The researcher must be alert for clues and deceptions. To go to the documents with preconceived mental pictures of decorative arts settings is to accept a forgery among materials

that are authentic. To allow the vagaries in your sources to establish precise images without further justification is capricious. Research on furnishings is an endless frustration. The object is a document in itself, and to attempt to trace and identify it in written sources is characteristically difficult.

To the eye of the appraiser who entered the "Two Large Velvet Chairs" on Mary Hampton's inventory, the description was perfectly adequate. The chairs described themselves to him on the spot. Reading that inventory a century later, and lacking both the objects and supporting evidence, we must conjecture what sort of chairs these were that appeared "Large" and "Velvet." Their mass and fabric somehow registered with the appraiser, so we might decide that the pieces were mostly upholstered. But knowing that several types of big upholstered chairs were familiar by the 1860s, we may ultimately acquire one in the Gothic-revival style, only to discover subsequently that Mary Hampton's was French Antique. Such honest mistakes are among the occupational hazards of researching historical rooms for restoration.

The Primary and Secondary List

When you arrive at the point of beginning to edit the collections list, and the list is quite large, your work can be greatly clarified if you split the list into two parts. Compose these two in such a way that you can study them side by side. When you are through, the lists are finally combined again. Let the first of the two lists consist of the objects that actually exist, whether you have them or not. The second list consists of objects you know only through written sources. The report has described the status of the occupants of the house, and the sources that supported that conclusion have supplied a local, regional, and national context upon which you will lean heavily in weeding out the second list.

Heading the primary list are the objects documented as original to your house. These may be dominant pieces, such as a bed or a sofa, or they may be transient objects, such as a tin candleholder or a book. Just how expendable they are depends upon their historical validity. Hearsay will of course carry less weight than a bill of sale; and you must always suspect hearsay at the outset. But if in all other respects the object supports the hearsay, its credentials are fairly strong. Even though you are unable to acquire historical objects actually used in the house, leave them on the list. Any substitutions for the originals must be considered temporary.

The other furnishings from the catalogue of objects may not be original to the house but are to the area. Their stability on the list depends upon how many original materials you can get. Naturally, second-best to the original is that which is documented as having been used locally at the same time. An elaborate "Recamier" sofa, however, should not be imposed arbitrarily upon the plain cottage of a tinsmith, simply because cottage and sofa were contemporaries in the same town. The assumption, once frequently heard, that "the tinsmith would have had a Recamier if he could have afforded it" is absurd. Obviously the furnishings, no matter how excellent their local pedigrees, must be at least probable to the historical circumstances of your house.

By the same token, when assembling numbers of objects from diverse sources it is important to maintain a clear idea of the tone these materials will project collectively, in a single place. One is strongly tempted to take practically anything that is well documented; but the house should not become mere shelter for documentary furnishings. There are other kinds of museums that serve that purpose better.

It is not, however, the documented objects that usually lead restorers astray from historical accuracy, but the "supporting objects."

These are the materials we noted earler as supposition. They have no local provenance but are merely "period" and become as a group a sort of thermostat with which you adjust the tone of the room to the accurate historical climate. Comprising usually a big part of the secondary list, these often anonymous objects are selected and combined only with the utmost care. They can be used to enrich or to simplify. They can create sharp contrasts, or they can blend into a decorated ensemble.

In building the secondary list, strive to give substance to any written references to objects by correlating them with actual objects you find in museums, illustrated in old graphics, and pictured and described in monographs on decorative arts. Although none of these sources may include objects from your locality, they provide useful points of reference in the general stylistic sense. You must remain absolutely aware, however, that what you are seeking is materials that are historically correct and not merely things that would look pretty in your house. Do not treat the various illustrative sources as furniture catalogues, nor consider yourself a customer about to place an order.

Selecting what we want from a large array—a "selection"—of furnishings is second nature to us today. When we decorate for ourselves we think in terms of making choices from the vast market of available furniture mass-production has laid before us. Various styles are popularized through advertising and in such magazines as *House & Garden*. Even when we furnish with antiques, a whole spectrum of styles comes to mind; a first-class antique shop today differs little from a furniture store in the predictableness of its stock. Through interior decorators, museums, and books has evolved a narrow series of types of historical objects which have become the trademarks of this or that period—the Chippendale and Queen Anne chairs of Williamsburg (Colonial), the French Antique par-

24 lor sofas of Natchez (antebellum). In restoring rooms we tend to think of certain furnishings as "right" for certain periods, thus applying to the past the same selectivity we apply to interior decorating in our own time.

The further back your restoration reaches in time, the more of a danger this selectivity becomes. Mass-manufacture grew from seed to flower between the American Revolution and the 1870s. Concurrently the market in household goods changed from a very limited one dominated by craftsmen and the man working at home to one of great proportions controlled by businessmen. This radically affected the decoration of houses, for in accepting the fruits of mass-production, the citizen forfeited the creative decisions he had once made in dealing personally with the craftsmen and tradesmen and in making the furniture and other objects himself. No longer did he participate in basic decisions on design. He began to accept more standardization in decorating his interiors than he had ever known. Standardization in the style and types of objects came to characterize his rooms, and while at the outset he tried to compensate for this with personal clutter and "artistic" devices, he was rapidly possessed by it, and by World War I the situation stood rather much as it is today.

It is characteristic of most restored interiors as ensembles to reflect the standardized taste, the selectivity created by mass-manufacture, even though all the individual objects may be authentic. We are so accustomed to this standardization in our lives that its presence in historic houses does not seem strange. And we have been conditioned to it by three generations of restored houses. For a house of 1895 or 1917 it is essential to study the advancing state of standardization as it was in those periods and to take it into account when the rooms are restored. But for a house of 1790 or 1820 or even 1835 standardization in that sense hardly applies at all.

Nevertheless, when you are acquiring furnishings for the historical interior, you are faced with locating objects that already exist. So you are making selections in a way that was probably not done when the house was originally furnished. Only remember that each house presents different objectives for furnishing. In the early periods, before mass-manufacture, or even later in areas of the country not affected by it, rooms were usually furnished slowly. All but the most basic kinds of furniture were hard to come by and often were acquired one piece at a time. Style was of the object, not the total setting. Things did not necessarily match or "go together." Contrasts in scale among furnishings were not likely to be co-ordinated with an eye to total effect. Most rooms were likely to be less the finished settings we have grown accustomed to seeing in restored houses than places with individual character, mixed in style, class, and quality.

On the second list, nothing should be considered permanent until your consideration of furnishings is well along. Most entries on this list will have alternatives. As objects are actually acquired for the house, the list diminishes and solidifies into an increasingly permanent form. For the dining room of a small Pittsburgh bungalow of 1900 the acquisition of a pressed-glass punch set may preclude the need for the painted china coffee service that was also on the list. An undocumented Sacramento parlor of 1869, blessed with the gift of a documented eight-piece parlor set known to have been shipped by rail from the Midwest to California in 1875, might be completed to feature the set, which would support a thesis based upon nineteenth-century California's close identity with older settled parts of the United States. The second list would therefore be shaped to support the idea, with the inclusion not only of other types of imported objects, but with local materials that would give contrast. Thus the message of the parlor set would become clear and more articulate, amplified by many other objects.

The collections list, its two parts at last united, develops from many kinds of historical investigation. It is an absolute necessity before serious collecting begins. To proceed without a collections list is dangerous, for, in the process of its compilation, the list accomplishes two things: it maintains historical discipline in an area where one can easily go astray; and it helps further to refine the vocabulary through which your historical objectives will be accomplished.

4

Restoration and Finishing of the House Itself

WHEN it comes down to making final decisions about the architectural changes you will make in the house, certain practical considerations may conflict with the objectives expressed in your report. One hopes that these problems have been self-evident from the start, ranging from the very basic question of whether your community can support a house museum (or whether the building might best serve part as museum and part for other purposes), to whether or not it is wise to rip away subsequent additions and render the structure "pure" to its original form.

Architectural Decisions

The most desirable decisions *architecturally* are not always the best *historically*. In other words, by giving architectural considerations top priority, you may cut off a treasure of possibilities for variety in historical interpretation. Since the beginning the architectural point of view has dominated historical restoration, and this has created an unfortunate imbalance. Presented with a crumbling house to restore, traditionally one turns first to an architect. If this architect is unfamiliar with modern restoration concepts—and many are—he may be inclined to base his decisions not upon the particular building but upon his aesthetic eye for academic typicals. To a trained professional architect, historicity is likely to be less important than how well the building represents a type of architecture. Even the relatively few architects who are

either schooled in restoration procedures or who have developed a field in it too often show surprisingly little feeling for interiors. "Restore the fabric of the building," one often hears. "Do what you please inside." The idea behind this is, of course, that furnishings, paint colors, and so on, are temporary, while stone walls and wooden structural elements are not. But this philosophy has been ruinous to the interior finishing of many museum houses that have been restored architecturally according to the best principles.

The interiors of such houses seem inevitably to become hypothetical specimens, three-dimensional plates from a history of design, rather than being particularly historical or individual. They show few traces of human living, except as they reflect the taste of the restorers themselves. And what do they teach about history? Restoring a house to illustrate architecture and decorative arts can have a validity of its own, in some cases, but in general, in point of content, it is a rather thin approach. The how and why of a certain place are just as important as any universalities about fine and applied art they may embody. In the historical interior, let the human factor take precedence over everything else.

Weigh all the alternatives before you make any decision about the house. Your conscientious research analysis qualifies the ideals expressed in your report. That these ideals are worthy objectives is in no way diminished by the fact that they may take years to realize. A house that has stood for a hundred years need not be rushed backward or forward. If there is some doubt about the wisdom of removing part of the building, then do not do it, even though you might, for the time, do no more than stabilize the questionable part, awaiting later decisions. If it is advisable to reserve a section of the house for organizational or commercial purposes, be certain that the particular function will not be detrimental to the building's historical and architectural integrity and that the museum areas will be treated according to the high historical standards reflected in your report.

To the historian it is nearly always most desirable to devote the entire building to the museum function. But since the late 1960s economic realities have increasingly favored varying uses for old buildings. The adaptive use of historic structures as other than museums has saved many a building that would otherwise have been lost. One would hardly be pleased to find a restaurant in Thomas Jefferson's parlor at Monticello; yet among the delights of Nantucket is the Jared Coffin House, the restored dwelling of an early nineteenth-century sea captain, in which the functions of house museum, restaurant, and inn mix happily. Captain Coffin was not president of the United States, nor a founding father of the nation: the question here centers in tone.

Chances are, the extent of your compromises will be in making portions of the house available for meetings and social functions. You may, further, open a shop of some kind, or reserve space for rental as commercial or civic offices or as apartments. There are good and bad points to each. What concerns us here is that adequate and significant space be devoted to historical rooms that will present a cohesive picture of the past. That can be accomplished in a few rooms, or you may need them all, depending upon the house and what you want to make it say.

Decisions involving the ultimate form of the restored interior spaces should not necessarily be predicated on the appearance of the house as it was originally built. Alterations may have so totally changed the character of the building that they interfere with your historical objectives. Then some tearing away and restoration is probably in order. How extensive this work will be depends upon the depth of your knowledge of the original fabric and its importance, and, of course, your budget. Sometimes

minor removals will accomplish what is needed, without involving you in a major overhaul. Think long and hard before you demolish additions that, no matter what they look like, might be put to practical use, or elements that, though fifty years later than the time you will represent, have virtues of their own and with a little sound logic on your part, might become assets instead of liabilities in the general scheme.

Where the exterior has been altered even by large additions, the changes can usually be explained, so they do not distort your presentation of the past. Subsequent alterations to interiors, however, present more difficult problems. A large part of the effectiveness of the restored room in a house museum depends upon the clarity of its historical theme. If the room's architecture is so changed as to bear little relation to the period in question, the theme will be nearly impossible to convey in a visual way. Interior changes in a house occupied for many generations by the same family must obviously remain. They attest continuity. But what of a house that has been sold many times, its interiors having been remodeled as often? Unless you are content to adopt a historical theme that fits the interiors as they stand—that is, after the last changes were made—the rooms will have to be revised. At its simplest, that can mean replacing a door or mantel; or at the other extreme it can mean a virtual gutting and reconstruction of a whole section of the interior. Whatever the task, you cannot expect to base your interpretation of the 1840s upon a sitting room, and be believable, when the space was joined with the adjacent hall in 1885 and embellished with picturesque Queen Anne decorations in varnished oak. Either your historical theme or the '80s elements in the room will have to be changed.

On the other hand, it may be clear that enough of the other rooms survive intact to carry the historical theme of the 1840s, or can

28 be more justifiably restored for the purpose, to permit you to leave the Queen Anne sitting room and hall. The mixture of periods may result in a house that is as it never was; your consolation is that you have preserved something that seemed worth preserving, and have broadened your historical scope. Perhaps the Queen Anne space will be left bare of furnishings, to speak only as an authentic example of Queen Anne interior architecture, to be used as an entrance or for gatherings and exhibit purposes. Yet it may actually be that the Queen Anne rooms cannot be reconciled in any way with your historical objective. The decision to pull out and restore is always a decision to destroy a document. Sometimes this must be done, and if it is so in your case, preserve all the elements as they are removed. While you may think you have no reason to keep them, you do not know but that generations to come may want to put them back.

After the solutions on the physical house are reached, you may be left with a single room to furnish or there may be twenty. The report has established the historical points the room will make and has suggested how they may be made. This will need some adjustment, if the number of available rooms is smaller than you had counted upon when the report was written. Already the collections list provides possibilities and objectives for furnishing. The actual work of bringing furnishings together may be complicated because what you want is unavailable, or difficult to find, or because your funding is inadequate. The last, one hopes, is not an insurmountable obstacle; in the lean years, be comforted by the lesson of some of America's most costly restored rooms, that poverty is not always detrimental.

Choosing a Time Period

Your house will represent either one or several periods. That is, the interiors will reflect a long or short span of time. In the latter instance, unless you are showing a moment in time—such as the day the treaty was signed—you may confine yourself, for example, to the decade during which a particular family occupied the building. Even though that family may have built the house, you should normally place greater emphasis upon, say, the fifth and tenth years of their residence than you do upon the first, for it is their lives as *lived* there that gives your story substance. If it appears that they repainted a room during the decade, perhaps the second color is more historically revealing than the first, since it was selected by the occupants after they had had the experience of living in the room. Likewise, if you are dealing with a long span of time, three or five generations, you obviously do not wish to peel the house back to the way it looked the day it was finished. Changes through the ensuing years chronicle the occupants' continuing dialogue with the house. Perhaps the family, or an interesting succession of owners, lived there between 1819 and 1961; the house would best be taken back to 1961. That does not preclude restoring different rooms inside to different periods, but it does raise questions.

Take, for example, the concluding date 1961 and assume that in that year the last of three aged sisters died, leaving their family house in derelict condition, even though the accumulated furnishings of a century of family living survived until that time, when they were sold at auction. In restoring the house today to 1961, will you be able to reproduce its faded state? And if you can, will the effort be worthwhile? Does the principal importance of the house lie in the fact that three people kept it intact? Probably not. You would be better off in this case settling on some earlier date that would allow you to interpret the family in a time when the house was more relevant to the world around it, rather than an anachronism. If, on the other hand, you had been able to get the place in 1961, prior to the auction, there would be but one objective: to "freeze" it; to preserve it as you received it, right down to the telephone books.

Old houses can be preserved for many reasons and put to many uses. When they or portions of them are set aside as house museums, museums of their own history, the justification narrows. The restored house can contain a collection of furnishings not directly relevant to its own past—but then it is not really a house museum. An example of this is the James K. Polk Museum in Columbia, Tennessee, where a remarkable group of President Polk's household and personal possessions are assembled in a brick dwelling that was the home of his parents. Here the importance of the collection supersedes that of the house, which must be considered a gallery, even though most of the furnishings are arranged in room-settings. If it were otherwise, the Polk memorabilia would be used more or less anonymously to show the lives of the parents. Then the Polk Museum could be called a house museum. The distinction must be clearly understood, that in a house museum the contents cannot be thought of as separate from the structure. Both combine, blending and contrasting, more to evoke a sense of wholeness about a time in the past than merely to illustrate its relics.

Finishing the Interior Walls

Decisions on finishing the interior spaces of the historic house should be made insofar as possible before the structural work on the building begins. The completion of this finish—walls, floors, ceilings, architectural elements in the rooms—is effected after the structural work is done, and gives the spaces a sensory impact that is extremely important to their success in evoking the past. That the structure itself has been returned to its state in a certain time is only part of the story. Buildings exist for human use, and if yours is to be used as a house museum, a physical presentation of a yet earlier use as a home, then the work of restoration continues beyond the structural stage in the sensitive surface finishing of the interiors.

This finishing follows historical evidence. The going is a lot rougher here than with structural matters, where the clues are usually bolder. There may be no evidence. You must then substitute justifiable possibilities for fact.

Interior Paint

There are usually traces of paint; so the paint colors, determined through scientific research, are restored accordingly. Now and then a room is still covered with an early coat of paint, a peeling or very dirty survival of a time later than what you wish to represent. Preserving it as it is may amount to pure antiquarianism; still, you have more to lose than to gain by scraping it away, unless an earlier coat be-

Paint chip under the microscope, from the Ximinez-Fatio House, Saint Augustine, Florida. —*Carole L. Perrault*

30 neath it, from the desired period, can be exposed again.

Well-executed paint surfaces dating from before about 1850 are nearly impossible to reproduce, for lack of adequate craftsmanship. This applies less to artificial wood-graining and marbling than to surfaces in plain colors, for those dramatic visual deceptions, carefully contrived, go far in concealing the absence of perfection in the more basic techniques of application. Our paints today—and for the past century—contain various kinds of vehicles added to the pigment that make the paint smooth as it dries, leveling out the brush strokes. Before these vehicles came into use, smoothness was attained by applying many coats or rubbing the dry surface with powdered pumice; apparently neither practice was common in the United States, perhaps because of the cost, although the technique was familiar to trained painters.

Instead, with a deft touch, the painter "drybrushed" over a coat or two, working his brush (which he usually called his "beater") in the wet paint so that the strokes were perfectly straight, and for all practical purposes perfectly parallel, tiny comblike lines that followed the plane of what he was painting. Thus on the surface of a door and the jamb, the delicate lines extended unbroken from the base to the upper corner, where they terminated precisely at the wood joint, to begin horizontally across to the other corner. On doors, the direction of the brush strokes likewise varied on the stiles, rails, and panels. Because painted surfaces got dirty, it was a practical custom by the last quarter of the eighteenth century to varnish painted interior woodwork, which could then, on wearing, be revarnished, thus preserving the paint.

Scientific analysis has shown over and over again the endurance of early paint work. Before the rather arbitrary date of 1870, a house of, say, 1800 might have had its woodwork repainted only once or twice; for the century after 1870, the microscopic cross-section may reveal twenty or more coats. In scraping the surfaces, one finds the old paint to be harder to penetrate than that which is recent. But for all the beauty of the old, entertain no notion that to uncover it is easy. It is a monumental task, and of course you never know how much of the old coat survives until that level is wholly revealed. Sometimes samples can be found still exposed in attics, cellars, closets, and the troughs into which interior blinds fold back, as well as the surfaces revealed when shelves, curtain and light fixtures, and other later additions are removed.

Plaster walls are usually more troublesome for the paint analyst than those of wood, if only because plaster in old houses has sometimes been replaced. The only recourse then is to try to find small pieces that escaped the rubbish-gathering. Even when these survive and retain color, they may give no hint at all of what they represent. Likewise, even walls remaining intact, whether plaster or wood or any other material, hold mysteries that cannot be solved in absolute terms. The analysis may detect traces of glue and the material the glue originally attached; but after all, this merely indicates the presence of an applied wallcovering, certainly nothing about its appearance.

Wallpaper

If your only recourse is to finish the walling in some "typical" way, take every documented possibility into account. Paint is not the only recourse. Wallpaper, for example, may be the answer. It was probably known to seventeenth-century Americans, but it is believed to have been rather common even in middle-class houses in the eighteenth century. A growing variety of wallpaper was widely available in the nineteenth-century, even before the mass-production of cheap, machine-made papers in the 1840s, which made its use almost universal.

On plaster walls the paper was often butt-pasted directly upon the surface. Wooden walls were covered best when the paper was overlapped. While the paper was frequently pasted on or even tacked directly on the wood surface, the best result was achieved by tacking a layer of thin canvas—called in the eighteenth and nineteenth centuries "screening"—or other goods over the wall and pasting the paper onto that. Changes in the climate cause expansion and contraction in wooden walls that can and will tear paper unless the canvas is present to absorb the movement. Wooden walls furthermore present irregular surfaces. Plaster walls provide a flatter and more stable surface, so here the textile foundation was usually omitted. Hairline cracks and crude repairs in plaster were often concealed by wallpaper; paper has always been an inexpensive alternative to calling in the plasterer for a new white coat. Plaster walls that were intended at the outset to be papered were frequently not given the white coat at all, but were left at the scratch stage, just previous to the final coat, and finished off with wallpaper. On a first-class job, lining paper was sometimes used as a base layer, rather as a blotter, to absorb most of the moisture from the paste, so that when the outer wallpaper was applied it would stick but its colors would not run. Pastes were concocted by the paperhangers; they were thick, cooked substances, composed usually of a flour base, often mixed with alum, stale beer, or port wine.

As the general availability of wallpaper spread, the variety of designs naturally multiplied. Before the late nineteenth century, wallpaper patterns, in most situations, carried few of the connotations of suitability we associate with them today. "Bedroom paper," "dining-room paper," and most such designations were apparently unknown in the eighteenth century, although there are references to "parlor paper" and "hall paper." We find mention of color, insofar as a customer ordering paper in a letter might specify a paper in blue or green or another primary color already present in his room. But while some ideas of suitability clearly existed, they cannot be taken as rules, certainly outside the upper class, until well after the middle of the nineteenth century.

Our strict classification of appropriateness in wallpaper design seems to be the product merely of generations of use. After the mid-nineteenth century, cheap, mass-produced papers tended to perpetuate the simpler, more informal patterns—the little flowers, the pinstripes, geometric shapes, ribbons, all in fewer colors. Richer designs ordinarily characterized the more expensive wallpapers: they were well into current style motifs, bolder and more formal, even architectural. These papers were of heavier stock, boasted variety in color and tone, and were sometimes embossed or flocked. That a better paper would be desired for public spaces—the main hall, parlor, dining room—is not surprising, nor is the use of cheap papers in bedrooms, sitting rooms, and the like. Quite possibly these economic considerations made us, through custom, arrive at what we take for granted about suitability in wallpaper designs today. Before the 1880s the distinctions were not so clearly drawn.

The co-ordination of the design of wallpaper with the other decorative elements in the room seems to have had little meaning before the middle of the nineteenth century, and even then, careful co-ordination as we know it today, including color-tone, was not the rule. Wallpaper served the decorative purpose of giving pattern to blank walls; it could also, in solid color, make a rough wall appear smooth and soft. Wallpaper was not necessarily an aspect of a studied ensemble but could be seen as a thing unto itself. Often old construction contracts specified that the builder would provide "paper of suitable quality" for the rooms of the unfinished house. One might suppose

32 that in such cases the wallpaper was ordered sight unseen, and perhaps the painter then mixed his colors to complement it.

In any event, a painter could always make an adjustment to the paper itself, after it was on the wall, if the color did not suit. Benjamin Franklin wrote to his wife from London in 1767: "Paper the walls blue & tack the gilt border round just above the surbase and under the Cornish. If the paper is not equal Colored when pasted on, let it be brush'd over again with the same colour . . . I think it will look well."

From the 1790s until after the War of 1812, French papers were the best papers used in America. English papers appeared again in America with the flood of British products that came after the war. Both the English and the French produced papers superior to those made in the United States, but the French paper, in the magnificence of its colors alone, excelled all others. Whatever the origin of available papers, and despite the broad area of wallpaper's use, the selection was relatively small before the triumph of the wallpaper machine in the 1840s.

Before the development in the early nineteenth century of machines for making "endless" wallpaper lengths, wallpaper was printed on rectangular sheets that varied in size according to the dimensions of the mould in which the paper was made. These sheets or "pieces" were painted all over with a "ground" color, over which the designs were stamped with woodblocks, using tempera paint. A different block was required for each color. Although the manufacturing process for making endless paper on rollers was developed in the first decade of the nineteenth century, the hand-made "pieces" were still well in evidence in the 1830s.

In 1841 the English perfected a steam-powered mechanism for printing endless wallpaper by rolling wooden cylinders over the length of the paper. The surfaces of the cylinders were cut back, leaving the design standing up like a cookie-cutter. The design was in turn packed with felt which, saturated with paint, made a solid imprint when rolled over the paper. Two colors required two rollers. This development of roller printing was the basis of the later sophisticated techniques for the mass-manufacturing of wallpaper.

By the late 1840s Americans could choose from a wide variety of wallpapers at mercantile establishments. Within twenty years the selection became so extensive that the average customer, with nearly limitless options, could find wallpaper suitable to his most sensitive decorating scheme. This particular situation, unknown before the 1870s, is still the case today.

When an actual wallpaper is documented as having been in a certain room in the time you wish to represent, and it is gone, you have a mandate to reproduce it, although your budget may make that a goal for the distant future. If an original paper still clings to the walls, by all means leave it; to justify replacing it with a copy, the paper must be so far gone as to be indistinguishable. Wood-pulp papers—as opposed to the more enduring rag-pulp papers—began to rise to domination in this country after the mid-1850s. If this is what survives on your walls, it is likely to be discolored to a dark brown. Be reluctant to remove it; its present inadequacies can certainly be explained.

Too often restorers purchase or commission costly reproductions of papers that have no documentary relevance to their house or locale. The money would sometimes best be spent on other things. When the particular pattern of the original is not known, and there are no likely documents from similar houses in the area, you are free to consider more economical solutions. Inexpensive modern papers reproduced from old patterns can sometimes suffice very well. Be certain that the original document was a paper, not a fabric. Prior to hanging the paper, check the colors. Some have probably been altered to suit modern tastes and may need to be retinted by hand. Use tempera for papers before about 1850 and watercolor for the mass-produced papers thereafter. For the ambitious and talented, simple patterns can be reproduced through hand silk-screening or the old techniques of wood-block or roll printing. Properly done, these processes give that conciseness and variety of color found in early papers but not possible to achieve through the rapid silk-screening process of commercial wallpaper manufacture—and, alas, most "reproductions"—today.

Borders were mentioned practically every time wallpaper was advertised, as early as the eighteenth century and as late as the twentieth. A number of borders are produced by wallpaper companies today, and while the broad and elaborate ones, with fruit, swags, architectural elements, and so on, usually need work in the area of color, some of the simpler ones can be used much as they are. A familiar practice throughout the first half of the nineteenth century was to use one or several borders; usually in rich colors, these were, at their plainest, merely narrow strips in contrasting color or colors. Plain or figured, these borders were pasted in various configurations around mantels, doors and windows, along the tops of baseboards and chair rails. They were pasted directly onto the paper that covered the whole walls, a practice that must have pleased the paperhanger, for he was thus released from having to fit the background paper so exactly against the ceiling and architectural elements, realizing that any irregularities would be covered by the border.

From about the 1830s, perhaps a little earlier, until the late nineteenth century, manufacturers produced both "velvet" and glazed paper borders, which in solid colors can be approximated today by cutting flocked or glossy paper into strips and either leaving the outer edge straight or cutting it in some ornamental outline, copied from an actual document.

As late as the 1880s both solid and decorated borders and combinations of the two were used frequently to enrich a room's formal architectural character; borders were applied in long panels on the walls, which sometimes framed colors or patterns different from the background. With care the effect can be recreated out of modern solid-color papers using, for example, a sea-green field with maroon or very reddish pink borders edged in an almost black-green.

Still, if your room is of the 1870s or as late as about 1895, you are frankly in trouble trying to work with modern papers. There was a span of time, roughly from the late 1860s until the turn of the century, when wallpaper enjoyed enormous popularity and was used nearly everywhere. Made for ceilings and walls alike, the majority of it was the machine-produced kind, with few colors and small repeats. Beginning in the 1870s there were inventive textures in pressed pasteboard, rubbery oil compounds, and *papier maché* imitating morocco which were still available in the 1920s. At the other end of the popular scale was the so-called oatmeal paper, the mottled design of which was inherent in the rag composition of the paper. Oatmeal paper, produced first in the 1830s, was the cheapest kind and was used by all classes. It found special preference among the Victorians; yet it was used into our own century for halls, closets, and ceilings. Except for an occasional small floral pattern and reproductions of the designs of such exceptional wallpaper designers as William Morris, Victorian wallpaper patterns, and even more so the colors, find little acceptance among the manufacturers today. For the years prior to the Victorian decades, and for the twentieth century, the problem is not nearly so great, because in this century there has been an interest not only in "period" wallpapers as compo-

34 nents of expensive "traditional" interiors, as well as a continuing popular attraction to "colonial" quaintness in the decorative accoutrements of ordinary houses.

Some approximations of Victorian papers, then, do exist, but they lose much more in translation and are harder to adapt than those from other times. What is more, you are likely to need for your Victorian house several patterns in one room, following the popular custom of using sets of papers for dado, field, and ceiling frieze or dropped border, as well as perhaps a ceiling pattern. These combinations were sensitively co-ordinated, according to ideas of both contrast and harmony, on the basis of color, texture, and design. By mixing glossy and solid papers—which because of color may need to be simulated using paint—with patterned papers, you may put together an adequate combination of your own. The odds, however, are against you. If a solid paper or a palette of colors in solids will not suffice, you will probably have to seek out a document to copy, or resort to another solution.

Fabric Wallcoverings

Fabric wallcoverings have never been much used in modest houses, at least for ornamental purposes. In his *Rural New England Inventories, 1675–1775*, Abbott Lowell Cummings notes that he found "very occasional" references to fabric wall hangings in seventeenth-century New England houses. In hot climates, where plaster is likely to hold moisture and rot, cheap cloth was in the late eighteenth and nineteenth centuries sometimes laid on the walls before the scratch coat of the plaster quite dried. The cloth was then painted. It is documented that in Galveston, Texas, in the late 1850s frame houses were ceiled with cotton domestic, which was stretched over the studding and sometimes also the ceiling joists; an example of this survives inland from the Texas Gulf Coast at Austin, in an old frame cottage of the mid-1840s known as the French Legation. Anglo-Americans in Santa Fe in the second half of the nineteenth century stretched cotton cloth over the ceiling joists of Mexican-style houses, to protect the rooms below from siftings from the dirt roofs.

Decorative fabrics were seldom used as wallcoverings in any American houses before the late nineteenth century. There is the well-known red damask placed some years ago on the walls of the eighteenth-century parlor at Gunston Hall in Virginia; leather, though not a fabric, is clearly documented as having covered the walls of the Middle Room upstairs at the Governor's Palace in Williamsburg. There is otherwise little documentation for such coverings until a period beginning in the late 1860s, through to the century's end, when old photographs show the presence of damask, satin, silk, velvet, tapestry, and even chintz on the walls of some fashionable urban houses.

Even so, fabric wallcovering seems not to have been particularly desired before the mid-1880s, and it was not an important feature of stylish interior decoration until the twentieth century. Fabric wallcoverings really came to the fore with the great interest in "European" interiors that accompanied the late nineteenth-century revival of interest in neo-Classicism in architecture. On a costly, though not a high-style level, an example of its use was in the Blue Room of the White House as redecorated in the "Colonial" style by President McKinley in the late 1890s. Here wide panels of figured silk brocade were set along the walls in deep frames of ornamental plaster. Several years later, in 1902, the New York architectural firm of McKim, Mead & White completely remodeled the White House for Theodore Roosevelt and covered the walls of the Red, Blue, and Green rooms in sombre tones of tightly stretched silk, with classical borders appliqued.

Through the twentieth-century decades of big houses, which ran until about World War II, fabric wallcoverings enjoyed a certain heyday that was not to reappear until our own time, when simulated fabrics in vinyl were introduced. Covering walls with rich fabrics such as silk was never a common practice, even in mansions, any more than it is today. Certainly before the time of climate control it was grossly impractical, as it could not be removed for the hot months, and it was hard to clean, being stiffened with sizing and accessible only from one side. Of the several techniques for cleaning fabric wallcovering, the most prevalent seems to have been to wipe the surface in long strokes with chamois, which was replaced when it got soiled.

The nearest a fabric wallcovering came to being used in a popular way was with burlap. Natural, dyed, or painted burlap was widely used from about the 1890s until the early 1920s, often above a wooden or plaster dado, which might be covered with Lincrusta-Walton or another heavily embossed wallcovering in imitation of fancy plaster or morocco. The burlap was available specifically for use as wallcovering and was hung much as wallpaper, with paste, and butted. It was practical, and it provided the desired texture and "warmth" current taste dictated. The same companies that produced it sometimes also manufactured lines of painted canvas wallcoverings; these varied from stenciled and embossed designs in oil paint featuring a plain field with a running border, geometrical or with stylized fruit and flowers, to long panels adorned with pink roses, cherubs, doves, nymphs, and the like, and intended to be set into panels of wood or plaster. By World War I there was not a town in the United States too remote to have access to such mail-ordered fabric wallcoverings.

Painted Walls

The finishing of plaster and wooden walls still seems to have been as often as not accomplished through painting, particularly before the mass-production of wallpaper began

in the 1840s. Even when the paint has been stripped from wood walls—a popular thing to do to old wood in the 1940s and 1950s—the careful sleuth can usually find a paint trace hidden away somewhere. When plaster has been cut out and replaced, it is probable that all of it was not thrown away, that some fell between the studs in the wall or clung tenaciously behind a mantel. If the present plaster walling is not to be removed, these renegade fragments will probably remain unknown, and unless you are fortunate enough to find a section of old plaster that was incorporated into the new, you must make hypothetical decisions about painting your walls.

Paint colors are simply too numerous to attempt to discourse upon here. The absence of specific evidence on your walls naturally suggests paint research elsewhere in the region, to discover colors actually known to your area in a more or less given time. It takes no expert to know that coloration is a very exacting matter. When an old volume tells us that the popular straw color of the 1820s is made from mixing whiting with yellow ochre or Dutch pink, and a dash of Venetian red, it does not really tell us much. There were commercial producers of paint in the United States in the eighteenth century, but not until the 1870s, when ready-mixed paints began to gain public favor, did the manufacturers begin to publish chips as samples of their wares. For the first three-quarters of the nineteenth century most painters bought their colors as dry powder or in solid form, which they ground, then mixed their paint according to any number of methods they had learned as apprentices. So your best sources for color lie in the scientific analysis of painted surfaces that survive.

Decorative painting on walls seems to have been far more familiar in American houses even in the first half of the eighteenth century than we often realize. At first mention of the term, "decorative painting" implies full-scale scenes and elaborate ornamentation perhaps more than it should. Decorative painters more

36   often created effects to enhance a room's architectural character. It is safe to say that in the United States, prior to World War I, most painters were decorative painters of sorts. That is, most knew how to pull and wiggle feathers and brushes and blend colors to achieve the look of marble; and most could create borders freehand or with stencils. While these particular effects were common for a century and a half in American houses, the demand was greater for different techniques at different times. And some painters were naturally more talented at certain of these techniques than others.

The anonymous painter who decorated the wood-paneled parlor at Marmion in King George County, Virginia, in the 1770s marbled the pilasters and painted flower-filled urns, leafy swags, and scenes on the flat surfaces. Whether he was an itinerant, just passing through, or a local resident, his presence and his ability to do such work are doubtless what inspired the owner to commission the decorating, for the room had already existed some thirty years without it. The same must certainly have applied to the modest interiors of the house of the tanner and tavern keeper John Jay French near Beaumont, Texas; here the painting, dating from about 1850, is simple in every respect, but for its brilliant colors: there are off-white walls, with ceilings and simulated baseboards in bright blue, all executed with the most sensitive brushwork, save the doors, which are crudely grained in several browns to suggest mahogany. Availability is always a determining factor. This is not to say that Mr. French would have commissioned murals, had a painter appeared who could do them; nor does it assume that Marmion's owner would have preferred something plain to what he got. But it does say to you that, in making hypothetical decisions about the treatment of your interiors, do not drift too far into the broad general field of decorative arts for inspiration, any more than you would

wholly abandon local history in your interpretation in favor of only national or world themes. Keep your anchor down.

For later houses, post-Civil War, you can resort to known sources when considering decorative painting. Some regions are known to have had ambitious free-hand wall decorators, and willing customers, but the painters of the second half of the nineteenth century and the first decade and a half of the twentieth ordinarily worked with stencils, to achieve an exactness of line similar to that in printed wallpaper designs. These stencils they either bought or cut for themselves, frequently using published patterns. By and large their designs were also in imitation of wallpaper, as borders or over-all patterns. As wallpaper, ever cheaper, grew in common use it was unfortunately very often necessary to scrape down or wash away existing painted wall decorations to assure a secure and flat base before the paper could be applied.

Wherever there were painters there was certain to be the availability of decorated walls, and they were executed in public and private buildings alike. The dark, rich colors of the Victorian decades were achieved better by painters than in all but the most expensive wallpapers. The dull finish that the "distemper" paint (glue, water, pigment) gave to walls provided the desired contrast to the shiny glaze of the varnished oil paint on the woodwork. What was more, walls decorated with paint seemed more organic to the materials of the house than did paper.

Although you may wish to take what seems to be the easy way out and paint your walls solid colors, you cannot rest assured that you are historically correct. Plain colored walls knew times of fashion, but as research deepens, the presence of decorated walls becomes more evident. Perhaps it stands to reason that if in the course of having an interior painted you could have the painter beautify parts of it with decoration, you would probably do it. This could mean, in 1830, "sanding" the walls by puffing sand over the wet paint, or mixing sand in the paint before it was applied, then scoring the walls while still wet to resemble ashlar; in 1840 it could mean picking out the elements of the crown molding in various colors and shades, including gilt; in 1890 it could mean stencilling an over-all pattern, then flocking the wet paint with cotton or linen lint; or at practically any time it could mean simply the framing of the architectural elements of the room with a free-hand pinstripe to give them importance, as one would outline a figure in a drawing.

Other Wall Finishes

For all the appeal of decorated walls and wallpapers, it must not be forgotten that many walls had very simple finishes or no finishes at all. This does not apply only to modest houses. Accomplished plasterers were familiar with a technique for creating a very smooth and uniform, marblelike surface that was meant to be left uncovered. This was done while the final or white coat was still slightly moist, and it involved sprinkling the surface with water and rubbing it to a polish with pumice stone. A well-executed plaster finish was beautiful to see. Many an interior in both town and country went a long time without paint on its walls, and some survive unpainted today, either exposed, or beneath later wallpaper. In all localities it was considered wise for the owner to allow the plaster to dry for at least one full year before paint or paper was applied. While this was not always followed, particularly by contractors building on speculation, it indicates that bare walls were not unfamiliar and that their decoration must sometimes have been attended to long after the house was finished and occupied.

In the eighteenth and nineteenth centuries, whitewash was used on interior walls, particularly in the country, where its use prevailed

until well into the twentieth century. Whitewash, though used practically everywhere on ceilings before the 1870s, when white ceilings fell into popular disfavor, was also widely applied to walls and tinted. It was usually kept stark white. Whitewash could be made cheaply at home, and one of its virtues was that it discouraged mildew. But it eventually flaked, and because of its coarse, irregular texture, it was never really satisfactory as paint. Where whitewash was used on interior walls it was usually applied to plaster and was, ideally, refreshed every year. The woodwork of the room would then be painted with oil paint and probably varnished. There were modest houses, of course, in which the whole interior, wood and all, was whitewashed, but this is certain to have been either because of isolation, as on a frontier, or the lack of money to have something better.

The likelihood of your using actual old paint formulas in restoring your interior paint is scant. Documented colors can be approximated in modern paints; a simulated whitewash is available commercially, or can be created by thickening white paint with a vehicle for texture. It would be best, of course, to compose your paint as it was done in the appropriate time in the past. Barring that, insist that in its application the paint resemble the work as it would have been. The texture is very important to the final effect. Where you discover evidence of graining or marbling, copy the original sufficiently to recapture the particular type it was; where it was crude it should be crude in reproduction, for as with all painted surfaces, the *manner* in which it was executed is quite as important as the fact that it was done in the first place.

Floors

The question of floors seems a simple matter. Yet the foul practices of restorationists make it a major one. Those who restore

38 American houses seem to wait in eager antici-
pation for that moment when the heavy sanding machines roll in to peel the floors to abject
nakedness, and utter flatness, whereupon one
of any number of tawdry finishes then renders
them "beautiful." There are two kinds of
wooden floors: those which are hardwood,
such as oak, hickory, walnut; and those of
softwoods, such as pine, ash, poplar.
Hardwood floors do not suffer so much from
sanding. But with softwoods, sanding can
bring disaster, not only because it eats deeply
into the wood, but because it cuts away
the tough sealer time and use have created on
the surface.

Hardwoods and Softwoods

Very few eastern or southern houses seem to
have had hardwood floors before the 1870s.
But before that decade, from Wisconsin west-
ward, since softwood was not available, the
hardwoods, hickory, chestnut, and walnut,
were the predominant materials for flooring.
Black walnut flooring was favored for very expensive houses in many areas from the mid-
1850s until the later 1870s, and was often
meant to be at least partially exposed. The
popular taste for all-over carpeting gradually
began to yield in the seventies to a new preference for large rugs and carpet sizes that left
the floor showing around the edges. The fashion for exposed flooring was slow in taking
hold, for Americans were long familiar with
the comforts of all-over carpeting. As the carpeting trend developed, so did the interest in
hardwood, and among the hardwoods oak rose
to predominance. The love of pattern found
expression in parquetry, at first a luxury for
the few, then by the 1880s, though still a luxury, available to many in inexpensive prefab-
ricated "parquets." Those were veneered
squares and lengths made to be glued down
on canvas over a subflooring. One of the usual
ways to spruce up an old house, before the

later "colonial" craze beginning in the 1920s
for "old pine" floors, was to lay hardwood
flooring over the earlier pine. This was done in
countless houses for the sake of appearance,
durability, and insulation. Where that was not
done, the pine floors were usually either
stained or painted—sometimes only on the
part that showed outside the floor covering.
And occasionally one finds a pine floor that
has been cut out for several feet around the
sides of a room and replaced with hardwood,
which would then serve as an exposed border
framing the large rug that concealed the remaining pine at the center.

Coloring for hardwood floors can be a problem. In the Victorian decades a great issue was
made of color, and particularly that on parquetry. Your paint analyst can probably determine the original colors, unless the
floors have been thoroughly stripped. If this is
the case, and you have parquetry, you are ad-
vised to adopt a stain-and-varnish scheme
from one of the flooring catalogues of the
period. Where there is no parquetry, the
hardwood was nearly always of one color,
sometimes light, sometimes dark, although occasionally the boards were alternated light and
dark.

The chances are that the finish will have to
be restored to your hardwood floors. If the
floors were not greatly lightened to yellow, or
even mildly bleached in the 1920s and 1930s,
or stained a very dark walnut color after World
War II, they are probably discolored by dead
varnish and dirt. Unless that has an appealing
look of old age that is worthy of preservation,
proceed with cleaning the wood. Paint and
varnish remover must be used in stripping the
thin, manufactured parquetry, and it is best,
though not always an absolute, for other
hardwood surfaces.

Ideally, a softwood floor, we have said already, was hidden beneath a floor covering of
some kind. Left bare, it splintered, it wore,
and it scarred. But before the advent of mass-

produced carpeting, particularly ingrains in the 1840s, most American floors seem to have been left uncovered. Nearly all were probably bare in the eighteenth century, and only after the War of 1812, really into the 1820s, do carpets and floorcloths begin to appear with some frequency in middle-class inventories. A floor covering remained a luxury to most people; floor coverings will be discussed in some detail later on. What concerns us at this point is what to do with softwood floors in historic houses, for being so often exposed in the past, their treatment in restoration will play a significant part in the effect of the completed historical room.

A house restored to, say, 1885 or 1910 or 1936 is likely to have its pine flooring painted, stained, varnished, or simply sealed with linseed oil. All those treatments have been well known for the past three-quarters of a century. If your house is to be restored to a time earlier than that, and you have pine floors that bear only the marks of age and use, count yourself the possessor of a document; leave them untouched. Alas, the situation is usually otherwise.

The restoration of softwood floors creates difficulties from the point of view of maintenance. Flooring of any kind was rarely varnished or stained, prior to the Victorians' attraction to those practices, and this is particularly true of pine, which was considered purely utilitarian. In the eighteenth and nineteenth centuries softwood floors were sometimes painted; few examples survive, but there are written references to their existence, and painted floors appear now and then in old paintings. When the floors were not painted in a solid color, they, like painted walls, were given stenciled or freehand designs, in imitation of richly figured wood, marble, tile, or, more often, carpeting. Fancy-painted floors must always be considered exceptional; they had to be constantly touched up and revarnished, and certainly by the 1820s the avail-

ability of ready-made floorcloths and carpeting must have made them almost obsolete.

There were other ways of treating softwood floors; for example, rubbing them with clay or brick-dust. Sometimes sand was kept sprinkled over floors; it helped smooth the surface, and ground out dirt. But by far the most common way to treat pine floors was simply to scrub them from time to time with lye-water. The lye, obtained by boiling wood-ashes, was natural to the material and worked as a cleanser and a sealer. When new, the floors were bright, close to white, and with age they darkened usually to a grayish-brown color— the combination of dirt and repeated scrubbing. Sometimes in better houses floors were oiled or waxed or both, but apparently not often. Today's finishes that make floors look like table tops were unknown, even in approximation.

When the use of floor coverings in a house is documented, replace them in some way. Softwood floors will thus be easier to contend with; otherwise, with heavy visitor traffic in prescribed patterns, paths will eventually begin to appear. In this case you are presented with the need for a sealer that will not interfere with the bare look of the floors, yet will protect them. Again, any stripping that is done should only follow the most serious considerations pro and con. It may well be that the floors, albeit lacking the bright, scrubbed surfaces they once had, should merely be waxed on top of what is there. Where there will be floor covering, as all-over carpeting, they can be left beneath the covering as they are. Stripping absolutely must be done with paint and varnish remover; it is slower, but does far less damage, and will not destroy the ripples years of wear have made in the surface. Leave the remover on the wood as briefly as possible; hand-sanding is permissible in tough spots. After stripping, scrub the floors with mild lye-water several times, allowing it to dry after each application, and if the need for strong protection

40 appears, which it may, coat them in the appropriate places with a clear, flat sealer. Continued light waxing of the areas where traffic is heaviest can serve the same purpose, although some experimentation should precede this to make certain that the wax causes no discoloration. Either way, you will lose some of the effect the original floor would have had.

Stone, Brick, and Marble Flooring

Before the mid-nineteenth century, floors of stone and brick were usually laid tightly without mortar on a bed of clean sand. The floor was then spread with more sand, which, when walked upon, ground and thus toughened and even slightly smoothed the elements and eventually worked its way into the cracks separating them, further securing all parts as a united whole. Sand continued to be applied for purposes of cleaning and absorbing moisture. In basements and ground-floor rooms where brick and stone floors are most often found, drainage problems that we today solve with drains and sump pumps were further justification for laying the floor in a bed of sand. Even within the foundation wall itself, various simple means were devised to allow for seepage beyond the exterior walls of the house. Plaster walls did not usually extend behind the baseboard; the baseboard intervened between the plaster and the floor. Otherwise the plaster (or even vertical wood sheathing) would induce capillary attraction for any moisture that might collect on, in, or below the floor. The practice was not restricted to basements but was the same in rooms above the ground, for the walls needed protection from water when the floors were scrubbed. Baseboards were, in fact, known as *washboards*, a term that seems to have died out with the practice of scrubbing floors.

Floors of hard materials were sometimes built up on a foundation comprised of a curtain wall filled with earth and sand. The material was then laid as though it were being put directly upon the ground. Marble was often done this way on porches; but marble, being subject to water-damage, and being a costly material, was probably more often laid over a very strong wooden framework or supported upon brick or stone vaulting. The marble pavers were cemented down and together, then the surface was kept polished, so as to make the most of its color and figuring. In the early nineteenth century, marble was cleaned with strong soap and powders of fuller's earth and pipe-clay. Today there are commercial cleaners for marble, but strong soap and hot water, applied with stiff brushes, will usually suffice. The marble should not be repolished, if to do so requires cutting the old surface; and because of possible breakage, resetting should be avoided if at all possible.

Tile

Ceramic tile flooring, lighter in weight than either brick, stone, or marble, was first imported to and later manufactured in the United States. There are a few instances of very early tile floors in the United States, but the vast majority of them fall between about 1865 and the 1930s, with of course the revived interest in recent years. Tile for flooring first became popular in the late 1860s after the introduction of encaustic tiles by British manufacturers. *Encaustic* refers to the mass-manufacturing technique of applying color to tile with heat and wax, a method adapted from ancient encaustic painting, hence the name. The dull-finish encaustic tiles, best known in earthy browns and ochre and in deep reds and bright blue, were relatively inexpensive and provided colorful and practical flooring. They were commonly set in geometrical patterns and were fashionable for halls, conservatories, bathrooms, kitchens, and any other areas where the floors were likely to need frequent cleaning. While the name *encaustic* was applied nearly universally

Victorian flooring and floor covering: encaustic tiles in the vestibule, with Brussels carpeting in the hall beyond, at the Leland Stanford House, Sacramento, California, photo 1871. —*California State Library*

to tiles set in ornamental patterns, it was actually more or less a trade name for the time-saving means of manufacture. The luxury market still provided a wide range of ceramic tiles that were not in fact encaustic.

The most popular use of tile flooring in America was for hearths; tile hearths and tile fireplace facings were used nearly everywhere in the last quarter of the nineteenth century. Tile was also widely employed as wainscoting in vestibules, kitchens, and so on. In the early 1880s glazed earthenware tiles began to rival the earlier dull-finish material and by 1900 had superseded it. These were sometimes decorated with transfer-printed scenes and figures,

but seem usually to have been in solid or mottled colors, often featuring a design in relief, such as a cherub or a flower.

When tiles survive intact, they are simple to clean and regrout. But survival is seldom the case, for settlement and dead grout, together with hard use, take their toll. Whether decorated in designs or solid color, the tiles are practically impossible to replace without resorting to specially commissioned reproductions. Should reproducing them at the outset be impossible because of the cost, leave your tiles as they are, however cracked and snaggle-toothed. Allow no more than the safety measure of pointing them up and leveling off the areas where tiles are missing with solid color tile or cement, when it is absolutely necessary. Realize that if you attempt to remove the tiles from the floor or the fireplace facing, you will probably lose many of them, and thus be worse off than when you started.

Earth Floors

Where dirt floors were used, they were packed hard and swept until a tough surface developed. Sometimes one finds references to their being oiled. When the liquid dried, it helped harden the floor. In Spanish and Mexican days in the West, the Latin settlers brought with them the custom of soaking the floor in animal blood, and there are also references to whitewashing hardened dirt. The impracticality of resurrecting these methods in a house museum are clear, particularly since the space is likely to be small, as in a cabin, an outbuilding, or a basement room. Colored concrete has been resorted to, its effectiveness sometimes mildly enhanced by a light scattering of sand. Canvas is a possibility, laid on a subflooring and painted some dirt-color, with abundant sand cast into the wet paint. Neither of these solutions is ideal, but unless the rooms can be seen only through doors and windows, or you are willing to build a dis-

42 tracting ramp, the visiting public will keep your floors so chopped up with their modern high-heeled and hard-soled shoes that the effect of old packed-dirt floors will be virtually impossible to maintain.

Modernizing

Before the actual restoration or reproduction work begins on the interior walls and floors, you will install such electrical outlets, heating and air-conditioning equipment, fire prevention and burglar alarm systems as seem necessary. Somehow these mechanical wonders always detract from a house museum that is supposed to represent an era when they were unknown. Heating systems original to mid-nineteenth-century and later houses can be adapted for use and become an integral part of the interpretation. Yet Victorian ventilation systems do not fulfill our idea of air-conditioning, so you will probably install a frankly modern system for summer. Forced-air heating systems can often be reworked modestly to serve both for heat and cooling. Hot-water systems cannot. There are circumstances where the equipment necessary for climate control ruins the historical quality of a building. The smaller and simpler the house, the more serious this becomes; modernizing may involve the virtual sacrifice of any feeling of authenticity so much that the equipment should not be installed.

Climate control is believed today to be essential to the preservation of old materials and finishes. In accepting that, also realize that it makes little sense to destroy or deface original parts of the building in the process of installing climate control machinery or any other equipment. Cutting plaster to make room for an air register is perhaps necessary; but say the plaster has an early wallpaper or fresco—is cutting into it then justifiable? Certainly not. Other means must be found. Unfortunately, many restored houses that have fine climate-control equipment are not equally endowed with the human expertise to operate it properly. Fabrics dry-rot and panelling splits. Some of the worst deterioration seems to take place in our age of protective interior climates than was known before, when people opened windows and performed other acts that now, in a museum context, are seldom done.

If the systems must make their intrusions, be certain that they will be managed as they should be, and that they operate twenty-four hours a day. Climate control in a museum is for the preservation of historical materials, not for human comfort during visiting hours. Before the system is decided upon, have a fair knowledge of what it is likely to cost to operate. Will you be able to pay the monthly bills?

Most restoration groups cannot afford the most expensive and advanced equipment and will be content with central heating and air-conditioning, with a humidifier, and in some regions, a dehumidifier. Air pollution and our modern demands for creature comforts make it hard for even purist restorationists to agree that the house should not have, if it did not originally have, any climate control at all. Furthermore, your house will probably have no fulltime resident. Even if someone lives there, he is unlikely to perform the daily adjustment of curtains and blinds, the building of fires, the rituals of caring for objects that were a part of life in the original house, before the days of climate control. You may deem it educational and a challenge to organize volunteers or staff to do those things. At best, however, they can accomplish only some of them; and still the house will be cold when the weather is cold, and hot when it is hot. Some have tried to make a house "live" accordingly, and the experience is delightful, in pleasant months. A certain recourse is to close the house during uncomfortable times of the year. But this has its drawbacks, too: in restoring the house as a museum for public education, you have made a commitment, and the house must be accessible to the public.

When planning for air-conditioning and central heating, listen to your engineers. Extraordinary—and sometimes unnecessary—contrivances to hide registers and ducts can obstruct the system's effectiveness. If the system cannot work efficiently, why have it, in the first place? You will obviously not permit the building of a duct in the corner of a room that is important in your interpretation; certainly registers do not belong over mantelpieces, or boldly set in the middle of a wall or beside an important architectural element. Neither will they be operative behind a bookcase or under a rug. These considerations you will be aware of, but you must also be willing to compromise. It may be that a room in some location strategic to the technology of the system can be removed from the interpretive function, and given the ductwork necessary to serve the other rooms. Lacking closets and other convenient locations for ducts, you are better off to lose a secondary room or even two than to disfigure spaces essential to your interpretation.

Any air system will require registers of some kind and probably return-air vents. Up to a point you can minimize their presence by putting them in the floor or making thin incisions in the ceiling or over the doors. Registers are always unwelcome, unless they can be fitted into the fixtures of an original heating system. When they are concealed in the chimney flue, you lose the fireplace for anything but its appearance, and one could question whether the loss merits the gain. If you must have climate control, you must accept registers as a fact of life. Keep them off the walls and ceilings if you can, preferably placing them in the floor. The room's cool temperature in July will make visitors scan about in search of the source of the chill; when the room is warm in January, with no flame on the hearth, the same curiosity is aroused. You will never really hide registers.

Electrical switches can be located unobtru-

sively without burying them in little covered boxes in the walls or hiding them behind doors. Central switchboards where the lights are all controlled in one spot are usually a dreadful inconvenience, though they serve a purpose for security. You must in any case have switches in the rooms, if electric lighting is used. If the switches need to be hidden, place them low on the walls, about twenty-eight inches from the floor, immediately beneath a chair rail or near the frame of a door. They will usually go unnoticed. Paint them to match the surface in which they are installed. Switches can also be set into the side of the frame of the doorway, against the wall, though it involves cutting into the woodwork. If the baseboards will be painted or stained dark, place the wallplugs in them; if not, sink the outlets into the floor and provide them with protective caps when not in use.

Electricity is, of course, very necessary to the museum house. One of its lesser purposes is for lighting, when you weigh that against its value in climate control, security systems, and simplified means of housecleaning. Illumination is the area, ironically, in which electricity most frequently intrudes on your efforts to create a historical ambience. It seems somehow comical to enter a restored room of, say, about 1820, that glows from the light of flamelike electric bulbs atop fake candles, then to note that the restorers have gone to extravagant lengths to hide the wires, cords, and switches. In adjusting your house to museum purposes, you will naturally resort to some deceptions in achieving the look of realism. But be cautious with your tricks. Things cleverly concealed or faked often draw attention to themselves more quickly than if they were left to be what they are.

The finished rooms at last are wired, or left wireless, climate-controlled or not; their surfaces are restored or preserved or both. Probably it is not, in its refreshed and protected state, the exact house it originally was. Your

44 research experience will make you sense that, and it may make you worry. The work yet to come must cover your necessary compromises, to fulfill the objectives of scholarly restoration. You have before you a vacant house, devoid perhaps of some of the romance that attracted you to it in the first place. The house is only a visual outline of what is to come. The outline will be expanded with material details of every kind into a historical essay.

5

About Furnishings

URNISHINGS means chairs, lamps, wood-boxes, curtains, bean pots, books—in short, anything more or less moveable that contributes to the liveability or beauty of life in the house. Rooms are containers for these things, in the course of being containers for people. For people do not live in rooms without objects, whether those objects be a prehistoric man's hunting implements in a cave, or the fancy appointments of a millwright's parlor of 1892. In historic houses, *furnishings* takes on the broadest meaning; the term also includes clothing, letters, the ubiquitous eyeglasses, and everything else that, though not furniture in the usual sense, enriches our understanding of how the house was used.

Furnishing a historic house successfully is more complicated than the restoration of the building itself. Structural investigation, paint analysis, and other detective work can unravel the mysteries of a house that has been changed beyond recognition; the original location of windows, the definition of spaces, the texture and the color can often be exactly documented, for at least traces of the substance are likely to have survived. This is hardly ever true of the interior furnishing. Even the most detailed inventories are not visual, and the survival of one or a dozen documented objects does not necessarily say much about how the room was as a whole. This is why so many historic houses have rooms furnished to represent styles in decorative arts. But there are other solutions.

The plan for furnishing the historical interior must evolve from the plan for historical interpretation. It is arrived at, furthermore, through a careful combination of specifics with historical generalities—both, of course, being

manifested in objects. This particular sort of mingling is always necessary when you re-create, for even when you are so fortunate that your specifics include most of the original furniture, you must still resort to generalities in deciding upon the other objects that will be used with it.

There are various kinds of specifics and various kinds of generalities. That your hall was once described as having a hall-tree is a specific, but also a generality, in that you know nothing about what the hall-tree looked like. Thus you will acquire a hall-tree of the appropriate date to *represent* the one that was there. Research may further indicate that most halls of comparable houses in the area also had

The room in use: Jefferson Davis's study in Biloxi, Mississippi, photographed in 1884 while he was writing his history of the Confederacy. —*National Archives*

46 a sofa, and the size of your hall suggests more furniture than merely the hall-tree. Then you acquire a sofa to *symbolize* the generality of most halls having sofas. The arrangement of furniture within rooms and the use of individual objects in the historic house is nearly always symbolic and must be determined through research and a careful accounting of historical possibilities, not whim.

In making the furnishings plan—which may or may not be "final," depending upon the availability of materials—you are doing what the interior decorator does when he commits his scheme for a room to paper. The difference is that the decorator's course is determined by his personal interpretation of an idea that may be his or his client's. Your course is guided from concept to completion by historical fact and implication. No matter the antiques he uses, the decorator's standards are those of the present; yours must be those of a past time and place.

You must seriously examine in terms of your own research any fixed visions you may have accumulated about what "period rooms" should look like, and be quite certain that your decisions are not influenced unduly by these. *Period rooms*, in the usual meaning of the term, are museum or other interiors of a historical type, in which the common denominator is style. This may be an eighteenth-century Philadelphia dining room furnished *en suite* with the similar works of one or two cabinetmakers, against a background of old Philadelphia paneling; or it may be a nineteenth-century Maine kitchen furnished with a great variety of kitchen wares. In any case, the prime purpose is to exhibit a type or types of decorative arts. Some of our best-known rooms are of this sort. But even if your rooms are of sufficient artistic merit, is the decorative arts story the one you want to tell? Will that story be strong and full enough to justify the rooms' existence? Very likely the answer is no. A large part of the historical room's vocabulary

lies in the province of decorative arts, yet the historical room should teach more than a lesson in that alone, even when it happens to be a splendid example of a style or type. Decorative arts should not appear to be the principal focus of life in your house—unless in fact it was.

Consider the rooms as they were or might have been by the time they were fully established, when they had come to fit the customs and habits of their occupants. This will usually mean that your rooms should appear to have developed piecemeal, instead of all at once. Thus they should show change within a certain span of existence, as rooms inevitably do, whether boldly through the addition of new objects and decoration, or subtly through a rearrangement of the same contents and changed patterns of use. A room of 1830, for example, lighted at the outset only with candles and oil lamps, would be greatly revised by 1850 with the addition of gas lighting, because this innovation created new possibilities in furniture arrangement. None of the furniture, however, might postdate 1830. Moreover, a family's fortunes may have changed; hard times may have left the rooms essentially incomplete: the "right" curtains never acquired, the old refrigerator never replaced. Money in another instance may have come along ten years later, at which time different circumstances and ideas of fashion made purchases for the house not at all what they would have been in the beginning.

By taking such historical questions into consideration, your rooms will lend themselves to varied interpretation. Contrast and incongruity are great tools of teaching. If your research has been done seriously, there are many historical perspectives from which the interiors can be seen. The interpretive versatility of the historical room is only as great as the human element the room represents. To evoke through room-settings the texture of life as it was lived in a particular place is a monumental task, the outcome of which boasts its successes or failures visually. The interiors may never really be as they originally were, and if they are you may have no way of ever knowing it.

Still, the well-executed interior, even lacking the specifics of what was known to have been there, is far more than a shot in the dark. Your background of research, with the resulting general and exacting theses, the objects catalogue, and the collections list, together with the vacant but otherwise finished rooms, provide rich raw materials and exciting ideas from which to develop, room by room, a plan for furnishing.

Begin by preparing sketch-plans and elevations of the rooms on graph paper. Cut out to scale in colored posterboard floor-outlines and elevations of any original furnishings from the house. On the graph plans and elevations, place these representations of your givens: if all you have, for example, are three framed engravings, place the scaled cut-outs representing them on one or more of the elevations. A wardrobe, on the other hand, is placed on both the plan and the elevation.

Following the items in the inventory, cut out in another color of posterboard approximate sizes for all the furniture mentioned, and assign these to the appropriate or probable room. Further list on a separate card for each room the transient objects—cups, bedclothing, books—which cannot be dealt with on the graphs. Reconcile original objects to those in the inventory. The result is that you have what is "in hand" differentiated by color from what is not. Your acquisition effort will be directed toward objects in the latter category. You will seek models in the objects catalogue— acquiring those if you can—and after exhausting that, from sources more remote. The graphs will more clearly focus your vision than mere guesswork in the empty room itself.

In the absence of an inventory and/or original objects, the synthesis of your research produces a hypothetical inventory. This will con- tain some givens and a wide variety of possibilities, which work with the graphs can help thin out. Make similar cut-outs of these furnishings in contrasting colors. With the givens in place, how much else do you need? There may be the decision between a clock or a mirror, a table or a lounge, a trunk or a chest; but these decisions, while you may have your preferences, might have to be determined by what becomes available. The usual rule is: the earlier the house, the less the quantity the better, except when you know otherwise for sure.

When there are old photographs taken at a relevant time, use these as you would a partial inventory. Only here, of course, you have, for as much as the camera's eye recorded, an image not only of some of the actual furnishings, but of their locations in the room. Even though the photograph may show only a vignette of the room, the transcription of this to the graphs using the cut-outs, sketches of rugs, pictures, curtains, lamps, and so on, will take you further along toward the completion of an accurate furnishings plan than any other source, for it will suggest actual ways of placing materials in the room.

Consider now the rooms themselves. Where and how does the light fall in them at different times of the day? Which were exposed to winter wind and which to the most summer sun? To what extent were they private from visitors and the daily life of the household? Or were they, like the "halls" in eighteenth-century American farmhouses, the centers of activity? What was their proximity to the kitchen, to the bedchambers, to the principal entrance, to the porch? Were they small and unpretentious, or, in the context of their time, grandiose? What does interior finishing do to play up or minimize a room's status among the other rooms? If the original use of the room is unknown, or varied, how and why did you arrive at this present designation, and what does it suggest about the way the room was lived in?

48   Many questions come to mind, but most particularly that of the room's original function. It is difficult to generalize on this subject, because while customs in room use follow certain patterns from time to time, they are also as likely to vary. We have been well accustomed in this century to rooms with specific uses—dining rooms, bedrooms, living rooms, "dens," and so on. This is largely a nineteenth-century phenomenon, which, though seen in the design of mansions early in the century, became known to any extent to the average family only in the Victorian decades.

It is true that house-planning, especially after the mid-eighteenth century, began to change toward the inclusion of more rooms and passages, creating more privacy. But old inventories demonstrate clearly that as late as the third quarter of the nineteenth-century, multiple uses of rooms remained in many instances the rule. Whether this is because the inventories reflect the habits of people too old to change their ways is not indicated.

Dining rooms, for example, often served also as sitting rooms; the same was usually true of at least one bedroom. Central passages sometimes contained sofas and chairs. The kitchen in a small northern house had also the communal function of the seventeenth- and eighteenth-century hall. In the South, where the kitchen, even of a small house, was likely to be in a completely separate structure from the main house, the communal room could be a bedroom, the dining room, or a parlor or sitting room in the winter, and the central passage or a porch in the summer. Furniture seems to have been moved about among rooms more than is customary today. And the configuration of furnishings within interior spaces was determined in a large degree by sunshine and shadow, by heat and cold, which is all the more reason for you to be very familiar with the "nature" of your rooms.

By the 1820s the use of rooms in urban houses of fashion and some of their suburban and rural counterparts, particularly in the East, would not surprise us very much. The double room, divided by "folding" doors, was the transition between the old multiple use of spaces and the new tendency toward rooms of more limited function. Double rooms normally contained the dining room at the rear and the parlor, or sometimes the library, in the front. Thus the dining room, the fireplace of which was lighted soon after that of the kitchen, became very warm during breakfast, and, when the doors were opened, shared its heat with the sitting room in front, where the fire was not begun or at least so advanced. For subsequent meals the process was reversed, with the dining room gaining warmth from the sitting room. The summertime saw double rooms equally convenient as places where the breeze could blow through the house uninterrupted, a special virtue in city houses, where there might be no porches.

In very large houses, and in many others toward mid-century, especially with the advent of central heating, the double rooms were both used as sitting rooms—that is, a formal parlor in front, and a less formal one or library to the rear. Apparently "double parlors," the term commonly used for those double rooms, does not describe the use of most of them. They rarely functioned as a pair of drawing rooms before the 1870s, and even then only in big and costly houses. Double rooms were obviously a great advantage for social and ceremonial occasions, when crowds were present. That must not, however, be considered their first purpose. Our modern eyes find it hard to accept a bulky dining room table or a bed in full view through a double doorway from the parlor, but that is often the way it was.

The largely nineteenth-century development of rooms as having single functions helped create a market for matching sets of furniture, which reflected the distinct functions of rooms. Matching suites of furniture, long associated in Europe with wealth, boasted a room's limited purpose quite as much as fair hands indicated a lady of leisure. And they were desired as any other marks of success by those with the money to afford them.

In America, though many early manufacturers such as Duncan Phyfe made suites for the parlors of the rich, the suite was not really available to the middle class much before the later 1840s. Within twenty years the "set" was a familiar package on the American market of mass-production, and its presence seems to have hurried along the demise of the multipurpose room wherever the size of the house and the pocketbook permitted. By the last fifteen years of the nineteenth century, even a remote farmhouse of three or four rooms might gain a five-piece parlor set and thus transform the old living room with its "company bed" into a parlor, curiously useless to any immediate need other than perhaps the satisfaction of living with the times.

Lay out your graphs in the appropriate rooms, and with room-use and daily living in mind, simply play with the furnishings. This is not an idle exercise; it will help you think about the rooms in terms of your research and objectives. To do all your planning off-site is quite as silly as to imagine the material historian making final judgment on an object entirely from a photograph. Your room is, at the outset, your foremost object, and you must know it very well.

Imagine, for example, the father and mother and eight children gathered in the hall on a night during the Revolution and what the room must have been like, regardless, for the moment, of the individual character of the objects. Was the war being fought nearby, and was the family anxious, or were the battles so far distant that any news was such old news it made little difference in the household routine? Were the people clustered before the fire? Where would the furniture have been placed, to accommodate such a scene? What sort of transient things would have accompanied them at this moment—logs for the fire, books, something to eat? Local inventories suggest no curtains, but twelve chairs, an oval table, a desk, and odd lots of china. Was the china being washed now at the table and being put away in the built-in wall cupboard, which is still in place?

The importance of having a historical imagination about your house is essential to the successful furnishing of its interiors. Your research, if it has been full, will both check and broaden this imagination, causing it to solidify at last into strong and varied images of life as it was lived in that particular place at another time. The furnishings plan must evolve from this picture also, beginning with general impressions, then, step by step, filling out the details.

6

Furniture

IT WOULD be a physical impossibility to describe in one book what is appropriate in furniture and what is not for three hundred years of American houses. Even to undertake such a task would be presumptuous, for there is yet another generation of scholarship to be done—and it will be a busy generation. A book of that sort would be misleading, except in the most general way, for, since interiors have personalities of their own, one can go only so far with hypotheses. Your furniture collecting must be devised specifically for your interiors, taking into account where they were individual to themselves and where they partook of the median of the age. What you turn up will become part of the growing scholarship on the subject. Copies of your findings and conclusions should be placed on deposit at an appropriate state and local library, as well as at an institution where they can be shared by the general field of scholars, as at the Avery Architecture Library at Columbia University, the Athenaeum of Philadelphia, or the Henry Francis du Pont Winterthur Museum. Eventually these materials should be published, if at all possible.

Given empty rooms, the objective—alas, too often—is to fill them up, and the largest objects, the tables, chairs, bureaux, beds, and so on, naturally carry matters along more quickly toward that end. As a result of the popularity of "antiques" in our homes, we are accustomed to thinking of historical settings largely in terms of furniture. Most restored interiors are overfurnished and thus broadcast the modernity of the standard of selection that created them. A piece of furniture should be acquired only after a coldly critical appraisal of its role in the historical tone of the room as a whole. In the historical interior the furniture must conform to the historical concept, whether it be an ensemble based upon a version of a style, as known both to the Victorians and in our own century, or a combination of many forms, contrived to represent the mixtures that characterized rooms before the industrial age.

One of the questions paramount in collecting furniture for the historical interior is whether or not to use pieces that predate the occupation and use of the house. Only now and then do inventories specify or even suggest the age of furniture: "1 old table" could mean, in 1830, an eighteenth-century Queen Anne type of tea-table in mahogany, or it could mean a ramshackle kitchen table in pine and not five years old. It is generally wise to assume that not everything in a house was new when the house was built; however, to be safe, this requires some elaboration.

There would be few "antiques" around today if someone had not preserved them. Families of many generations' or even a few years' residence in a locality are more likely than not to take along furniture they already have when they change houses. These old things might become a minority in the new domicile, relegated to a dark corner; yet they are present, and as long as they fill a functional or sentimental need and do not obstruct the desired look of the place, they remain. When a move involves great distances, however, it is quite another story. Before our time of efficient cross-country freight services, it was usually a practical necessity to leave most if not all furniture behind. Furniture is heavy; it is vulnerable to breakage. Nineteenth-century documents are filled with references to crated furniture being shipped by water and later by rail, but the vast number of those crates unquestionably contained new furniture from the burgeoning manufactories. Transportation hazards and costs, though discouraging, seem not to have been the sole reasons people di-

Still in use, the house of many generations: 6 Gibbes Street, Charleston, South Carolina, photo 1899. —*The Museum of Charleston*

have been influenced by the twentieth-century affection for furnishing with antiques. Even the Victorian custom of accenting decorated rooms with "relics" of the past was restricted pretty much to the eastern seaboard, where such furniture might be acquired through inheritance, an estate sale, or purchased in an antique shop.

A highly sensitive aspect of collecting furniture for the historic house is quality and class. You will have gained through research an idea, or exact knowledge, of what was available to the original inhabitants of your house; one hopes a few pieces survive that reveal something about the class and quality of what they owned. Beyond the record of your particular house, learning to judge class and quality for the period you wish to represent takes an intense study of the documented examples on your object list, in comparison, through publications and museum collections, to documented specimens of the best of that sort which have undergone vigorous scholarly investigations.

Class and quality are most clearly revealed in the realm of style. Here for comparison you will find numerous illustrated books and exhibition catalogues, particularly for the eighteenth and first quarter of the nineteenth centuries. The material, unfortunately, becomes thin through the succeeding decades until just before the beginning of the twentieth century, when you are at last able to resort to advertisements in the popular home furnishings magazines of the day. What you are trying to determine is where on a hypothetical scale of quality fall the few or many objects of documented local use. Are they "high-style," being equal to the best examples produced anywhere at the time of the style's reign in fashion? Are they similar, but not so well designed as the best? Are they modified versions, clearly made long after the style's peak, and do they show characteristics of a subsequent style? Do they represent the radical

vested themselves of most of their furniture before long moves. There was the matter of preference. Why transport the old when you could have something new? And perhaps new furniture made sense with a new life, in a way difficult for us to understand today.

Unless you have precise documentation to the contrary, do not use furniture in early rooms that you know predates the occupants' settlement in the region. This is essential when in point of time your interiors could not

52 departures of an erratic local cabinetmaker?

There is a certain uniformity in furniture style that, according to how it is translated, is a good indicator of class and quality. Apart from "style" furniture, however, is furniture in the vernacular, which was, in the last quarter of the eighteenth and for most of the nineteenth century, called "common" furniture—a designation appearing with great frequency in inventories. Vernacular furniture's form and design were products of custom and function. Produced at home, built to order by the local cabinetmaker, or even manufactured in quantity, vernacular furniture was ordinary and everyday, usually made from a softwood, and very often painted. Its forms are many, they vary from place to place, and they are deeply emblematic of the ethnic backgrounds of—and influences upon—those who produced it.

One of the greatest weaknesses in the general picture of furniture study in America is in the vernacular, and any solution is complicated by the diversity among regional types. Your most abundant sources for comparison of vernacular furniture types will tend to feature the vernacular mainly as it showed influences from formal style; works on "pure" vernacular forms are scarce. Most of the studies you will find concentrate upon the eighteenth and early nineteenth centuries. The best of these will necessarily, by the nature of the material, be directed toward one geographical area. For most regional vernacular furniture the scholarly sources and documented collections are rare, where they exist at all. Yet up until the age of mass-production after the Civil War, vernacular furniture predominated, even though certainly by the 1840s style as popularized by the manufacturers was likely to be reflected in it.

The first reaction to the challenge of acquiring furniture for the historic house is to want only the best examples. This is noble indeed, if by "best examples" you mean pieces that in quality and in combination with one another could quite possibly have been used in that specific place. But if you mean only furniture that is aesthetically pleasing to our modern eyes or furniture that falls into that list of acceptable antiques associated with residential decorating today, then you are all wrong. For in so doing you will unquestionably lose that magic of contrast that characterizes houses where people live.

There is good documentation for elegantly furnished rooms in American mansions of the eighteenth and early nineteenth centuries. Latrobe's "Oval Saloon" in the White House of 1809 must have been spectacular to American eyes, with its matching suite of Grecian sofas and chairs, its tinted wall and ceiling coloration, and the abundance of its scarlet velvet, which covered the furniture cushions and draped both the windows and two mirrored niches. Foreign travelers now and then exclaimed over the interior decorations of mansions in the cities, indicating that some Americans lived in high-style surroundings, but also showing, by their surprise, that the number was very few. Without actual documentation for such settings, the restorationist of interiors is foolish to plan them, although to do so is always tempting, because from our modern perspective we feel more comfortable with them; they are easier to understand.

Historical sources prove that American houses, even mansions, were rarely high-style in any international sense before the end of the nineteenth century. Our "American" high-style was even then largely in architecture and not in interior decoration—as a look at original interior photographs of some of our celebrated 1880s and 1890s domestic architectural specimens will clearly show. Excellence in architectural design and execution can never be taken as a green light to proceed with collecting furniture of the same quality; in so doing you would be making the least safe bet.

There is a curiously homey feeling to American interiors, which perhaps reveals itself most in exceptions to formal norms. What is "right" becomes in American interiors less the issue than how well the rooms reflect the private lives of those who live in them; more important than the show of wealth or education is most often the show of decency and an awareness of the comforts of good living, be it high or simple. This can be consistently traced back to the colonial epoch, through many phases of household taste. Where in Europe this domesticity is readily associated with the rise of the middle class, here it speaks not of one aspect of society, but is the dominant characteristic and ideal of the whole.

The careful co-ordination of your furniture collection will be the first major step toward realizing the essential humanity in the historical room. If your sources indicate that the room was as rich as Latrobe's at the White House, be alert and do not jump to conclusions; Latrobe, after all, decorated the Blue Room with the greatest difficulty because of the limitations of American craftsmen and materials: its elegance was, to his cultivated English eye, slightly tawdry. If a restoration of his Oval Saloon failed to provide that particular look, it would deprive the room of a vital part of its history. Every historical interior deserves that same exacting sensitivity toward tone in the selection of its furniture.

From the detachment of years, achieving an articulate mixture of quality and classes of pieces of furniture takes serious consideration and perhaps even trial and error, which can be costly. You are fortunate when there is an inventory to lean upon, or at least a synthesis of many inventories. Without either, and with only sketchy sources, bear in mind that elegance is and has always been achieved in many ways, and comfort and a certain beauty sometimes exist where circumstances might make it seem impossible. Do not go either way into clichés: remember the simple wooden

shelf that held the marble statue in Mary Hampton's drawing room; take note of the manufactured pieces, plain and fancy, bought all at about the same time, that make up the middle-class "prettiness" of Lincoln's parlor in Springfield; and at Mount Vernon observe how the mingling of vernacular furniture with the sophisticated works of urban American and a few foreign craftsmen helps us sense the contrasts in the life of this Virginia planter and his world.

Acquiring what you must have in furniture for the historical interior is always a case of catch as catch can. With documented pieces this becomes even more the case. When you buy or accept as a gift a piece that is documented as having been used in your house or even an appropriate piece used at the same time in the community, you are seldom wise to hesitate simply because the object is in poor condition. If it fits your museum needs—or will, when it is restored—take it. With other pieces you can be more selective, but not foolishly so. For example, authentic American furniture of the colonial epoch is rare enough to justify the expense of restoring nearly any object, no matter the condition, as long as the parts are there. Furniture of the early twentieth century, on the other hand, is more abundantly available, and you might feel safe in passing up several pieces in disrepair to await one that is perfect.

Upholstery

Restoring furniture can be very expensive. About upholstery this book will say very little, except to call attention to a few general areas of consideration. The range of upholstery fabrics is, and has been, almost limitless—wool, silk, linen, cotton, horsehair, leather, and in our own time, the various synthetics. If an upholstered item has its original covering or one from a time early in its history, you should try to save it intact, if only to preserve the docu-

54 ment. If the piece is original to your house it is mandatory to make every effort to keep it on the furniture. Sometimes the condition of the fabric makes this impossible. To then reproduce the material will be expensive, though it should be done. The simplest alternative, however, is to select from a manufactured line something similar, retaining all of the ruined original for reference.

In the absence of documentation for upholstery in the room, consider the widest spectrum of possibilities. In other words, do not marry yourself to silk damask, when on reflection colorful furniture calico might better serve the historical tone. Will the room be upholstered *en suite*, with matching curtains as well? When research suggests this treatment, apprise yourself of what so much material would have cost. Relative to other household costs, is this an expense the family would have justified? If the family lived in the house a long time, should your selection of fabric represent a time somewhat later than the style of furniture, to show that the rooms were spruced up after a certain time? Was the upholstery in the rooms a mix of patterns and colors and a mix of upholstery and slipcovers? In a house furnished over several years, variety is more likely than not.

The manner in which your upholstery is applied should be carefully researched by studying illustrative documents, such as prints, paintings, and photographs. Today's tight-stretched and overlapped upholstery would have horrified an upholsterer in 1800; part of his craft was the ability to cut and stitch material to fit, to avoid overlapping except where it was ornamental, and thus to be able to stretch tightly enough for a trim, smooth appearance, without putting undue and destructive tension on the fabric. "Elastic wires" or iron springs came into increasing use for chairs and sofas in the 1830s, having been patented in England in 1828. With springs gradually came visible expressions of their hidden attributes of comfort: deeper seats and backs, tufting, furniture forms determined as much by the upholstery as by the wooden structure—and sometimes more. The fabric coverings tended to be slack, as opposed to clinging. By the mid-1850s this looseness was taken up not by being tightened but by being more fully stuffed. "Comfortable furniture" or simply "comfortables" described the deeply upholstered pieces of the 1850s and 1860s. The trend developed to its ultimate in the 1870s with the "Turkish" and "overstuffed" modes that, through a changing succession of forms, led to the comfortable seating furniture so familiar everywhere today.

As there has always been furniture of differing qualities, there have been upholsterers of differing abilities. Mass production brought about shortcut techniques that became acceptable characteristics of styles. That the Victorians covered up some of these shortcuts with trimmings, that the subsequent generations found the shortcuts unobjectionable and left them exposed is a quite natural evolution. But it shows us that the manner of upholstery has

A romantic image of 1809: drawing room, Locust Grove, Louisville, Kentucky. —*Locust Grove*

changed. The upholsterer who will restuff and re-cover furniture for your historical interior should be shown documentary examples that indicate what you must have; before any work commences, the furniture should be photographed; and with overstuffed pieces, it should be carefully measured. These steps are necessary precautions against unfortunate—and expensive—mistakes.

Wood Surfaces

Of equal importance in preparing furniture for use in the historic house is the restoration of structure and exposed wood surfaces. Reproducing the wax finish on eighteenth-century furniture has been perfected, to some extent, by many years of trial and error; quite another matter are the varied treatments—the lacquer, gilt, bright and dull varnish and paint—often in combination in one piece of the better sort of Victorian furniture.

It is best to refresh the object of furniture by cleaning and minor repairing. Even a chair, say, that is all to pieces might be joined again, cleaned, and used as it is. Stripping to the bare wood should not be considered if the old finish remains, although there are exceptions. Painted surfaces that appear to be original should be left, regardless of their condition, and only "touched up" where new materials are added. An unfinished surface, grayed with age and scrubbing, should be left alone, and certainly not peeled and given one of the popular "natural" finishes achieved through stains, varnish, oil, or colored wax that have been the curse, particularly of old vernacular furniture, for the past forty years. The usual recommended remedy for the dark, muddy finish one often sees on old pieces consists of the gentle rubbing of the surfaces with a combination in equal parts of denatured alcohol, turpentine, and boiled linseed oil. This will gradually cut through the build-up of wax and grime and revive to a sufficient degree the

color and figuring of the original surface. Currently, however, even this once-infallible treatment has many defamers, who point to gummy surfaces and oil-darkened finishes. Whatever method you use, you will need to experiment with it first; see that you are informed well in advance on the latest approved formulas employed by museum conservators. These can be learned either through *recent* publications, or letters of inquiry.

Rubbing down and cleaning, however, are not always adequate. Sometimes there is the need to cut through varnish, which will require abrasives of one kind or another. The practice of varnishing natural wooden surfaces of furniture in this country can be fairly well dated from the early 1820s, when the "French Polish" was introduced to the United States from France and England. Long familiar as a protective coating for paint, though not normally used on any but painted furniture, varnish was made by dissolving a resinous substance in linseed oil, alcohol, or turpentine; French Polish was a further refinement incorporating shellac, which was not unfamiliar to Americans when used by itself as a coating for furniture.

Great were the practical advantages of varnish over the previously prevalent wax, which became gummy with use, and oil, which darkened and dulled the wood. Neither oil nor wax, nor even shellac provided the tough protection or the glassy shine of varnish for an age increasingly enamored of flashy wood-grain. Varnish was especially necessary for Americans, whose houses, being smaller, received heavy use.

Varnish grew in such popularity that it was applied not only on new surfaces, but was enlisted to recoat old ones, thus presenting problems for the restorationist. Sometimes varnish deprives furniture of the original effect it was meant to have. If a return to this effect is wanted, obviously the varnish should be removed. Dead varnish can obscure the original

56 richness of painted pieces. Certain types of furniture, which were originally varnished, have surfaces so layered with successive coats of varnish and so blackened and textured that they too must be either cleaned, where the dead varnish is melted and scrubbed off, or stripped and revarnished. The treatment will depend upon the condition of the object and the class of workmanship available to you. This especially is true of the Classical furniture in the style known in its day as Grecian—now called "Empire"—the design of which relies heavily upon fiery wood-grain for animation and ornament. It is also true of some furniture types from the Victorian decades, especially when the material is oak.

Whatever the condition of the furniture you acquire, preserve the original finish if you possibly can. Restoration work is valid only when the state of the object interferes with the integrity of its design. But by the same token, you would be unlikely to remove padded arms added by Zachary Taylor in 1848 to a Philadelphia side chair of 1735! That a piece of furniture is worn and dark with age is no reason, necessarily, to restore it to the way it may have looked when it was brand new. Chances are it *would* have looked new originally in your house; but then, your house might have looked new, too. However, both are old, and the tracks of time are usually treasures to preserve. An essential aspect of the historical power of old houses and furniture is that they are real, that they were there in the time, if not in the actual place. When they seem too slick, they lose some of their credibility.

With furniture—and furnishings—there are instances where it is simply not possible or wise to use original objects. Reproductions of furniture have their uses in the historic house. Rooms that the public will use to any great extent, such as halls where people sit awaiting tours, are better off provided with reproduction chairs than with good historical pieces. In other cases, where the consideration is not vulnerability to damage, but historical accuracy, reproductions are also sometimes in order. The National Park Service has furnished the famous Surrender Room at Appomattox with reproductions, for the original furnishings now belong to the Chicago Historical Society. That room in the McLean House, so well known, so well documented, would have been trite furnished in any other way than with the original objects, which were unavailable, or exact copies.

What then of rooms not of such historical importance, but which are documented in great detail by photographs? In furthering this question, two series of photographs come at once to mind: those of Norwalk, Connecticut's, Lockwood-Mathews House, taken when it was new, in the 1860s, and those taken inside Iolani Palace in Honolulu variously between about 1883 and 1893. Both buildings were under restoration in the 1970s. The likelihood of finding exact duplicates of the furnishings from either house is small, although except for Iolani's throne, none were one-of-a-kind. Normally, with only an inventory and no photographs, one would proceed to acquire furniture contemporary with the original, being careful to follow the indications of research: that the Connecticut mansion represented high style, while the island king's representative selected largely from Davenport's manufactured line in Boston. Under ordinary circumstances, without photographs, you would never know the difference. But in these two cases, you would. So the result would be a sort of parody on the original, housed in the actual house, but not true to the visual documentation. Would the fact that everything was "period" carry the day? Or would your best solution have been to reproduce the furniture as it appeared in the photograph?

7
Transient Objects

WITH furniture, you build the basic framework of the historical room. After the furniture, but co-ordinated with it in your planning, come the transient objects. In a sense all household furnishings are transient objects, for they can be moved about. The term *transient object*, however, is more usefully defined as an object that is placed in a room for a special purpose—either use or ornament—and that would not be there otherwise. This does not include furniture, such as chairs, tables, sofas, and beds, but it does include needlework frames, andirons, vases, ceiling fans, and the other sorts of accessories that contribute to liveability or enhance the room's appearance. Transient objects are often small; they can be very plain or elaborate; they can be mechanical; they can be as enduring as a marble statue or as perishable as a dish of chocolates. Many of your historical themes in interpretation will be developed through transient objects. Each object tells a story in itself, and also, by its presence, implies a role in the life of the household.

Objects of Use

Among transient objects, objects of use are more numerous in houses than objects of ornament. How they are distributed through the various rooms determines whether they are predominant or secondary in one's over-all impression of the place. A farmhouse sitting room of 1840 will certainly contain more objects of use than the formal parlor of an urban mansion of the same time; yet, relatively speaking, differences between the kitchens, cellars, and bedrooms of the two might not be so great.

Inventories, it seems, frequently fail to include objects of use, and one suspects that this is because they were so ordinary as to have no value. For example, bandboxes of the early nineteenth century are known to have been visible in rooms, as receptacles for storage. Yet these bandboxes, wallpapered or painted boxes of thin wood or pasteboard, an equivalent of weightless luggage, are seldom mentioned in inventories, though many early boxes have survived. Kitchen equipment, on the other hand,

Object of use reused: milk crock, ca. 1840, becomes an ornamental object in 1978. —*Haworth P. Bromley Photo, James Giraytys Collection*

58 particularly of metal, will be found listed nearly every time—before the last quarter of the nineteenth century, when mass-production of such materials made them cheap and abundant and diminished their transferral value. Even those kitchen inventories, however, that provide the largest listings of objects of use, rarely mention mousetraps, scrub-boards, brooms, or the many ordinary things that we can be certain were there.

In assembling objects of use, be cautious not to make aesthetics your basis for acquisition. In their obsolescence, objects of use from the past can be very appealing to our alien eyes. Decorating with them, consciously or unconsciously, can be deadly to the historical room. Spinning wheels, bedecked with bows and ribbons in Victorian parlors, were no longer objects of use, but had been born anew as quaint ornaments. Do not make ornaments of pots and pans, spectacles, fly-swatters, and chamber pots. Always bear in mind that objects of use, no matter how well designed, are in rooms first because they are useful; if they are purely the features of a decorative scheme, then they are ornaments.

Preliminary to deciding which objects of use will be used in your rooms, review what research has turned up about the entire operation of your house and daily life in it. What were the details of living there that created functions for objects? Comfort, convenience, maintenance, health, and pleasure all required objects to facilitate them. What useful objects might be in a bedroom of 1840, along with a bed, a dresser, and a chair? Probably many things: a chamber set; medicines; hair oil, combs, brushes; a toothbrush; soap; clothing, perhaps folded on shelves behind a curtain strung neatly across the fireplace reveal; a trunk and bandboxes; linens, quilts; a box of letters. All these express the functions that created them.

Once you have developed a list of specific functions within your household, begin to as-

sociate these with objects. In the absence of precise references or surviving artifacts, you must turn to scholarship in the general field. Many possibilities may then present themselves. For an example we will discuss the basic function of heating in some detail.

Through time, the objects of use for heating have been many. Some are small and moveable; others are as large as pieces of furniture. The open, wood-burning fireplace was the most common form of heating in the United States until well into the second half of the nineteenth century. In our pursuit of objects connected with early fireplace heating, we find that only in about the last decade of the eighteenth century did the "draft" chimney come into widespread use; and even so, contemporary accounts reveal that smoky fireplaces were not obliterated. "Chimney cloths," plain or fancy valances hanging from the mantel shelf, were familiar companions to smoky fireplaces in the eighteenth and nineteenth centuries, serving the same purpose as today's metal hoods. Thus a chimney cloth, an object of use.

Fireplace equipment in iron and brass is well documented for the eighteenth and nineteenth centuries. Inventories suggest that there were more andirons, pokers, tongs, and shovels of iron than of brass. Yet they show, too, that by the 1830s even a rather modest household was likely to possess a pair of brass andirons. Fireplace furniture, being in great demand, was an early fruit of mass-production. Brass, cast-iron, and steel implements were usually manufactured to be sold as sets, which by the Victorian decades might mean an entire matching ensemble—tools, andirons, fender or screen—in an elaborate "French" design, or, beginning in the later seventies, in the "Colonial" mode, which prevails today. Your fireplaces should be outfitted with both fuel and implements. It may not be necessary to use all possible types of implements on every fireplace, but there must be enough to facilitate the functions of laying, maintaining, and extinguishing a fire. In the summer sometimes all this equipment was stacked in the fireplace and the opening covered by a board, plain and painted, or decorated with painted designs or some configuration of fabric; whether this was done or not, the sooty interior of the fireplace was usually whitewashed.

The wood-burning fireplace was not the only means of fulfilling the function of heating. In other means lay other objects, and the restorer, having turned to the general subject of heating, should take these alternatives into account. There were early efforts both to improve the fireplace and to replace it with something better. Firebacks of iron reflected and held the heat; a step beyond that was the stove.

Stoves came into use in many public buildings and in some affluent private houses in America early in the eighteenth century. While there were several kinds at that time, the most familiar seems to have been the "close stove," an upright, enclosed box made of iron plates and usually mounted on a frame or legs. The efficiency of stoves over open fireplaces was well known in 1744 when Dr. Franklin introduced his open-hearth "Pennsylvania Fireplace." Subsequently modified by others, the so-called Franklin Stove took hold after the Revolution, when the use of stoves in general became more popular.

Stoves were of two kinds: those that were part of fireplaces and those that were not. The object was to produce the maximum heat from the minimum fuel, and this was done either by means of reflection or by bringing the whole firebox into the room. Franklin's stove was set just outside the fireplace, its back-plate bricked tightly into the opening; the Rittenhouse Stove, an early improvement on Franklin's, was set directly into the fireplace. The chimney opening was masked down, leaving only the stove's opening visible.

Warming and cooking: stove broadside, 1855. —*Courtesy of the New-York Historical Society, New York City*

Six-plate stoves, in use in America at least by 1744, required no chimneys, only stovepipes. They were oblong boxes made of six iron plates pinned together and set up on legs. They extended directly out into the room. The ten-plate stove, not so common nor so ornamental as the six-plate, included an oven, which accounted for the four extra plates; it was the forerunner of the free-standing cookstove, to come later on. Another kind of stove stood upright, instead of being horizontal and it was often called a "cannon stove" because it consisted of one or more cylindrical drums resembling cannon. Versions of six- and ten-plate stoves and cannon stoves are still sold on the market today, but they are continuations of simple sheet-metal models from the later

60 1880s, not those heavy iron ones of the eighteenth and earlier nineteenth centuries.

If your period is from about 1780 to 1800, there is a possibility that a stove was present in your house; if it is forty years later, and the family was middle class or higher, you can be almost certain there was a heating stove at least in the most frequented sitting room. The tall kitchen fireplaces that we so often see today fitted out with andirons, spits, and so on, were sometimes built to accommodate ranges, not open-fire cooking, as is commonly believed. Certainly after 1815, and in a good many instances before that, the iron cook-stoves or ranges were characteristic of kitchens in wealthy households. By the early 1830s they were rather familiar to the middle class, if by no means to the extent that they would be after 1850.

For the restorer, early heating stoves are not ready finds, and early kitchen ranges have all but vanished. The sources for stove designs are profuse, so you may at last resort to commissioning a reproduction. Reproduction costs are, of course, exorbitant, even for the simple, boxlike ranges of the early 1800s that fit into the fireplace. When the time and expense is given toward securing a reproduction, see that it is in working order; you may hesitate to use old stoves for reasons of safety and their preservation, but when these considerations are not in the way, the stove can serve a useful function in interpretation.

Wood was the fuel most widely used in the early years of the United States. Coal was also burned by Americans throughout the eighteenth century, particularly in Virginia, because the principal source for it in America was the James River region. Virginia and English coal were not unfamiliar to eastern mansions. But not before an increasing wood shortage began to be felt in the cities, and the discovery of coal in 1808 in western Pennsylvania, did coal become a major source of heat in the United States.

Coal fires required a smaller fireplace opening and less depth than wood. Coal fires had to be elevated. The ordinary way of accomplishing this was to build brick hobs out from each side of the firebox and fit an iron grate between them, with the rear of the fireplace brought forward either with masonry or an iron fireback. Hob-grates could also be bought as a unit. A number of eighteenth- and early nineteenth-century hob-grates from England survive in American houses; the finest consist of an iron grate—a sort of basket—contained in a superstructure of ornamental brass or brass and steel. Somewhat similar hob-grates were manufactured in America. The business gained considerable impetus in the absence of superior British goods during the War of 1812.

By the 1820s all classes of American-made coal fixtures were available. There were sets for the purpose of adapting wood-burning fireplaces; there were grates made especially for small fireplaces built to burn coal. Generally speaking, this earlier coal equipment is very scarce today and may have to be reproduced for the historic house that requires it. The later and improved models, made from the 1850s on, linger in some abundance. These were cast, as opposed to being wrought, iron with a slightly protruding grate, beneath an opening through which the smoke passed to the chimney. Their basic design changed very little from then on.

Central-heating systems were known to a limited extent in early nineteenth-century America, most notably in the United States Capitol and in other public buildings. It is stretching a point to call central-heating systems from any period transient objects; yet parts of them—ducts, registers, pipes, radiators, and so on—are visible in rooms. They are superfluous to the design of the room and can be considered objects of use.

Original fixtures from early central-heating systems are nearly impossible to find. If you need them, you will almost certainly have to copy surviving examples or diagrams in old pattern books (usually English publications). Hot-air central-heating systems began to be desirable luxuries for American mansions in the 1830s. The earlier examples, first appearing about 1810, were mainly in factories and public buildings; but the principle, though improved, remained much the same. The earliest and simplest consisted of a closed cellar chamber, heated by an iron stove built into the brickwork. The room filled up with hot air, which found escape through ducts into the rooms above, attracted by the draw from the fireplace chimneys. The draw increased if a fire was built in the fireplace. A natural improvement, to protect those who had to enter the suffocating heatrooms, was the encasement of the stove in a large "box," usually built of brick, to which the ducts connected at the top. As crude as the system seems—and they were denounced as unhealthful in their day—the all-over warmth they gave to rooms, stale smell and all, must have been a delight and a novelty as well.

A great improvement on this idea took place with the development of the gravity system in the 1850s. This system introduced an efficient, self-contained furnace, built on the principle of the earlier devices, with an inner combustion chamber of iron encased in an outer chamber of brick. The difference was that cold air was drawn directly into the outer shell. When the air became heated, it rose and was pushed up into the ducts by the cold air that continually entered below.

Various hot-water and steam-radiator systems were patented in this country from the 1850s to the 1870s, but neither type came into popular use in private houses until the 1880s. Their radiators and pipes were objects of use new to American domestic rooms. Where the more discreet hot-air registers were usually richly ornamented, to appear not so utilitarian, it followed that radiators, occupying as much

space as a piece of furniture, should be even more so. Radiators, far more than hot-air registers, are the symbols of the spread of central heating in American houses.

A hot-water or steam system was more practical to add to an existing house than a hot-air system, because merely pipes and radiators were required (and could be left exposed) instead of cumbersome ducts. Hot-air systems, though now rivalled by water and steam, continued to be improved, most notably with the addition by the late 1880s of electric fans to move the air along. Countless air, water, and steam systems survive from the late nineteenth and early twentieth centuries, though nearly always their sources of heat were changed from coal to oil or gas around the time of World War II.

The accouterments of heating are prime examples of objects of use. Being functional, they serve a purpose in their time, and when that has passed, they are adapted or replaced as soon as possible with something more useful. Some objects of use do not become obsolete; indeed, it is far simpler to find early fireplace equipment for your house than it is to find stoves, hob-grates, iron registers, or even radiators. A skillet may survive several generations in a family because it seems indispensable to the preparation of one food, while the other kitchen implements are discarded along the way. Finding authentic objects of use often takes more time than money. You will want real pieces; but in many cases—as with little things like soap, for example, and corn-husk brooms—you are sure to have to resort to some reproductions, which you may even have to make, yourself.

Ornamental Objects

Ornamental objects are not thrown out so quickly. Consequently, they are easier to locate. Objects of use can become ornaments, like the spinning wheel mentioned earlier, or a

62 lard-oil lamp that is kept long after electric lighting is installed. Objects of ornament are for decoration; normally, they serve no other function. Because they say revealing things about the occupants of a house, they should be selected with the greatest care.

Our personal taste attempts to assert itself more forcefully in the collection of ornaments than in anything else. From the perspective of today, most of the objects of the past are ornaments, whether they were originally so or not. While one hopes only restorers of interiors of the 1950s will opt for pepper mills with chintz lampshades or bidets planted with tuberous begonias, equal caution should be

Object of ornament: "leader of the monkey band," Chelsea, English, ca. 1780. —*The Colonial Williamsburg Foundation*

taken with treatments less obvious. Firearms, for example, are sometimes arranged in early houses as wall-decorations and over-mantel ornaments, when they usually belong out of the way in cabinets or closets.

The objects of ornament in a historical room will, to a greater or lesser degree, make a statement about the taste of the occupants, their financial capabilities, perhaps their creative talents, and their motivation to acquire such materials. These same objects of ornament will furthermore illustrate individually and in combination an aspect—or several aspects—of the ideas of beauty of a period in time. So before you begin to collect, you must be well informed in all these areas, as they apply to your house.

It does not necessarily follow that because people were rich they filled their houses with the finest. The acquisition of household ornaments may not have held the slightest appeal to that wealthy farmer who, on the other hand, spent lavishly on agricultural equipment. Perhaps in another locality, where there was an interest in fine houses and domestic appointments, and some healthy competition in building, he would have changed his attitude; but you will not want to change his ideas for him one hundred years later! In some houses, particularly in the country, there might be only enough ornamental objects to illustrate occasional bursts of enthusiasm on the part of families otherwise preoccupied with practical matters. Other houses may be laden with decorative materials, the owner's particular interest.

With the coming of the industrial age, the quantity of ornamental objects in houses began to increase on a rising scale, beginning early in the 1820s. This is not to say that the houses were suddenly crammed with material of this sort; the contrary is more often the case, but of the objects present, those of ornament become more of an issue than previously. Inventories indicate that at first the difference was probably very small in modest houses. But it is fairly safe to assume that, except for the poor, everybody had a place in the consumer market, according to how they stood in the growing cash economy of the United States. "Pretty things" were quite as much a blessing of manufacture to the common man as the objects that reduced work or provided comfort. Mercantile houses in city and town retailed the goods of manufacturers; improved transportation by steam and rail opened a thriving mail-order trade; and traveling salesmen moved wagonloads of goods among the villages and farms of New England and the South. Manufactured goods thus found their way into American houses in the form of clocks, chalk statuary, fancy oilcloth table and floor coverings, and an endless number of other items once known only to the few.

It should be remembered that the novelty of this new availability of ornaments sometimes overpowered what we rather bullheadedly insist is "good taste." The gaudy chalk parrot on the farmer's mantel was something nice in exchange for money that might otherwise be buried in everyday expenses. Purely an ornament, the parrot was beloved for that very fact. A richer man, with a little more suavity, might purchase an alabaster urn; but the reasoning was the same. It is understandable that city people, who dealt more regularly in cash than did farmers and were daily exposed to mercantile temptations, would have objects of ornament in greater abundance. But it is still dangerous to assume that what they bought would fit our definition of what is right and proper. Certainly, until the mid-nineteenth century, the market was still limited enough to preclude the selectivity we today call good taste; and even so, the strict standards of *ensemble,* so familiar to us, were then only in their infancy.

The watersheds to keep in mind when planning for objects of ornament are the War of 1812 (1812–1815) and the Civil War (1861–1866). Prior to the first event, manufacturers

produced largely for regional markets; afterward, they began to seek customers on an increasingly national scale, as transportation permitted, and as law began to favor American entrepreneurs. The Civil War hastened the development of the means of production, and by the close of the decade of the 1860s, manufacture was indeed mass-manufacture on some levels, needing only a few years' time to expand into nearly every facet of American life. Without the consumer, there would have been no manufacture; the nineteenth-century home's contents were expressions of the state of manufacture as it applied to their particular localities. In a cottage in a Rhode Island hamlet in 1740, no more than the product of a local pottery or a bit of English china would likely ornament a shelf; sixty years later, the work of a Boston printmaker could probably be found on the wall; a century later, a pair of Philadelphia girandoles might enrich the mantelshelf; and one hundred and fifty years later, one could behold in the same room a glazed pottery jardiniere made in Chicago, among many, many other objects from sources even farther distant.

For preindustrial times, the average house had few ornamental objects that were not essentially decorated objects of use. Framed prints are the ornaments most continually mentioned in eighteenth-century inventories. The situation was somewhat the same in expensive houses, with the difference conspicuous in the presence of objects of use of a finer sort—silver teapots, porcelain dishes—and such ornaments as porcelain vases, portraits in oil, and a greater profusion of prints. Many of the cheap ornaments of the eighteenth century, such objects documented to American rooms as paste figures made in England and decorative vases made in China, have awesome market values today; this situation clouds our understanding of them as ornamental odds and ends available to colonial citizens with the money to buy them. Similarly the

64 ordinary earthenware coffeepot of 1770, with its incised banding and rich glazed color, stands out in the restored room as a treasure, when originally it was not at all.

Unless you have specific information that dictates otherwise, be even more restrained in the number of ornaments you use in most houses of the preindustrial age than you are with furniture. In any case, do not pack the mantels, cabinets, and tables with groupings of export porcelain, oriental pots, and small figures. The effect of rooms in which this is done is far closer to that of the late nineteenth- or twentieth-century "Georgian" or "Colonial" interior—both late Victorian—than what sources indicate eighteenth-century rooms were like. Pictures may be quite another matter, as they were sometimes used in large quantities. Prints were in a sense mass-produced, early on, as were books; this early production was nothing to compare with the output that began in the 1820s. Indeed, inventories attest the value of books as late as the 1840s by often listing them title by title. A rich man's inventory of 1785 might list twenty prints in one room and sixty books in his library, but nothing else in the house in such plenty except kitchen and tableware.

Understandably the rise of the consumer market had its main visible effect in houses. We have already discussed this phenomenon in furniture and wallpaper; it was the same with ornaments, and ornamented objects of use. From the 1820s, improved tools and methods of production and marketing brought to the average citizen an array of products more extensive than he could ever have imagined before. He supported this vigorously with his pocketbook. Through successive decades, the feast of objects swelled and was devoured by a population that grew not only in size but in its appetite for material manifestations of prosperity. Even the negative reaction of the 1860s and 1870s to "machine-made" objects was largely lip-service, which the entre-preneurs superficially accommodated through "honest" design, all the while increasing their use of machines.

In addition to manufactured ornaments—such as sets of mantel vases or candleholders, framed looking glasses and pictures, carved images, picture pins, table covers, center-pieces, and so on—houses contained ornaments made at home. These could be nearly anything. Polished seashells, decorated letter baskets, woodcarvings, and an infinite variety of needlework increased in volume in rooms through the nineteenth century to rival the flood of manufactures. Nor were these personal creations by any means exclusive to the Victorian decades. There are early literary references to such ornamental materials, which appear almost without fail in old drawings, prints, and paintings that show interiors. Sometimes these were fancy decorations for homely things, such as a velvet cover for the brick used as a doorstop, or a chintz skirt for a trunk. More purely ornamental were the arrangements of dried flowers and waxed fruit, stuffed birds in nests, blown eggs in a basket. Artificial flowers were made from hair, feathers, shells, wax, paper, and silk, and prior to the Victorian affection for things "real," seem to have been the most popular dinner table decorations where flowers were used. Pictures painted at home or at school commemorated family events, illustrated something or someone, copied other prints, or, more often, recorded a sublime scene from the painter's imagination. Live things, such as plants in pots, birds, and sometimes small animals in cages, also found places in some American interiors long before the last quarter of the nineteenth century, when one expects it.

As a general rule, consider ornaments the accessories a family would gather over time to add beauty and interest to a room. Implicit in acquiring ornaments for the restored interior is the need to understand the ideas of beauty in the given age, and the nature of their application in the locality of your house. Because the house is an example of Greek Revival architecture does not necessarily mean that the rooms were outfitted with Grecian-style ornaments, though they certainly may have been.

Some families were, in the past as is true now, extraordinary collectors, and amassed numerous ornamental possessions. Whether they were accumulators or collectors is a matter for historical analysis. At any rate, you may have the house of such people; and if so, your program of collecting will have to be based upon an approximation of their original intentions and probable changing tastes, in the absence of the actual collections. In considering your interiors, always draw a careful distinction between fine art and decorative art. When the house is described as palatial in its ornamental accessories, be certain whether this meant handsome embellishments to contribute to an over-all effect, or if it actually involved a collection of works of art that could stand isolated on their own as individual pieces of merit in their own time. There can be no doubt that there have been throughout American history houses of elegance and richness. This is always relative, of course; what was elegant in Boston in 1790 might not be particularly elegant for London, yet a contemporary North Carolinian might have held it in awe.

Do not be misled by white columns or turrets, records of great financial returns, or the ecstatic memoirs of the local minister. Stay close to your characters, to their locality, and to the world they knew in preparing a point of view toward collecting objects they would have thought were beautiful.

8

Lighting

A type of transient object that deserves separate attention is the device for artificial lighting. Basically, lighting devices, attached or moveable, are, like stoves, objects of use. Yet, also like stoves, they can be so ornamental as to influence the character of a room. Subject to obsolescence, they sometimes remain for their ornamental assets, even when to adapt them to more efficient service is impossible.

There are essentially four types of artificial lighting to contend with in restorations: candlelight, oil-lamp light, gas light, and electric light. All are implemented by devices that vary from the simplest holder to the most elaborate hanging fixture. The first two can be moved about while in use; the latter two remain connected to an external source of fuel. This, we will see, influenced enormously the manner in which the rooms were used.

Even in the early decades of electric lighting, the great brightness we demand from artificial light today was unknown. Artificial light is to us a substitute for natural light; before the universal use of electric light, artificial light was merely a supplement to natural light—and an expensive supplement it was. Lighting in rooms was relatively dim, and the further one goes back in time, the dimmer it was. People in the 1880s and through the 1890s complained about glaring electric bulbs even more than their ancestors in the 1840s had about gas jets; Argand lamps must have seemed blinding in the 1790s. In illuminating the historical room with electricity, it is absolutely necessary to use no greater an intensity of light than would have been possible in the given period, with the actual lighting devices at work. To bathe a room in brilliant light when it would have known only an oil lamp is to take away something integral to its historical character.

This is sometimes more easily said than done, especially when your room was lighted by devices with exposed flames. You cannot effectively electrify "Betty" lamps, the lamps most commonly associated with simple houses of the seventeenth and eighteenth centuries. The Betty lamp looked a bit like a one-eared ashtray with the oil—fish oil or animal grease—uncovered in a small iron bowl, the wick running from that to the flame through an uncovered, troughlike spout. Nor will you be very effective at electrifying candlewood torches, split from resinous pine and fixed sometimes in iron holders, or simply stuck at an angle into a receptacle on the wall. In such cases, when you cannot rely upon natural light, pale indirect light will have to suffice. It should be directed to certain areas, so that the room will still remain partially shadowy; there must not seem to be an all-over bath of light.

Somewhat the same problem exists when your room must be lighted to suggest candlelight. Those queer little electric bulbs one so often sees mounted on imitation can-

"Betty lamp," or grease lamp. —*Smithsonian Institution*

66

dles are a poor solution; they are not convincing, keeping them lighted during the daytime is absurd, and they call attention to themselves very loudly.

For two centuries before the Civil War the basic unit of artificial lighting in America was the candle, if you do not count the light from fireplace fires. There were various kinds of candles. Rush-lights, reeds soaked in fat, were a homemade variety in the seventeenth, eighteenth, and early nineteenth centuries. Other types of candles were made either by a process of dipping or with candle moulds. Farmers' wives made tallow candles, usually in the autumn when animals were slaughtered in preparation for the winter supply of meat. The purified tallow was skimmed off boiling animal fat, then made into candles, which were used sparingly through the rest of the year. Beeswax, bayberry, and spermaceti (from the head of the sperm whale) were preferred substitutes for tallow, but did not exist in such abundance. Already in the eighteenth century candles were produced in quantity for sale. Candles were frequently advertised in urban newspapers in the later eighteenth century, but as purchases they were luxuries, and as late as the 1850s particularly those made of beeswax were still expensive.

The almost universal presence of candles naturally called for candleholders, which were made of many materials—iron, tin, pewter, wood, brass, glass, porcelain, earthenware, and silver. As with andirons, clocks, and similar objects of use, there was more often than not an effort to make candleholders attractive, if not beautiful, and to make them serve their function to the maximum. The simplest candleholder was equipped with a base of sufficient weight to keep the device steady; a socket was provided to secure the candle (prickets, though familiar in seventeenth- and eighteenth-century England, are not documented as having been used much in America). Beginning in the eighteenth century

there was usually a drip pan, a rim to catch drippings, and when there was not, a portable one—a *bobèche*—could be added; candleholders—even chandeliers—were usually moveable, whether hung on a wall, from a ceiling, or used on a table or on the floor. To conserve candles there was sometimes an ejector, incorporating a spring or other mechanism to push the candle upward until the last particle was used. In many instances glass, as the material of the candleholder or applied as prisms, magnified the strength of the light, as did mirrors and lenses.

With candleholders, as with other historical objects, it is the fine pieces that most numerously survive. Sticks of earthenware, iron, or pewter, or the even more ordinary manufactured tin ones that were available from the eighteenth century through to the twentieth, are rare. No matter the opulence of a house, somewhere it was bound to contain specimens of these simple candleholders. Brass candleholders, a step up the scale, were imported from England through the eighteenth century, and while it is known that they were produced in the colonies, it is difficult to identify American examples simply by their appearance. American manufacture of brass candleholders began to compete with the British imports only during the War of 1812. An ever-increasing variety of styles became available to the buying public, from the chambersticks of the 1820s to the prismed girandoles of the 1840s, created as sets consisting of candelabra and flanking single candleholders. It is important to realize that though brass candleholders came in various qualities and were very familiar objects in American houses, such houses would seldom have been any lower on the scale than middle-class.

About the same can be said of glass candleholders. These were originally produced in an apparently limited quantity, notably after about 1780 by the age-old method of blowing. Glass manufactories were going con-

68 cerns in New England, western Pennsylvania, southern New Jersey, and Ohio early in the nineteenth century; usually such objects as candleholders were peripheral to the production of bottles and windowpanes. A development in 1827 at the New England Glass Company, Cambridge, Massachusetts, introduced a practical technique for moulding glass that permitted the manufacture of glass objects in greater number and at cheaper cost. "Pressed glass" found immediate application to candleholders. The first principal manufacturer was the Boston & Sandwich Glass Company, Sandwich, Massachusetts, where the moulding process lent itself to such highly imaginative forms that "Sandwich Glass" enjoys as much popularity with collectors of antiques today as it did with customers when it was new. Such ornamental glass is, of course, not always "Sandwich," as it was produced in other parts of New England and the Midwest. Most of the decorative nineteenth-century forms—the caryatids, the dolphins, and crucifixes—have been reproduced in the twentieth century. Just how extensive a national market the New England and Midwestern glass works enjoyed in pre-Civil War America is uncertain; but already in the 1830s on the East Coast and throughout the Midwest they seem to have been everywhere, providing handsome candleholders, among other products, at prices the middle class could afford.

Silver candleholders existed, of course, in much smaller numbers than those of either brass, glass, or pottery. Silver candleholders cannot be considered ordinary to American houses before the 1870s, when imitation silver and cheap plate began to abound on the market. Though manufactured in urban centers and distributed to retailers already in the first quarter of the nineteenth century, silver candleholders, no matter how thin the plate, were readily identifiable symbols of prosperity. The restorer can profit from a splendid body of American scholarship, both in print and in museum collections, on American silver

and foreign silver used in America. Other than for its aesthetic appeal, silver has attracted scholars because it is usually marked and can therefore be researched more precisely than most brass, glass, or pottery, not to mention furniture. Silver candleholders appear in documents of wealthy American families from the seventeenth century on. In the first four decades of the nineteenth century, the silver market was democratized considerably by the production of silver-plated candleholders and candelabra, which, being much less expensive than the same products in pure silver, came at least within the reach of the middle class.

We have seen that the oil lamps of elementary kinds, such as the Betty lamps, were used in American houses very early. Oil lamps maintained an important place in American lighting until the domination of electricity, which occurred in different places at different times, but which can be considered rather complete, even in the country, by the late 1930s.

Animal-fat and some fish oil (which stank abominably) continued to be used in lamps through the eighteenth and until the middle of the nineteenth century. Most often these fuels seem to have been burned in unshaded lamps, which consisted of a font with the wick running through a watering-canlike spout; this wick spout, the first device for enclosing the

Varieties of grease lamps with different means of holding the wick but the same devices for hanging. —*The Smithsonian Institution*

wick, began, like the wick of the Betty lamp, on the side, but was customarily mounted by the 1790s on the top of the font. Whale oil, which was more desirable than animal fat but had to be purchased, was used in lamps as early as the late seventeenth century; it rose to popularity in the later eighteenth century and was only eclipsed when kerosene took the field in the 1860s.

Argand Lamps

Whale oil was a finer oil and cleaner to burn than lard. Both were expensive to buy. The devices for lighting using the various kinds of oil were steadily improved in the years after the Revolution, beginning with the Argand lamp, invented in 1783 by Aimé Argand, a Swiss, and in limited use in the United States in the 1790s. The Argand burner employed a hollow cylindrical wick instead of the traditional flat, solid one. This wick was encased to the *side* and slightly below the level of the font, so that an uninterrupted draft of air could rise up through the cylinder; the draft up the cylinder was created by a glass "chimney" that surrounded the circular flame and rose to an opening above it. Oil was fed to the wick by a gravity system. With the circular wick there was not only a greater area of flame, but the draft of air, warmed, created enough oxygen to consume the carbon smoke that would normally have accompanied such a big flame. Thus the Argand burner gave brighter artificial light than anyone had ever seen before, and it was smokeless.

Through the first half of the nineteenth century, when there were Argand lamps of every class on the market, from Japanned tin to bronze, there were constant efforts to improve the principle. As an efficient burner, it defied improvement, but the main complaint about the Argand lamp itself was that a shadow was cast on one side by the font, thus wasting valuable light. The double Argand—a single central font with a burner set to each side—was

Argand lamp of brass, tin, and iron, manufactured ca. 1840 by Thomas Cox of Birmingham, England, and marketed in New York by John and Joseph Cox. —*The Henry Francis du Pont Winterthur Museum*

one partial answer; the Argand chandelier was still another. For single-burner lamps, however, two of the many improvements found practical application in manufacture: the Astral lamp and the Solar lamp. Both lamps had Argand burners, but the obstructing font was placed beneath the burner.

Other Oil Lamps

The Astral, invented in the late eighteenth century, refashioned the font as a tubular ring, set Saturnlike around the flame, so that light could fall on the surface of a table as well as more generally brightening the room. In practical application, the Astral lamp in America was based upon the English Sinumbra or

Argand sconce of tin, ca 1790. The mirrored reflector has peeled away from the canteenlike font, and the glass chimney and wick are missing. This sconce belonged to George Washington. —*Mount Vernon Ladies' Association of the Union*

and on down through the font to air-holes in the base.

Simpler devices for burning whale oil, as well as lard, were prominent on the market. The tin lamps, like the tin chambersticks for candles, were the most numerous; sometimes they were Japanned in bright colors. And when the various glassworks in New England and the Midwest began producing candleholders, they also produced lamps, which were sold cheaply nearly everywhere. Brass lamps, sometimes fitted for paper shades, and brass sconces and chandeliers for oil burners fill the records of public buildings. Peg lamps were small lamps of tin, glass, brass, or even silver, with pegs instead of bases underneath, so that they could be secured in the sockets of candleholders. Britannia metal, perfected in England toward the end of the eighteenth century, knew extreme popularity with Americans, for lamps as well as for tableware, from the 1830s through the 1880s. Like pewter, Britannia metal was composed principally of tin; unlike pewter, it contained no lead. Britannia metal very nearly put the pewter trade out of business, for its gloss and texture was more like that of silver. Besides being innovators in lamplighting, the English found a great market for their lamps in the United States, and a number of surviving lamps with American labels are doubtless English, their labels merely indicating the names of the American jobbers or retailers.

Whale oil was rivaled on the popular market beginning in the late 1840s by the highly explosive fluid camphene, made from turpentine. Camphene lamps used a solid wick that, for protection, ran from the lamp to the flame through a tight metal tube. There were often several wicks, and the flames burned very brightly. But neither camphene nor whale oil, nor any other liquid fuel, could match the efficiency or cheapness of kerosene, which took the market beginning in the 1860s.

shadowless lamp, patented in Britain in 1820. This was an improvement on the earlier Annular lamp used extensively in France. Astrals, which appear with some frequency in America by the 1830s, were too cumbersome to carry about and were usually situated in some semipermanent spot, such as a center table.

Patented in America in 1843, the Solar lamp was portable. The font, a bulbous affair set below the wick, was pierced vertically by a casing that extended the draft from the chimney down through the usual Argand burner

Kerosene Lamps

Kerosene—also called "coal oil"—burned brightly, was relatively clean, and could be had in abundance. Its lamps nearly always employed the wide, flat wick that, unlike the Argand, but like all other types of oil lamps, dipped directly into the font. There were various improvements in kerosene burners through the late nineteenth century and into the twentieth, some based upon the Argand principle. During those years it can be safely said that no matter what other sources of light were used in American houses, kerosene lamps were present, too. They were prominent on the market of houschold goods until World War I in forms both plain and fancy, but most notably from the 1880s on, as the simple, clear-glass or metal base with the tall chimney and as the decorated china vase-lamp today called the "Gone-with-the-Wind" lamp, after its inaccurate use in the movie.

Gas-Lighting

Gas-lighting was developed in England in the 1790s, but did not begin its rise to popular use until the great surge of public improvements that followed the defeat of Napoleon in 1814. It was used first more in factories and for public buildings and street lamps than in private houses. Coal gas was created by burning a quantity of coal in a furnace, usually of iron, from which the volatile gases were thrown off, purified, and by means of pipes conducted to gas-lighting devices fixed in the rooms. A bright light and clean, gas-lighting was in widespread use in England by the close of the 1820s.

Not so, however, in the United States. There was a parallel interest in gas-lighting here; experimentation in the United States commenced in 1796 at Philadelphia, and the first commercial gas company was established in 1816 at

Kerosene lamp, ca. 1865. —*Collections of Greenfield Village and Henry Ford Museum*

Baltimore. Still the use of gas-lighting in private residences was not well known in America until the 1840s, when businessmen became aware of the potential for profit in coal gas-supply companies. Even then, and for the next twenty years, domestic gas-lighting was a luxury largely of urban life and for those individuals elsewhere who had private gas plants in their houses. Its heyday in the United States ran from about 1875 until World War I, by which time electricity had all but taken its

72 place. Coal gas was subsequently replaced by natural gas for cooking and heating; the natural gas flame was not as satisfactory for illumination.

The gas-lighting device had its "works" elsewhere, so at its simplest it was nothing more in a room than a pipe protruding from the wall, with an upturned end for lighting, and a thumbscrew cock to turn the gas on and off. It was utterly stationary; the closest a gas fixture ever came to being moveable at all was when a lamp was appended to it by means of an India-rubber hose. Because gas fixtures were fixed in one place, they were situated with two purposes in mind: concentrated light and general lighting. Sconces or "brackets" accomplished the former purpose, along with lamps, which were fed either by the rubber hoses or by iron pipes. A bracket installed beside a mirror and given an elbow so that it could swing in front of the mirror had the added advantage of reflection. The same device had long been used with candles, oil lamps, and natural light.

General lighting of a room, however, came into being as never before through the gasolier, which was more often than not simply called a chandelier. Overhead lighting was by no means common even in fine houses before the age of gas. There were earlier chandeliers of all sorts, for candles, lard, whale oil, camphene, and so on, but they were far more often than not for public buildings. A few fine eighteenth-century chandeliers have documented American use, particularly in churches. Simple domestic or shop chandeliers of iron, tin, and wood have also survived. The chandelier was frequently but not always present in the formal rooms of costly houses throughout the first half of the nineteenth century; chandeliers were manufactured in the United States, but before about 1850 the better ones seem to have been English. Yet the overhead lighting device most familiar to Americans before gas came along was the lantern, which, in various forms, was usually designated a "hall" or "passage" lamp, even though it was often used in other rooms as well.

Gas changed the situation substantially. The unlikely presence of so many chandeliers in restorations of earlier periods is due to hindsight colored by the intervening eras of gas and electricity. Overhead gaslight was used from the outset and not only prevailed but became nearly universal for rooms that needed general illumination. The gasolier could be a very simple inverted L or T of pipes, or it could be a sumptuous creation in cast metal with a dozen burners. Where the chandelier had been moveable, often fixed with counterweights and pulleys so that it could be lowered for lighting and extinguishing, the gasolier was stationary. Some gasoliers had lower sections that could be raised or lowered, or branches that could be dropped, again made possible by a flexible rubber hose. Otherwise, gasoliers were serviced with long-stemmed lighters or were reached by ladders. The success of overhead gaslight created a great demand for overhead lighting devices that could be used in the absence of gas. Hanging oil fixtures, and particularly those fueled by kerosene, were used by nearly all classes from the 1870s to the takeover by electricity, and probably play a greater role in the spread of overhead lighting, and all the changes it brought, than the gasolier itself.

A great asset in deciding upon the types of gas fixtures to use in restorations are the catalogues of manufacturers who produced them. Moreover, the many improvements in gas-lighting and devices—all of which were eagerly embraced by the public—further help you narrow your range of choices, from the built-in mechanisms with pull-chains for adjusting the level of the flame (ca. 1900) to the incandescent mantle (after 1887). Finding authentic gas fixtures is quite another matter. Elaborate hanging fixtures can usually be located; if you need a matched pair or a similar

Gasoliers of the 1870s, Decatur House, Washington, D.C. —*A. Robert Cole Photo for the National Trust for Historic Preservation*

"parlor pair," the problem compounds. Late nineteenth- and early twentieth-century brackets can, with persistence, be found, while those of the 1840s to the 1880s are scarce. Plain to middling gasoliers and lamps seem to be the rarest survivors of all. Reproductions will be increasingly necessary, if not of the basic fixture, certainly of its parts, such as shades and shade-holders, and its special effects, such as ornamental chains, fire gilding, and bronzing.

Electric Light

Electric light made its appearance in domestic interiors through existing gas devices or as bare bulbs. Since you are not likely to commission bulbs made as those of the 1880s and 1890s were made, but will use modern ones instead, you had best adopt shades of some sort, so that the look of the light bulbs will not intrude upon the accuracy of your room. The problem of shading glaring electric-light bulbs produced some curious solutions. Electric lighting fixtures and lamps are richly documented in illustrated advertisements and books on electricity, especially after about

1890, when the use of electricity really began to rival that of gas. When an existing house was wired for electricity, the wires were usually exposed, if they were not fished through gas pipes. This you may wish only to simulate, for safety reasons. But the proper accouterments—the china and porcelain wire supports, the light switches—should all be there, anyway. They are as important as the lighting fixtures themselves. Finding such materials in a hurry is an impossible task; by taking your time and scavenging junk shops and storerooms of long-established electrical shops, you might find wonderful things. Housewreckers can sometimes direct you to what you want.

In concluding the subject of lighting, we return to the subject of electrifying devices that were not meant to be electric. This boils down to the simple question of whether the flame was shaded or not; clear shades can sometimes be replaced with frosted ones, or there are metal and paper shades that can sometimes be employed on candle or oil devices from the late eighteenth and early nineteenth centuries. Lights were often screened, using little free-standing screens of fabric or paper, which presents still another limited possibility. As long as the bulbs are concealed, their wattage appropriate, and the fixture's working parts are not ruined in the adaptation, there can be little objection to electrification. Fire laws in many places oppose the use of open flames, but enough restored houses use them successfully—those at Williamsburg, for instance—to point out their great value.

There is the final question of how many lighting devices to use in a given room. With gas, or, sometimes, with electricity, evidence usually survives in the structure itself. With other types of lighting, without an inventory that specifies, you must base your decision, as with everything else, on the nearest relevant sources you can find. There are some general observations, however, that apply. Do not

74 overload the rooms with lighting devices. With lighting, it is usually a situation of less being more. Treat only the ornamental devices, bronze Argand lamps, for example, or stationary devices, as fixtures of the room's decoration. In the prime of their use, most of the portable oil lamps and candleholders would probably have been kept stored somewhere until needed for a specific reason. When they are present in the room, let it seem to be that they are there for a specific purpose.

Since lighting is always so important, show how it functioned. This can be accomplished by providing a glimpse of gas pipes or electrical wires in the basement, if not along the walls, or by showing the place usually in or near the kitchen where the oil or candle supply was kept, along with the extra wicks, chimneys, and candleholders. We take lighting more for granted today than was ever possible before electricity. We neither fear it nor have to trouble ourselves beyond paying the bill, changing a bulb, or flicking a switch. The complicated story of artificial lighting teaches us that lighting was once the object of daily effort and concern.

9

Textiles

*T*EXTILES, sometimes objects of use, sometimes ornamental, often both, are a singular category for consideration in furnishing the historic house. In some inventories, they nearly dominate; in others, they do not merit mention, although we can be certain some examples were there. To the Spanish inhabitants of eighteenth-century St. Augustine, they must have been very important, for they dominate the inventories of houses of the "better" sort. Textiles were easier to transport than other sorts of furnishings. They could be folded away in trunks. Anglo-American inventories do not usually go into such detail listing textiles as Spanish ones in America do. But the Spanish took better inventories, anyway, following prescribed rules, where Anglo-American records of this sort may vary from place to place.

Most inventories, however, tend to specify such major textiles as floor coverings and window hangings. Bedclothing, not so much; but bed furniture—mattress, curtains, the other readily visible materials with monetary value—nearly always. Whether or not clothing is listed varies. Before about 1850, clothing may be included, but it is less likely to be mentioned much after that, suggesting that its value for reuse diminished with the advent of ready-made articles of apparel.

We will not deal with clothing here, nor with bed and table linen. Our attention will go to floor coverings and window hangings. As for the other sorts of textiles, it is difficult to generalize. Your local research and objects catalogue will reveal regional characteristics of what was used and how. Where you usually run into voids is in the area of quantity. Satisfy this question by studying appropriate illustrative materials, early prints, drawings, paintings, and photographs of interiors. Further employ your historical knowledge of what was available. Were most textiles likely to be homemade? Or could materials be bought at the store?

Take great care to outfit your rooms properly with accurate presentations of textiles, even when the originals may have to be kept off-exhibit for the sake of their preservation. The wardrobe should not be empty; the dining room cabinet should, if sources direct, contain tablecloths and napkins, and perhaps even cotton screening; sitting rooms may be furnished with tablecovers and shawls, as well as pillows and examples of needlework. Prior to the 1840s, clothing was usually pressed, meaning it was folded and kept on shelves, creating a function for clothes "presses" and the shallow closets, called "presses," that filled the reveals beside fireplaces. The practice of hanging clothes was established by the time of the Civil War, but formal photographic portraits of women as late as the 1880s show orderly creases in the dresses that indicate folding was not a thing of the past even then. The "wardrobe," as opposed to the press, was for hang-

New England textiles: counterpane and pillowcases in a plain bedroom of about 1810. —*Old Sturbridge Village Photo by Donald F. Eaton*

76 ing clothes and was equipped with hooks or pegs, not poles. As the quantity of manufactured clothing increased, and people had more clothes, the closet as we know it began to be a household necessity. To accommodate this increase, the hooks and pegs of other times grew, like Pinocchio's nose, into closet poles.

According to old prints, textiles were conspicuous features of American rooms, even when you do not count floor coverings and window hangings. Clothing, quilts, yardage of goods, and the like were often stored in open view, where there was neither an enclosed press nor the inclination to hide such cloth items; there were infinite uses as well for bits of cloth, which further increased the quantity of textiles. It was this comfortably familiar presence in houses of the earlier nineteenth century that we can suspect the Victorians interpreted in their own rooms with their numbers of ornamental textiles. The mantel lambrequin, for example, though purely ornamental, unquestionably enjoyed the comfortable heritage of the once-familiar chimney cloth.

We dealt with the treatments of bare floors in the chapter on restoring the house. The age of carpeting—for such it can well be called— did not come until the 1840s, when its mass-production on power looms placed certain kinds of carpeting within the reach of the average American. For obvious reasons, carpeting was immensely popular; its flourishing parallels that of wallpaper. Do not assume, however, that after the forties nearly everybody had carpeting or carpets, any more than you would feel safe in assuming that because some citizens of eighteenth-century America owned Oriental carpets or "Persians," many people did; for, as an absolute, they did not.

Straw Matting

The floor covering with the oldest tradition in the western world is straw matting, if you will accept as its ancestor the rush-strewn floors of the Middle Ages. Straw matting is documented as having been used in American houses from about the mid-eighteenth century; this was not the heavily braided variety known in Tudor England, but a thin, dense matting, woven in strips and imported from the Far East. Known as "Canton mats," "India mats," or, simply, as matting or straw matting, this material was by the 1820s a typical floor covering in comfortable American houses. China remained the principal source. Straw matting was cheap, and when new it was fresh-looking and smelled sweet. The usual way of fixing it to the floor (and it did tend to travel when unattached) was to tack it down, the strips laid side by side, overlapped perhaps a half-inch. Matting could be sewn into a carpet and not tacked down, in which case carpet-weights were probably necessary. It was frequently laid as carpeting, wall-to-wall. The latter practice was the usual mode by the 1830s, and by the 1870s, at least, a mat of newspapers was sometimes spread on the floor with the matting tacked down over it.

The closet's secret: painted border and wallpaper of 1895 remain uncovered in the upper part of a closet added ca. 1900. —*Haworth P. Bromley Photo*

Straw matting is normally associated with summer use. That is, the wool carpeting or carpet was rolled up and stored and the matting laid for the duration of the warm months. Many inventories taken in the winter prove that this was not necessarily the rule. Matting was considered a perfectly acceptable year-round floor covering; with rugs or a carpet over it, matting helped insulate the floors, and presented a handsome background for the floor coverings it bordered. Sometimes matting seems to have been used as a protective cover for carpeting in the summer or in times of heavy use, although because dirt and dust filtered quite freely through matting, this practice makes less sense than its reverse.

At this writing, straw matting of the "Canton" sort is nearly impossible to find for the restored interior. Some have tried sewing the short Hong Kong, Japanese, and Korean mats end on end to make strips; but this is not a good compromise. If walked on, this makeshift matting will not last long. Straw rugs with a flat or criss-cross weave will sometimes suffice, if mainly to give the desired straw color. There are patterned straw rugs, too, in natural and either red, green, brown, or blue, which may in some respects approximate colored mats of the sort that are documented as having been used in the United States in the first decade of the nineteenth century and thereafter. Old matting is very rare, for, since matting gets dirty and will take only so much scrubbing, it wears out and is thrown away. Occasionally one finds a tattered length of plain Victorian matting or some that is stencilled, perhaps with a heron at the corners and a border of palmetto leaves. Even if very early matting did survive, it would serve, like the ordinary Victorian kind, simply to reiterate the inadequacy of the substitutes to which we must resort.

One questions—with small hope for an answer—whether any type of floor covering in America was in as widespread use in America between about 1830 and World War I as straw matting. There were many other types of floor coverings. Sand, which might be called the "matting" of the less-prosperous country folk prior perhaps to about 1860, was used in the seventeenth and eighteenth centuries; there was a time, as we have seen, when sand was nearly universal on domestic floors in America, even in town. Before the age of carpeting, there was yet another floor covering, which came close to being a common denominator and which, in a somewhat different composition, is still with us today. This was the "oilcloth," or "floorcloth."

Floorcloths

Floorcloths were probably used in America in the seventeenth century, but their documentation thus far goes back no further than the first quarter of the eighteenth. The technique of painting canvas to make it tough and waterproof was well known in the practice of building. Prior to the appearance of tin, a cheap alternative for lead, copper, and other costly roofing materials suitable to low pitches was painted canvas. Tacked down in strips and carefully turned under and overlapped, the canvas surface, painted with three or so coats of oil paint, had its external uses on ships and buildings alike. With the painted surface varnished, the practical advantages of a floorcloth for a domestic dwelling, whether on an interior floor or that of a porch, were numerous: it was washable, did not absorb grease, it insulated the floor, and it was durable, requiring only an occasional revarnishing. The painted floorcloth was the forerunner of linoleum, which is, in fact, a floorcloth.

It was no less in the nature of the floorcloth to be beautiful than functional. Painters decorated them to resemble fine flooring—tiles, marble, parquetry—and all kinds of carpeting. Floorcloths were both simple and elaborate. The decorated examples we see in old Ameri-

78   can portraits might often be demonstrations of
the painters' abilities at the floorcloth art, instead of actual floorcloths the sitters owned. In
any case, the designs of eighteenth- and
nineteenth-century floorcloths, which we
know early Americans had, are preserved in
the largest number in portraits, and most of
these have New England provenance. Inventories and advertisements tell us that they
were also widely used elsewhere.

Floorcloths, like straw matting, were used
both as carpets and carpeting. It can be supposed that all wall-to-wall floorcloths were
made at home or executed on commission;
rug-size floorcloths could, of course, be had
the same ways but were also widely available
ready-made. The advertisements of painters
who could produce floorcloths are abundant in
American newspapers in all regions from the
last quarter of the eighteenth century until
about the 1850s, by which time they were
rather universally called "oilcloths." There was
probably a greater business, however, in the
manufactured floorcloths in large and small
rug sizes. From the 1750s, English floorcloths
were imported in quantity for sale in American shops. While this trade seems to have continued into the nineteenth century, as long as
there was a demand for floorcloths, American
manufacturers had fairly well taken the market
by the close of the War of 1812. Floorcloths
were standard wares in mercantile houses
throughout the nineteenth century. After
about 1845, they seem to have been more
commonly used in halls than in parlors, but
were often preferred over carpeting for dining
rooms, where there might at least be an
oilcloth crumb-catcher laid beneath the table,
over the floor or carpet.

Floorcloths began to be rivaled in popularity
in the 1870s by the more durable linoleum,
patented in England by Frederick Walton in
1860 and probably imported to America already in that decade. Walton's "oiled linen"
was, like his later wallpapers, covered with

Advertisement for a marble mantel factory, 1851.
—Smithsonian Institution

rubbery oxidized linseed oil, a cheap and
satisfactory substitute for the expensive India-
rubber coating that had characterized the most
expensive manufactured floorcloths since the
1750s. Before the close of the nineteenth century, linoleum had taken the market; with
linoleum still made today using Walton's basic
idea, "floorcloths" are still a part of our lives.
Floorcloths of the more traditional sort, however, did not disappear until probably the
early twentieth century. They were still practical when made at home. Victorian household
guide books told you how to make oilcloths,
using a base of muslin, tacked down and
sized, upon which chintz or wallpaper was
pasted, and then heavily varnished.

If your documentation calls for a floorcloth,
the chances are what you will use is a reproduction. Original floorcloths surviving from
any period are scarce; they are of such great
historical value as documents that they must
not be exposed to foot-traffic. Reproductions
of old floorcloths are expensive and usually
must be made to order. There are instances
when restorationists have taken on the task of

making reproductions themselves, tacking the canvas down, sizing it with a coat of thinned paste, and painting and varnishing it according to old practices. The resulting surface should be smooth and slick, showing very little of the fabric's texture. Reproductions are usually most successful when the floorcloth is plain or has a simple design, such as a stripe-border or an uncomplicated checkerboard. Elaborate, many-colored designs are quite another matter, requiring the work of a talented illustrator or a delineator who can copy old designs and colors exactly. Anything in this line less than the best and most accurate reeks of being an "adaptation," which, in the historical interior, amounts to an error.

Carpets

Carpets and carpeting were seldom available to any but the rich in the seventeenth and eighteenth centuries; their democratization in the nineteenth century marked the beginning of our modern idea that they are indispensable to the well-furnished interior. Floorcloths predated the use of carpets on floors in colonial America, for until the 1750s carpets were used as covers on tables and beds. While the whole range of English carpet-types could conceivably have been acquired by an eighteenth-century American of great means, Oriental carpets—called "Turkey" carpets—seem to have enjoyed preference. But there are unquestionably far, far more of these scattered among historic house museums today than were ever in the colonies in the entire eighteenth century. The popular affection for Oriental carpets and rugs laid upon highly polished floors is a lingering fragment of Victorian taste.

Transportation, small quantity, and cost were the factors limiting the use of Oriental rugs and carpets in America. The designs were copied at home in a dissimilar hand-stitching on canvas, the results called "Turkey-work." In the later eighteenth century, manufactured

carpets imitating Oriental or "Persian" designs were called "Turkey-work carpets." The term *Turkey-work* appears now and then in documents as late as the 1870s to describe abstract geometrical carpet patterns.

The English carpeting industry, which began to flower in the mid-eighteenth century, produced but was not restricted to Oriental designs; in fact, toward the end of the century, the English largely abandoned them in favor of floral and classical motifs and over-all patterns based upon French Aubusson and Savonnerie models. Carpeting manufacture was a thriving business in the British Isles by the fourth quarter of the eighteenth century. The various kinds of English carpeting appeared in America almost as soon as they did on the British market. But again, they were in the homes only of very rich people, with very stylish ideas.

These English carpets varied in quality and cost from the ordinary pileless "ingrain" carpeting, produced in strips, to the sumptuous cut-pile Axminster carpets, which were made in one piece by hand-knotting on vertical looms. Brussels carpeting, made in twenty-seven- to thirty-six-inch strips, had a pile composed of uncut loops; produced in Wilton, England, after 1740, the Brussels weaving process allowed for a profusion of colors and elaborate patterns. The "Wilton" carpeting, also woven in strips, was an improvement on the Brussels type, having a cut pile instead of loops. Wilton carpeting, in solid color or rich design, also found application as upholstery. "Scotch" for ingrain (after the location of its principal manufactories), "Brussels," "Wilton," and "Axminster" became the names universally used for *types* of carpeting. Although short-cuts in modern machine manufacture have watered down the quality considerably, the names have prevailed, and Wiltons and Axminsters are still on the general market today.

Peter Sprague's Philadelphia Carpet Manufactory was making Wiltons in the 1790s, as

80 well as some Axminsters in Turkey patterns. Carpet stores also opened in some cities in the East in that decade. Like many other American industries, carpet manufacture gained impetus in the absence of imports during the War of 1812. The sudden flood of imports after the war led to the protective tariff of 1816, which, with its 25 percent duty on imported woolen goods, was a distinct boon to the domestic manufacture of carpeting. Tariffs continued to rise sharply in the 1820s, yet the carpeting industry, though it developed steadily, did not grow as rapidly as one might have expected.

Already in 1813–1814, the first power looms for weaving cloth had appeared in the cotton mills at Waltham, Massachusetts. The time, however, when that principle of mass-production was applied to the manufacture of carpeting was slow in coming. Encouraged by the protective tariff of 1828, carpet manufacturers in that year combined the hand loom they had traditionally used with the Jacquard attachment, an apparatus that employed perfo-

rated cards to "program" a loom, thus making it possible for unskilled weavers to weave complex patterns. New mills opened; innovations continued to be made. By the success of the trade it is obvious that more Americans were buying carpeting, but carpeted floors were by no means typical of the house of the average citizen. The controversial protective tariffs declined from the hotly contested Compromise Tariff of 1833 until 1842, yet continued to provide a healthy climate for carpet manufacture. Through those years, sizable mills prospered, producing ingrain, Bussels, and, to a lesser degree, Wilton and Axminster. The industry did not emerge as a big business in the United States until 1844, when Erasmus Brigham Bigelow put into operation at Clinton, Massachusetts, his power loom for weaving ingrain. Bigelow's success soon persuaded him and others to undertake the mass-production of Brussels carpeting. By the late 1840s, manufactured carpeting, particularly ingrain, was readily available to the average American.

It is not remarkable to find carpeting listed in a middle-class inventory of the late 1830s, though it is surprising if the quantity was large. Parlor carpeting was a likely purchase, either ingrain or perhaps even Brussels. It was usually laid wall to wall; the strips were either sewn together or tacked side by side, and almost invariably the whole was tacked down around the edges. Elsewhere in the house some of the floors might also be carpeted. Stair carpeting was held in place by rods, which did not rip through the material as tacks did, and also allowed one to shift the runner readily for even wear. Bedrooms, offices, and so on, were often provided with cheap, flat-woven "Venetian" carpeting, usually striped, or homemade "list carpeting" woven from rags and string. Both of these were woven in strips of from twenty-seven to thirty-six inches' width, sewn together and tacked down around the edges.

In the 1790s, all-over carpeting—Scotch, Wil-

Tea table of Chippendale type, Philadelphia, ca. 1785, anonymus. —*Courtesy of New-York Historical Society, New York City*

ton, Brussels—was familiar in the homes of wealthy Americans. Axminster carpets, being extremely expensive, were rare. Of the fine carpeting, Brussels was apparently the kind most frequently used. It was first produced in the United States in 1807. Like Wilton, but less costly, it had strong colors (which would be stronger still with the introduction to carpeting of aniline dyes in the 1850s and chemical-base colors after 1869), and it was produced in intricate designs. Brussels and Wilton were produced also as borders, which could be sewn around carpeting in a solid or pattern, giving it the finish of a fine carpet. Borders were nearly as common with carpeting as with wallpaper.

The American carpeting industry continued to grow in the second half of the nineteenth century. Production per capita in 1870 was slightly less than one-half square yard; by 1900 it was one square yard. Once ingrain became commonplace, the production of Brussels reached a point where it, too, could be sold cheaply. By the 1890s the various types of "pile" carpeting and rugs had all but ended the reign of ingrain, though it continued to be produced as late as the 1920s.

The Victorian reaction against all-over carpeting must not be taken to suggest a complete turning away from its use. In the 1880s, manufacturers did turn to producing more rugs than before, and carpeting sewn to carpet-size became popular. But all-over carpeting was too well established as a luxury by the late nineteenth century to allow its complete abandonment. The dazzling floral "art square" rugs of the 1880s through the early teens began to be rivaled already in the late 1890s by simpler, deep-colored rugs and "American Orientals," which are still manufactured today. Carpeting and carpet-sizes, giving the seamless appearance of rugs, were entrenched by 1900 in "broadloom" carpeting, which, as its name implies, was produced in broad widths. In the twentieth century, machine-woven broadloom

Victorian textiles: bedroom at Terrace Hill, Des Moines, Iowa, photo 1899. —*Old Capitol Collection, University of Iowa*

carpeting of the Wilton and Axminster sort eclipsed the once-dominant Brussels, and survives on a small scale today in a market that has been almost overwhelmed since the early 1950s by "tufted" carpeting.

Carpets in the Recreated Room

Carpeting and carpets are a matter of great concern and expense on any restoration project where the documentation calls for such floor covering. If original carpeting survives, it should be carefully preserved, of course. Sometimes the original is so far gone, so rotten, worn, torn, and faded, that there is not much left to preserve, but there is the evidence from which to make a reproduction. Having carpeting, or a rug, reproduced is costly; there are companies that do this work well, albeit using, in most cases, modern methods of production. When reproduction is out of the question until a later time, leave the document on the floor, no matter its condition. Protect it from traffic and show it as what it is.

More often, you will have only a reference to a carpet as having been there. You may then

82 be so fortunate as to find a document from the area either to use or to copy; either of these possibilities is second-best but perfectly valid. As an alternative to commissioning a reproduction, you can, for Brussels and Axminster piles, try to find a suitable pattern in a commercial line (usually from an English manufacturer) and if necessary have it specially run in the colors you need. This will cost only a bit more than expensive modern carpeting. As a last resort, you can select from the very few appropriate commercial products on the market. There are several reproductions available today; one might hesitate about buying them because they are so widely used already that they seem to be "restoration props." Possibilities for carpeting of the period type on the general market are scant for the years 1790 to 1890. While the field is still sparse for carpeting appropriate for certain times after about 1890, there are patterned carpet styles that will suffice—usually the scattered, all-over designs featuring the repeat of a little flower or leaf. Few of the modern floral patterns with big roses, et cetera, have any relevance at all. Solid colors are seldom muddy enough for the 1870s and 1880s, or deep and vibrant enough for the years 1890 to 1917. Still, by searching with a critical eye, you can usually find at least one carpet style that will suit your house.

Antique carpets should not be considered for purchase without the assistance of an expert on carpets, as well as someone who is aware of the quality of carpet that is historically appropriate to your house. Such help will usually need to be sought from two different people. It is easy to overfurnish with floor coverings—to use the improbable Aubusson where an English or American Brussels is more likely, to use Oriental rugs where there was probably matting. Nothing can quite compare to the historical feel an authentic floor covering gives a room, if it meets the credentials of accuracy; nothing can demolish that feeling more quickly than the wrong floor covering. The

An object of use reused: a bed revised as a settee, photo 1900. —*Michigan State University Archives*

long search for the right antique carpet and the high expense of a proper reproduction are seldom regretted, if the historical basis was there in the first place.

Curtains

The curtains in restored interiors are quite as likely to be reproductions as the floor coverings, for, like carpeting and rugs, curtains are usually used until they are worn out. Some go to the attic and are forgotten; but, alas, the twentieth-century mobility of Americans has made ancestral attics so rare that the chances of finding anything tucked away below the rafters is small. Curtains sometimes survive as packing material. Most, however, are torn into rags or go to the trash pile. The thrifty world that was able to keep such things, thinking they might someday be of use, is nearly gone.

Antique curtains that survive in their original form are very rare in America, although there are excellent examples from most periods. The earliest documented examples of American curtains are eighteenth-century bed hangings. Specimens of window hangings are invariably later, well into the nineteenth century. There are window curtains that prevail in fair to good condition and are the treasures of the houses they adorn; others, like Andrew Jackson's rust chintz bedroom curtains of about 1835 at the Hermitage, have had to be replaced by copies, and the originals put away for preservation.

Sometimes restorers copy documentary curtains from other locations. The green and yellow chintz bed hangings of about 1810 in the collection of the Essex Institute, Salem, Massachusetts, have been copied for the Decatur House in Washington, D.C. The giraffe-colored lambrequins of the 1850s in Lansdowne plantation house near Natchez, Mississippi, have been adapted in color but reproduced in form for the Belter Parlor at Houston's Bayou Bend Museum.

In basic terms of longevity, earlier fabrics—those made prior to about 1840 and containing pure natural fibres, be it cotton, flax, wool, or silk—last indefinitely if not abused, while the later mixed fibres that flowed and still flow from the mills will not last, under the most ideal conditions. Early fabrics acquired in quantity, such as those from the walls of seventeenth- and eighteenth-century houses in Europe, have been used to make curtains based upon historical designs. Many examples of these can be seen at the Winterthur Museum. But of course these do not qualify as antique curtains. Most restorers have no recourse on fabrics but to turn to commercial reproductions of old materials, or to select modern materials that are similar to what they must have. From the point of view of conservation, this is best, anyway; the historic house museum, when used as actively as it should be, can be a death chamber for old fabrics.

On curtains, mistakes are frequently made. Historic houses are usually over-draped; what is more, their hangings, made on modern-day principles, nearly always hang wrong. The smothering plethora of silk, damask, satin, and velvet that characterizes American restored interiors really reflects twentieth-century customs. Some of it has justification; however, too little is rooted in fact or even probability.

What we take for granted about curtains is as much to blame as thin research. Our twentieth-century point of view about curtains differs markedly from that of most of the nineteenth century and certainly from that of the two centuries of settlement preceding it. Curtains, in the style mores of our time, compensate for the lack of interior architectural detailing. Moreover, they can cover up undesired detailing, and thus neuter the room to simplify the rest of its decorating. Curtains are so familiar to us as appointments of style that to our eyes most windows appear naked without them.

So let us begin with naked windows. In the eighteenth century, beds seem to have been curtained more frequently than windows. This made it possible to contain a warm sleeping space in a room that became cold with nightfall. Conversely, we today curtain the windows but leave the beds uncurtained. Two factors helped over many years to effect this reversal: improved heating and improved artificial lighting.

There is a strong parallel between the rise to popular use of the innovative oil lamps of the late eighteenth and early nineteenth centuries and the increasing number of curtains for windows listed in American inventories. Better artificial lighting made it pleasanter to stay up longer into the night; curtains at the windows blocked drafts and peering eyes from the outside. Stoves gave rooms a more complete heat than fireplaces. Curtains over the glass of windows helped contain that heat and were

84 even better draft eliminators than floor coverings—which, we noted earlier, increased on the market at the same time.

Project the trend through gas-lighting to central heating to electric lighting in understanding our common idea today that windows must have curtains. Different regions, different houses, stood at different places in the development of this use of curtains. In 1835 the Grimké sisters of Charleston, South Carolina, writing their letters by an Argand light, probably had their windows curtained; those of the candlelit room of Abraham Lincoln, far away in New Salem, Illinois, probably were not. Such differences still existed by World War I. By World War II, contrasts in this area were fewer.

Consider this less a hard-and-fast rule than a way of approaching the subject of curtains for your historical room. Being transient objects, curtains fall into the categories of ornament and use. A documentary reference of 1780 to "4 setts window curtains" for a richly architectural drawing room does not necessarily mean equally rich window hangings, though, of course, it may. An 1845 account-book order of "10 yds blue damask" could more plausibly refer to material for dresses, in some regions, than to window hangings. In looking over sources on window hangings, take special note of *where* the particular specimens appear: there is seldom an analogy between the gallery of an English country house and even a mansion in America until the 1860s and 1870s, and then the comparisons are very few. Those complex and sumptuous drapery designs published in France in the late eighteenth and all through the nineteenth centuries must have been an inspiration to some big-city upholsterers in America. But did they copy the designs or simplify them, as was the usual practice in the other branches of decorative arts in the United States? The draperies that survive suggest that they usually did the latter, until the burst of mansion-building that followed the Civil War.

Now and then the written documentation on curtains is highly indicative of the form the original window hangings took. Thomas Elfe, the Charleston, South Carolina, cabinetmaker, makes, in his account book of 1765–1775, frequent references similar to this one for November 27, 1773: "To 3 window Larths with pullies £4.10—to putting pullies in a set of Bed larths. . . . " He is referring to fixtures for bed and window curtains that open and close up and down—instead of by being drawn aside—through the configuration of rings, cords, and pulleys. A century later, an inventory might refer to "a lambrequin and lace curtains." This meant, usually, a flat valance of some opaque fabric, concealing the heading and devices from which lace curtains fell to the floor. "Three pairs of curtains" in a written document of 1830 is certain to mean two panels per window, which would have been opened to each side in some manner; "three curtains," however, could mean that for each of three windows there was a single panel that pulled aside in one direction or, before about 1840, a single panel that pulled up. For the entire nineteenth century and into the twentieth, the reference to a single curtain can also mean a window shade.

Festoons

In considering the various types of curtains that had widespread use in American houses up until early in this century, several characteristic forms become conspicuous at different times. Curtains that drew up by means of cords were quite familiar in eighteenth-century America and survived in some quarters three or four decades into the nineteenth century. Draw-up curtains were practical hangings for the English type of sash window, in which the top sash was usually fixed in place: the maximum use of the window's function could be had from such rising curtains. In books, these curtains were referred to as "festoons," but the word so seldom appears in personal documentation that your only clue will be when their fixtures are listed, as in the Elfe reference above, or when there are evidences of their former presence on the window itself.

The festoon forms were used widely on beds and windows throughout the eighteenth century. Festoons conserved material; yet when the curtains were drawn up, they provided a lively-looking bunch of fabric at the top of the tester or window. The average festoon must not be confused with the "Austrian shade," which, though similar and also technically a festoon, is more tailored and controlled, has more cords, and is shirred in scallops from top to bottom. The usual festoon was a simpler affair.

To make a festoon, one cut a size of fabric the dimensions of the window, measuring from the outer edges of the architrave, and from the extreme top to the bottom, allowing about six inches overage at the top and enough along the sides and bottom for binding. The festoon was tacked across a wooden lath, which was attached to the lintel of the window; the fabric, when it fell from this lath, totally covered the window and the entire architrave. Rings were spaced along tapes that ran in vertical parallel rows on the window side of the fabric; there was one row at each end, and one or more in between, depending upon the width of the window. Cords were run up through the rings and across the lath through pulleys to one side, where, when drawn at the same time, they caused the curtain to rise. A cleat (usually a pair of picture pins) secured the cords when the curtain was open.

The surviving American festoons are bed-curtains. These show us that festoons could be very ingeniously devised. Of course on a bed, which had a tester lower to the floor than the top of a window, curtains might function better when they did not rise straight up. Thus the rings were sewn on the side curtains in a

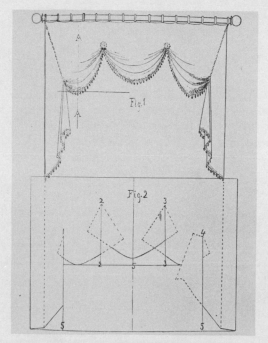

Pattern for making a flat valance, 1890.— *Frank A. Moreland,* Practical Decorative Upholstery *(1890)*

diagonal arc; when pulled open, the curtains then had the effect of being tied back, the grace of the resulting drape of the fabric depending upon the cleverness of the upholsterer in situating his rings. Window curtains made similarly amounted to split festoons, consisting of two panels. When the cords were pulled, the curtains swept up elegantly, giving the effect of a swag, with scallops at the center and tails cascading down the sides. Valances may not have been common with festoons, but there are eighteenth-century English documents that show them, short and either cut straight or with a fancy edge.

There is every reason to assume that in American houses festoons were more often than not made at home. The restorers who have done likewise in recent years have come up with the best specimens, actually resembling what is seen in old prints and paintings.

86   In making festoons, amateurishness with the needle seems to be a real asset. Like most types of curtains before the high Victorian 1870s, festoons were not tailored-looking. Old prints show them as being loose, hoisted irregularly, and folded into festoons that are sometimes wild. They are not suited to an exacting, trim look, and while a rod or lath was sometimes run in the lower hem, they were never equipped with parallel laths all the way up, as with the "Roman shades" of the 1950s.

Window Shades

Although the festoon's popularity was fairly well gone by the 1830s, another type of rising curtain, already in existence for quite a while, took its place. This was what we call the window shade. The earliest use of these in America is undetermined, but they seem to have been in evidence here by the War of 1812. Probably they were in use in the eighteenth century. Commonly called "curtains," they went also by their English name "roller blinds," and "spring-roller blinds." The latter refers to those with the spring-raising device similar to what we know today and apparently in use in England by the 1750s. Some of our eighteenth-century inventories that refer to "window blinds" may well mean shades, instead of Venetian blinds. By the 1860s the term *window shade* was in common usage in America, although the term also sometimes meant an external awning.

The British occasionally called window shades "Holland blinds," after the thick Holland linen especially woven for that purpose—and in the eighteenth century also used for sheets. Window shades in America are often described as having been made of cambric. The commonest kind of window shade was operated by means of cords. This shade consisted of a wooden dowel—a "roller"—with pivots on each end; the pivots were set into iron or tin sockets. These receptacles were little eyelets, sometimes fixed inside the window reveal, but usually held out from the window facing on triangular brackets at a distance of about three inches. The curtain itself was tacked along the roller, and hung to the base of the window, where it was weighted and kept flat by a lath run in a hem. One end of the roller was equipped with a circular notch, which was either a cut in the wood itself or in the rim of a small stationary metal wheel. A cord ran over this in a continuous loop, and through a pulley fixed at the base of the window. This lower attachment was not an ordinary pulley but what was called a "pulley rack," a vertical ratchet about four inches long, made of tin or brass, into which the pulley could be fixed at different levels. The loop of cord had to be kept taut, so that, when pulled into action, the roller would turn with it and thus collect the material. To tighten the cord, the pulley was lowered in the rack, until finally the cord was too greatly stretched and had to be reknotted.

The main purpose of the cords was to raise the shade. While the cords also functioned for lowering, it was simpler to pull down on the shade itself. Since this was what was commonly done, a tassel (or two) was often attached to the hem, both to make pulling convenient and to encourage pulling at the right place, insuring that the shade rolled evenly.

Manual roller shades, like festoons, were relatively easy to make at home. The fixtures—pulley racks, metal pivots, rollers, and sockets—were stock items in the stores. In spring rollers, from the eighteenth century to the late nineteenth, the spring mechanism, located in one end of the roller, was activated by a cord that hung from a lever on the device down one side of the window. When pulled, the cord released the spring, which caused the roller to turn; this action was stopped by releasing the cord. While spring shades were very convenient, they were more expensive than the manual kind with the pulley rack, hence the latter seem to have been far more common. The "automatic" spring shade universal today is counterbalanced, and has a built-in stop that appeared probably not much before about 1880 and was everywhere by the early 1900s.

Most window shades were probably left plain, but a fashion did develop in the 1820s for making window shades into "transparencies." These transparencies were painted in colorful designs or scenes and varnished heavily, to keep the paint from cracking. In the daytime they were bright, like stained glass, with light from behind; at night the artificial light glistened on them, as it did on oil paintings. The advertisements for decorated window shades abounded in American newspapers from the 1830s until about the 1880s. With some painters, perhaps the same ones who painted floorcloths, they seem to have been a specialty; there was also an American market for transparencies manufactured abroad. Painting the cambric shades, however, was also a home art, accomplished by some member of the family with a penchant, if not a talent, for painting pictures.

For the years 1840 until the late 1870s, one wonders whether any other hangings were as popularly used by Americans as window shades. They were used with other curtains, but as often, it seems, by themselves. Enveloping bed curtains were less and less numerous as functioning accessories. Ordinarily, "curtains" had come to mean window curtains. Many inventories that specify curtains undoubtedly mean window shades. If the Grecian fever of the early nineteenth century thrived on drapery, let it be remembered that it also favored simplicity and bareness, perhaps more so. The roller shade alone doubtless adorned many a Greek-Revival window, leaving the broad classical architrave unobstructed. For its practicality, the roller shade (or, as we know it, the spring-shade) has remained

in use. Its history is more continuous than that of its wooden counterpart, the Venetian blind, which was used to a limited extent earlier than the roller blind, in the eighteenth century, but which was rendered unnecessary by moveable external blinds in the 1840s and only reappeared to any extent in the 1930s.

The careful restorationist can reproduce old roller shades without much trouble, making sure that the fabric is linen or cambric, that the hem and lath at the bottom are twice the one-and-one-half-inch depth customary in modern shades. Pulley racks will not be likely to turn up and must be copied or simulated. The cord that is used with the roller shade must be coarse, not the waxed curtain cord of today, which will not grip the roller's groove.

Other Window Hangings

An elementary sort of window curtain that has been in use since at least the eighteenth century consists of a pair of panels of simple fabric either run on a thin iron or wooden rod through a sewn heading or rings, or tacked directly to a lath. These were opened by being pushed apart or tied back. The latter was accomplished using string, cord, or cloth tiebacks or "loops," or by knotting. Old drawings, prints, and paintings frequently show plain curtains of this sort neatly draped to the sides by being tied in a knot at about the same height the usual tie-back would be. Knotting curtains is practically a lost skill; it involved making a partial knot, something of a secure fold, from which with one tug at the hem the curtain could be freed. It is quite a feat to accomplish this knotting in the traditional way, using one hand.

"Sash" curtains or half-curtains served perhaps more universally for insect screening than for anything else. They covered only that part of the window which was moveable, the lower sash, and are frequently illustrated as being not full but almost flat, a very simple

88 material, usually white, running on a string, and hanging loose at the bottom. Called "short blinds" in the early nineteenth century, they gave city houses privacy from the street without cutting out the light. When used in parlors they were almost certainly of finer stuff, dimity, for example, than the cheap domestic and screening we see in most prints and paintings. Very little is known about sash curtains before they reappeared in twentieth-century houses as quaint "cottage curtains" in the 1920s and "cafe curtains" later on, named for their continued use in street-level restaurants and shops.

Window hangings, and particularly ornamental ones, were revolutionized at about the time they really got going in the United States by the appearance here, probably not much before the early 1820s, of the so-called French rod for draw curtains. Where the English used up and down sash windows, the typical window in France was a hinged casement, opening like doors. As the festoon made sense as a curtain for English sash windows, curtains that parted to each side were naturally better suited to casements, hence they were universal in France. In England, the taste for "French" curtains developed in the last quarter of the eighteenth century, when the festoon was still predominant in fashion. Side-hanging curtains had always existed in England, but they were difficult to open and close, particularly if the window was tall. The innovation of the French rod made them practical by making it possible to open, close, and overlap two panels by simply pulling a cord. This was not only convenient, but it saved wear and tear on the fabric.

The parts of the French rod resembled more closely those of a stage curtain than they did any feature of our modern traverse rods, in which the mechanism is encased. Adjacent to one end of a rod of iron, plain or painted brass, or gilded wood, was fixed a single pulley; at the other end were two pulleys; down low on the architrave of the window, as with a

Object of use: the punkah, or fly-fan, Fair Oaks, Natchez, Mississippi, 1822. —*Mississippi State Department of Archives and History*

roller shade, was a pulley rack. The cord extended from the pulleys to the pulley rack in a continuous loop, its two close parallel lines, when moved, running in opposite directions. The curtain itself was run on a heading of rings, and each of the two center rings was attached to one of the two cords that extended beside the rod. Thus when one of the cords on the side of the window was pulled, the rings were carried in opposite directions, sweeping the rest of the rings, and the curtains below, with them. To keep it from jumping the pulleys, the cord had to be kept taut.

Not always does a reference to French curtains mean that the actual rod mechanism was present. The name seems to have been freely applied to any dressy sort of window hanging in which the curtains hung in long panels, usually full, and were drawn to each side of the opening. French curtains sometimes had valances to conceal the rod and further ornament the window; at other times, the rod was exposed and quite decorative itself, with finials at the ends and great curtain rings of gilded wood or brass. The banks of fabric the open curtains made at the side usually required further tying back, which was accomplished by cord loops or by "curtain pins," usually made of hammered or pressed brass.

With or without the French rod, curtains tied back with a flair gave not only the softness of drapery, but they shaped the light, where it would otherwise have been a bold rectangle at the window. The history of window hangings in the nineteenth century is dominated by curtains that are tied back, from the crimson silk of 1810, bordered in galloon and tied back waist-high, to the white lace of the 1860s, tied back knee-high, making deep, sweeping folds. French curtains and French rods were ordinary terms for fine double-panel curtains until the mid-nineteenth century.

Ornamental window hangings were usually made by upholsterers, who also covered furniture and dealt in upholstery, curtain fabrics, and fixtures. To make curtains well was an art as well as a skill, particularly when drapery was involved. Before our own century, when the word is used indiscriminately for its prestige value, drapery meant valances or any feature of a window hanging sewn to hang in a stationary configuration of folds. There were many forms for draperies; some were flat and were cut in decorative outline, others were "piped," also hanging straight, but pleated, and yet other kinds were gathered up into elaborate swags, which, though stationary, seem to have been inspired by split festoons.

Little specific documentation exists from the eighteenth century for the gorgeous window "treatments" that are the usual props of restored colonial houses. Rich materials were imported to this country and do turn up in the account books of wealthy colonial citizens. There are a few instances where window hangings were ordered by Americans from London drapers. What these looked like is not known, but remembering that hanging curtains was also part of the draper's job, they were probably not very complex. A bed ordered from England, as a few were, might come equipped with drapery. Such orders from London, and the availability of American fabricators in the colonial period, must be considered, at the most, extremely limited. When the windows of colonial mansions were elegantly dressed, they likely had festoons of fine materials and trimmings, or, on occasion, side curtains with shaped flat valances of the sort that survive mainly in bed curtains.

The trade of upholsterer—and, less commonly, that of draper—began to be in evidence in American cities toward the end of the 1790s and really came into its own in the 1820s. Many of these upholsterers were foreign-born, some French—immigrants to America during the Napoleonic wars. They found a new urban society ready to buy the special elegance they could provide. Draperies became indispensable to stylish drawing rooms, particularly as a feature of the new Classical style, the ambience of which they enhanced immeasurably. At least by the early 1830s, window curtains of fine material could be bought ready-made and shipped anywhere. They were expensive, and being produced for a consumer market, were made big enough to accommodate all, so often must have seemed ill-fitting and over-sized. Tying back could correct the latter, and ready-made curtains may account for the predominance of that practice.

The Classical taste dominated fashionable window hangings until the later 1840s. In 1833 the now-famous illustrated broadside of the

90 New York-based Joseph Meeks & Sons, "Manufactory of Cabinet and Upholstery Articles," advertised furniture mostly in the Grecian style, and three types of French curtains one could order by number. Though the illustrations do not show it, the three must have been run on French rods. They were similar in featuring full, loose panels tied back to each side, swags at the top, and thin material behind, tied back low in one direction. It was the swags that set them apart as being from an upholsterer: these were so cut, gathered, and sewn as to appear to drape over fanciful rods and spears, which, presumably, were included as part of the package.

Simpler forms, which did not require an upholsterer's skill, may have been more typical. Two long panels of silk taffeta, hung from a single rod and tied back with a pair of ready-made tasseled cords, could be prepared by most any seamstress; while the lining and interlining called for some ability, dresses were lined, so the practice was not wholly unfamiliar even to a novice at curtain-making. Lining also helped make American-made fabrics seem heavier, like the more costly and better grade of English imports. Ornamental curtain rods, rings, "pins," and "bands"—also for tying back—were sold rather commonly in furniture and upholstery warehouses by the 1830s. When an ornamental rod was not used, the heading of the curtain was usually hidden. It took an experienced draper to make swags properly; but there were other solutions. Painted wooden cornices were made from millwork. They could be simply painted, or pasted all over with fabric, like a coffin, and decorated with gilt-metal stars and moons and cut-out borders, or with drapery rope and fringe. Carved wooden cornices had been used in costly window decorations in the eighteenth century, and even then there were cheap imitations made of cast plaster glued on a wood backing. These last were on the market in the United States in the 1820s, probably before. By the 1850s the idea had found expression and wide popularity in broad gilded cornicing of pressed brass, which was bought by the foot and tacked to a wooden frame. Natural wood or paint-grained imitations rose to fashion in the 1870s, but there was still a market for gilt cornicing until the early 1890s.

Fabrics for Curtains

The fabrics and trimmings for ambitious curtain designs were legion. A variety of tassels, gimp, fringe, borders, galloon, and braid were available in most cities, beginning in the 1820s. Of all the curtain materials, silk was always the most costly and luxurious, and included damask, brocade, satin, lampas, taffeta, and silk velvet, among others. But there were other, cheaper curtain materials that were also used in the better sort of window hangings. Dimity, a cotton woven in stripes, appears in American inventories from the late eighteenth century until the 1840s; linen was considered suitable perhaps more for bed curtains than windows, but it was used on windows; woolen moreen, plain or watered, grew in popularity in the 1830s, and merino damask in the 1840s; cretonne and sateen knew enormous popularity in the Victorian decades.

Printed calico, imported from England in the late eighteenth century, was successfully produced in the United States in the late 1820s. Colorful and available in many patterns, calico was used for furniture upholstery and curtains alike. Chintz was another popular cotton for curtains; more expensive and finer-printed than calico, it could be had with a polished or flat surface. Thin muslin became standard under curtains from the early nineteenth century to the 1850s when lace curtains became popular. This muslin, thinner than what we know as muslin today, is analogous to our cotton lawn or to a batiste without a sheen. Trimmed in fringe, a crocheted edging with little tassels, or with a border, and hung from a

Bathtub, ca. 1895, the Christian Heurich House, Washington, D.C. —*A. Robert Cole Photo for the Columbia Historical Society*

gilt rod, or beneath a drapery valance, bleached muslin could be quite elegant by itself. Fine muslin hangings were usually of the softer, thinner quality known as mull, which was sometimes embellished by being embroidered on the tambour frame.

For all the documented window hangings that exist from American houses, the real era of elaborate curtains did not begin until the 1860s. Then the interest, like that of architecture, was in romantic designs. When that time arrived, the lace curtain and the lambrequin already reigned supreme as the preferred hangings. Controlled and architectural, the lambrequin began to appear in the late 1840s and its life span trailed on three decades into the twentieth century. It was, at its simplest, a flat-hanging piece of opaque fabric usually stiffened with buckram lining. It could be a mere valance, not hanging very low, with some drapery; but ideally it was more than that, hanging long and cut out fancifully in its mid-section so as to shape the light from beyond it. Lambrequins were made in every material from silk damask to calico; they were nearly always in a color, which was trimmed—if not in a fabric, with a pattern.

Requiring less fabric than any other curtain form, the lambrequin was at once decorative and practical. Ladies' magazines suggested designs that could be executed at home; upholsterers' services were probably required for the most complicated styles. Lambrequins are sometimes illustrated as hanging over muslin or lace curtains, and sometimes over heavy curtains. Surviving examples indicate that, in the South, muslin and lace were frequently the only curtains used with lambrequins, whereas in cold climates both lambrequins and curtains were usually of the same material. In national publications of the day, however, you will find both, with those of the 1850s and 1860s more often featuring lace or muslin curtains without heavy side curtains.

Romantic window hangings of the Victorian decades were countless in variety. Books were published on the subject, and merchants offered ready-made curtains for sale. The bare windows found in many middle-class houses of the earlier nineteenth century became fewer, if we are to rely upon old photographs, inventories, and what is suggested in advertisements. By the 1870s ornamental window hangings in mansions could be so detailed and intricate in their designs as to seem to wall out the outside; some, equally elegant, were quite simple, being made of light-colored prints with bright trimmings. Chintz, velvet, damask, and brocade found their way from the market of mass-production in the 1880s not only to middle-class windows, but to mantels, tables, doorways, and practically any other place that, when "done," helped to fulfill the Victorian delight in drapery.

The common denominator by about 1880 was lace. Rivaled only by window shades and used usually in combination with them, lace curtains varied in quality from the least expensive cotton sort, woven on machines, to im-

92 ported silk lace made by hand and sold for handsome sums. Lace was as indispensable to the elegant drawing room of the 1870s as it was in the 1880s to the pretty parlor of a modest row house. In the first it was probably used with heavy side curtains, which were tied back, leaving the field of lace to pattern the light from the window. In a simpler house the lace might hang by itself, either run on a rod through a casing or rings, or banded at the top by a cornice.

Though lace curtains were provided with cords, bands, or pins, they were, at their most proper, left hanging straight, for it was the effect of light passing through them that gave them their special magic. To preserve this quality, and yet tie them back to give the animation of drapery, there were several techniques. One was to tie them back with oversize loops about eighteen inches from the floor, which parted the curtains at the bottom but allowed them to cover most of the opening. Another means was to "tack" them, either with a stitch or a curtain pin, which is simply to say that at each side of the curtain, about twenty-four inches from the floor, the fabric was pinched and lifted perhaps fourteen inches where it was fixed in place, leaving waves of folds, but not obliterating the lacy pattern. Finally, there was the very popular practice of attaching a long-stemmed curtain pin to each side of the window on the architrave; the hem of the curtain was then laid atop the stem, exactly at mid-point, and the curtains hung in luxurious folds.

The Victorians, presented with a vast market of fabrics and imbued with a love for curtains, were not as predictable as their ancestors, where curtains were concerned. This may be because we have photographs of their houses and thus know them better; but that is not really an answer. Curtains and drapery were integral aspects of the "personal" interiors they loved to create. They were fascinated by texture and pattern in fabric, and liked to play

Historic house interior, ca. 1910: old kitchen at the House of the Seven Gables, Salem, Massachusetts.—*Essex Institute*

one off against the other toward a "harmonious" whole. Theatrical gauze, a coarse netting somewhat heavier than screening, was a popular and cheap material for curtains. Embroidered or plain, bleached or left in its natural brownish color, it was enormously popular in the 1880s and 1890s, especially for bedrooms and as a summer substitute for other hangings. Swags were revived in the late 1880s, somewhat modified, and they were sometimes described as "old-fashioned curtains."

The popular fancy for inventive window curtains and the use of drapery elsewhere began to wane in the 1890s and was generally gone by the end of the first decade of the twentieth century. Curtains remained an important feature of household decoration, but there was a new preference for simpler hangings. Even lace, which was still widely available, was being replaced by thin, flat-hanging "glass curtains"—those against the glass—devoid of pattern and having a sheen. This, together with dark green window shades, was deemed sufficient in many a house. A step beyond that was two long side panels, not full enough to close. Usually they hung straight, their heading often the "French pleat" so familiar to us today. The lambrequin prevailed, not as the exotic of other times, but as a valance cut as a horizontal rectangle or given a very restrained, usually sharp-cornered lower edge, with a border perhaps of tapestrylike material, if a border at all.

These later curtains presented a conservative, tailored look not common in earlier hangings. They reflected, perhaps, the exactness and thrift of the machine age, as curtains have, ever since.

Curtains in the Restoration

In planning window hangings for the restored interior, your precise documents are likely to be few, forcing you to turn for designs to general historical sources. As in every other case where you must do this, bear firmly in mind the status and character of the occupants of the house and the level of style current in your locality. Restoration budgets so often suffer unnecessarily from the cost of dressing windows, when there are more probable alternatives in simple solutions or less expensive fabrics.

The range of reproduced fabrics is surprisingly large, though what you are usually buying is appearance, for the quality is not likely to match up to that of the original. You will want to be certain that the color in a reproduced fabric is true to the document; a reputable manufacturer will provide that information. The design may be very faithful, but the color adapted. Certain companies specialize in reproducing fabrics, and can, at very great cost, perform that service for you. This should always be considered a possibility where you have a document, even if it must be in the fu-

ture, and for the present a similar material must suffice.

Commercially produced fabrics in period styles can sometimes be used to great advantage. This takes considerable searching, not only of retail stores but of remnant places. Chintzes, muslin, velvet, and printed cottons, while not dignified with the claim to being "reproductions," now and then have quite ac-

Neo-Classical stove, ca.1810, the Octagon House, Washington, D.C. —*A. Robert Cole Photo for the American Institute of Architects*

94 ceptable period looks. Compare these always to documents that you have or find pictured in books. In the absence of a specific document describing or illustrating the original window hangings in your house, do not bind yourself to one historical form. Learn what is available in fabrics, and trimmings, then decide upon a form that suits your house in terms of that fabric.

Special attention must be paid to the way in which your curtains hang. If your interior predates the 1890s, reject any effort on the part of the fabricator to use French pleats. This makes the curtains gather too precisely and fall too regularly for correctness in earlier houses. In the 1870s and 1880s, some fine curtains were pleated in a small box pleat, stitched only at the upper edge, to which the curtain ring was attached. There was, from the 1830s, a style of valance that was piped in this way, using broad box pleats (the heading always concealed) to make the fabric fall in an effect of cone-shaped cylinders, sometimes with deep rope-fringe along the bottom. Before the late nineteenth century, even grand curtains were more typically headed by a shirred arrangement on a rod of thin iron, or by rings, which were spaced along the ungathered upper edge of the panel and run on a rod. Thus loose, and not so controlled, the curtains awaited only that finishing touch, tying back, in which the fullness could be adjusted according to taste.

The same feeling for accuracy applies to all your window hangings, plain and fancy. Festoons should appear loose, probably not shirred, and they should not be so contrived as to rise in exactly matched scallops, unless you know the originals were fabricated by an expert draper. Swags made by a good draper were not the stiff, orderly valances we see today but theatrical, animated, and abundant. Simple farmhouse curtains, on the other hand, should appear to be just that and not the work of London drapers. Roller shades should function as they would have; modern traverse rods are no substitute for the French rod with its pulleys. Attention to this sort of detail helps the historical interior to succeed.

10

Putting It All Together

$\mathcal{T}$HE final consideration in furnishing the historic house is the arrangement of objects in the room. At a glance, this might appear to be the simplest task of all. You have worked with diagrams on graph paper; from these you have developed an idea about what the rooms will look like. But while the finished rooms may echo the plans, they are not likely to follow them exactly, nor need they. The placement of actual objects raises questions not apparent in two-dimensional drawings.

Arrangements and uses of furnishings represent periods in history more accurately than do the furnishings themselves. When the parlor of 1831, intact in every respect, is rearranged in 1915 to feature conversation groupings of chairs, side-tables, and sofas, it suddenly becomes a room of the twentieth century. The living room in the new house of 1928 in Larchmont, New York, with its antique American furnishings of the 1740 to 1780 years, its authentic eighteenth-century woodwork, its carefully selected accessories, is betrayed as much by its arrangement as the antiquarian taste that assembled it. The room clearly serves a 1920s way of living. Furnishings arrangements are virtually inseparable from lifestyle; one creates the other, and one is mirrored in the other.

From your historical research you have at least some specific knowledge about the customs of the occupants of the house and of their local contemporaries. To interpret how their daily lives were translated into furnishings arrangements, you will need verbal and pictorial descriptions beyond the bare listings in inventories. Useful information may be preserved in a letter. Someone may even recall things as they were. Rooms are very personal; in their arrangement and regardless of the style or styles of their contents, rooms also take on the character of the age. For enlightenment in this very important area, return to the illustrative materials, the paintings, drawings, prints, photographs that you turned up in your research, and relate them to your particular interiors, as well as to the objects you have collected.

Consider the ways of living that the arrangements in these illustrations represent. The interiors of the small-town New England house of 1800 probably share few major characteristics with those of the suburban Philadelphia mansion, which is its contemporary. Yet there are general comparisons in the way the pictures hang, where the bed is placed, how (as opposed to with what) the mantels are ornamented.

When used judiciously, interior views of houses in foreign countries can also be useful. These are more numerous. The ones that bear the closest comparisons to American houses are those depicting rural England in the eighteenth century and bourgeois interiors in nineteenth-century England and Germany. There are also regional parallels, as between late eighteenth-century Louisiana and provincial France and Spain at the same time and a bit earlier. Such early illustrative materials show furnishings arrangements that were current in a certain time in history, even though the locale may be remote from yours. Foreign sources will be valuable, however, only after they have been compared to your own specific materials, as well as to contemporary views of American houses. The vines may be relevant, for example, planted in pots and growing over the windows, where the great porcelain stove in the corner obviously is not.

There are a few general points about customs in furniture arrangement that can serve as a guide toward solutions for your historical interiors. Before our technological age of climate control and electric illumination, heat,

96 cold, and light strongly restricted the way in which rooms were arranged. Two hundred years ago, the "setting" as we know it, with furniture carefully placed over the floor for both visual attractiveness and use *in situ* was in effect unknown. From the eighteenth century to the twentieth, customs in furniture arrangement completely changed. In this evolutionary process, the vanguard was practical innovation, not style.

That most revolutionary eighteenth-century invention, the Argand burner, introduced by the late 1790s a period of about twenty years that can be considered a first watershed in American furniture arrangement. The change was not radical, but significant. We have already discussed in connection with curtains the effects the brilliant light had on the use of rooms at night. In the daytime people still relied upon natural light from the windows, as they always had, and while it is obvious that everyone did not share the luxury of Argand lighting, its presence, in altering attitudes

Combination electric and gas bracket, Heurich House, Washington D.C. —*A. Robert Cole Photo for the Columbia Historical Society*

about living in rooms, began to affect basic customs in mansion and cottage alike.

The traditional manner of arranging furniture was to line it up against the walls. This was not an artless exercise; the most numerous pieces being chairs, they stood in neat rows, side by side, and were interspersed with tables, sofas, et cetera. A room thus arranged was "straight," which may perhaps account for that expression's being used to mean a room is in order. When the furniture was needed for use, it was moved to whatever situation was satisfactory. For an afternoon gathering for sewing, for example, a settee, the necessary number of chairs, and a small table might be arranged in a little circle near the fire, in the fall of light from a window, or in the path of a breeze that swept through the door. A desk frequently used for writing might be kept angled across a corner to take advantage of the light from two windows; it could just as well have been angled before one window, to make similar use of the daylight. The dining table was by no means a fixture in the center of the room. It too was moved about for comfort, and in large houses it was sometimes kept in an adjacent hall when not in use, leaving the chairs and sideboard or side table lined around the walls, and the center of the room open.

Objects of ornament were not placed about in such profusion in rooms where furniture was moved about as they would be later in the fixed setting. Ornaments were fairly well restricted to the walls, the mantel, and to immoveable furniture: those on the latter two sometimes appear to have been arranged in an orderly manner, other times they seem only to be stored, certainly not displayed, awaiting use.

Light's intensity varied at different windows throughout the day. But with the new Argand, evening light was more stationary, whether through sconces screwed fast to the wall, or from lamps, which tended to be cumbersome and were not moved about any more than was necessary. It made sense then to keep certain pieces of furniture near the light, if you had reason to believe that is where they would be used over and over. Hence a sofa pulled out into the room; hence an ever-so-slight beginning toward fixed placement for continual use.

Oil lamps, we have noted, continued to be improved. The Astral lamp made the center table indispensable. Having a table in the middle of the room was not unfamiliar, but it was never really characteristic of interiors before its advent as a practical means of making the maximum use of the shadowless lamp. Chairs were pulled up to the center table, which was often round, like the fall of light, and the family sat in a circle, reading, playing games, doing work of one kind or another, and talking. When the room was straight, the center table remained in place, with its lamp, while the chairs were shoved back against the wall. Because of the fear of fire and the daily need to clean and refuel lamps, small lamps and candleholders were removed to one central place after being used, if not carried off at night to bedrooms, from which they were collected the next morning.

By the 1840s, furniture arrangement was a combination of the old manner and the new. With improved stoves, the winter season might see seating furniture left near the fire; at other times, a large part of it was still placed against the walls, with, in sitting rooms, a table in the center. Only with the spread of gaslight, and especially overhead gaslight and that from kerosene, did the seat furniture and other tables begin to move out from the walls. Fixed arrangements more or less as we know them followed naturally, finding their first fashionable expression in America in the 1850s with manufactured ensembles in the "French Antique," a historical revival style that had been in evidence since the 1830s.

The arrangement of objects in a room was of major interest to the subsequent generations of Victorians. Their efforts were in a sense experimental. Many of our own modern concepts of arrangement are theirs. A room's arrangement, as a whole more than any of its parts, was to them an essay in personal preference—a manifestation of "good" or "bad" taste. Style was what you bought at the store; taste was how you put it all together. Furniture ceased to be the dominating feature, dictating the room's theme. It now had to share center stage with many other sorts of objects, some the purchased fruits of mass-manufacture, others made at home as further emblems of taste and sentiment. The decorated interior was to the Victorians a kind of altar to stability in a world in which old domestic symbols were dying very fast.

The taste of the nineties: Oriental rugs laid over Brussels carpeting, in a setting that features gilded rocking chairs in the style of Louis XV. The Heurich House, Washington, D.C. —*A. Robert Cole Photo for the Columbia Historical Society*

98   After about 1870 the arrangement of furnishings became an integral part of a room's ornamental quality. The germ of this idea was not new. What was new was the placement of furniture all over the floor in stable configurations, with the introduction of numerous transient objects, toward a decorated whole. This was in evidence to a limited extent in the symmetrical "French" arrangements of the 1850s, but not until the 1870s did the practice come into general popularity. By then, asymmetry was fashionable.

In the early 1870s the illustrative sort of historical revival styles in furniture were largely replaced by new and more abstract styles, which were not readily identifiable as "historical" Creative furniture designs suited the new concept in interior decoration, which replaced boldness in theme with subtlety. The conformity of the "French Antique" and "Renaissance" interiors was superseded by a taste for rooms in which the central element was— theoretically, at least—less style than the personal judgment of the individual who had created them. The notion was democratic up to a point; one did not have to be rich to exhibit good taste in this way: paper counted as much as silk. Good taste, however, did assume good breeding, which was often manifested in the exhibit of family crests and the use of antiques (that they be inherited was desirable but not mandatory).

As arrangements, these Victorian rooms were personal essays, composed of diverse objects in combination. At the outset, this was not achieved necessarily through the clutter we associate with Victorian houses. Indeed, both "cottage" and "mansion" interiors of the 1860s and 1870s could be quite uncluttered, even rather bare. Large numbers of objects did not begin to be brought in for the express purpose of decorating until the later 1870s, after which the quantity increased, then diminished after the early 1890s.

Certain preferences and customs naturally developed in the manner of arranging so many objects. From the late 1870s through the 1880s and early 1890s, fashion favored the grouping of furnishings into visual units. There could be many units in a single room. The units were complete "pictures." Take, for example, a square parlor in which a small sofa is placed across a corner with plants rising behind it, chairs to each side, and to its immediate left a table on which is carefully arranged a family album, a cigar box veneered with sea shells, china statuettes of Paul and Virginia, and an arrangement of dried flowers. Before the fireplace is an ottoman covered in the same Brussels carpeting that covers the floor, and nearby is a lounge upholstered in horsehair, with a fan of odd-shaped pillows and a paisley shawl that trails on the floor. Both these arrangements are art units; though in the same room, and contributing to the total, they are also separate and self-contained. Sideboards, tables, bureaux, mantels, pianos, and any other

Dining room with fancy chairs and Wilton carpeting, Decatur House, Washington, D.C. —*A. Robert Cole Photo for the National Trust for Historic Preservation*

flat surfaces created stages for art units composed of small objects. Whatnot shelves were adorned with pots, fans, and pictures. On the practical side, hall-trees held hats, coats, scarves, and umbrellas in a sort of artistic bouquet.

Art units as an idea may have been inspired by the fact that gaslight fell in circles, thus suggesting groupings within the light. Even the glaring incandescent mantle introduced to gas fixtures at the close of the 1880s did not give the consistent light that followed with electricity. In any case, the demise of the art unit and the rise of electricity were contemporaneous events. No longer split up into u-nits, objects were now spread uninterrupted around the walls. When there was a quantity of material, the effect could be one of over-whelming clutter; well arranged, the same number of things seemed to contribute to the room's architecture, as a part of its walls. Small conversation groupings of seating furniture opened up into fewer and bigger arrange-ments, thanks also to electricity. The quantity of objects used in rooms diminished in the late nineties and the first decade or so of the twen-tieth century. But the same striving to achieve a personal "statement" remained very much a part of room arrangement and prevails today.

By weighing the general chronology of fur-nishings arrangement in the historical context of your house, your final decisions in this area should become evident. There are, to be sure, exceptions to all rules of arrangement; some interiors were part this and part that. It would be difficult to expect the Indiana farmer of 1852 to arrange his lamp and candle-lit Greek-Revival rooms in the "French" manner. On the other hand, once ideas of arrangement became part of a popular stylish syndrome, they were likely to be carried out to some degree whether the original catalyst was there or not. So the same farmer, having bought himself a new parlor set in Indianapolis in 1860, very proba-bly arranged it more or less according to mod-

The porch as a room: James Ross Todd's piazza, Louisville, Kentucky, photo 1910. —*Mrs. James Ross Todd*

ern dictates, lamplight notwithstanding. Would he eventually have effected such an ar-rangement with the old furnishings? Un-doubtedly.

Old graphics suggest that the bare look so popular in the classical interiors of the early nineteenth century and on through the 1830s was well established in simple houses before that. Inventories taken in the 1840s and 1850s show that the quantity of objects in rooms was already increasing radically a good twenty years before the flowering of the art-unit. This was not a matter of decoration, but the natural manifestation of the growing consumer mar-ket. Prints and paintings depicting rooms of the 1840s and 1850s illustrate that there was a period of confusion about how to arrange so many things. This was certainly resolved by the late seventies. In the light of our cus-toms of arrangement today, we would feel far less alien in an arrangement of 1880 than in one of 1830.

The arrangement of objects in your historical interiors is thus as important to the interpreta-tion of the house as the individual objects themselves. Here your mistakes probably will

100   not cost anything, so experimentation is in order. The rooms, first of all, must live, as they
would have when the house was occupied. Let
the room arrangements vary from time to time;
this breathes life into a house, and keeps the
interiors interesting to your interpreters and to
the community.

Changes can come from regularly moving
and alternating the transient objects, particularly the objects of use. With interiors after
about 1830, you have further possibilities with
plant and floral arrangements. For earlier interiors, flower arrangements are only thinly documented, except as decorations for special occasions, and it appears that they were not used
inside at all during the eighteenth century.
People seem to have preferred living plants,
but before the 1850s even those were kept out
of frequented rooms because it was believed
that they rendered the air unhealthful in
closed-up spaces. The engaging portrait
painted of Mrs. William Cooper in summertime around 1816, seated in the central hall of
her house near Cooperstown, New York,
shows rows of bushy plants in boxes banked
against the windows. More surprising is John
Lewis Krimmel's *Quilting Frolic,* which depicts
a simple farm interior of 1813 with flowers in a
vase centered on the mantel.

Diminutive flower arrangements begin to
appear with some frequency in illustrations of
rooms in the 1830s; some of these may of
course be artificial flowers of wax or silk, for
both were very popular. The big, loose flower
arrangements, following rules about color and
form, belong to the last three decades of the
nineteenth century. It can be expected that a
predominantly agrarian society would be interested in plants. Perhaps it is true that the
Victorians' extravagant use of plants, which
even exceeded their use of flower arrangements, was a subconscious clinging to the
fast-vanishing agrarian way.

Seating groupings suggesting special occasions, such as tea time, a houseparty, or even a

The house of many generations, "frozen" in time:
double parlor at Kingscote, Newport, Rhode Island,
photo 1977. —*The Preservation Society of Newport
County*

funeral, are fascinating alternatives to the
usual arrangement, and they enhance interpretation. A room can also be temporarily arranged and stocked with appropriate objects to
illustrate a documented historical moment—
such as the day the particular household heard
the news of Gettysburg—or an everyday family or local occurrence, as recorded by one who
was present. Often this sort of information,
which may be too ordinary for a history book,
can become very exciting when recounted on
the actual scene, which has, in turn, been specially arranged to give it visual fulfillment. A
description of a family wedding, for example,
might be quoted by the museum interpreter
and supported by appropriate decorations, the
furniture set up to receive a crowd, hats hung
thickly on the rack in the hall, abundant food,
the family Bible that was actually there, a
waxed linen or canvas "crash" laid over the
floor for dancing, and any other touchstones
that will carry the story on to greater detail.

Still further possibilities for change lie in
seasonal modifications to interiors. So accustomed are we to modern climate control and
closed-up houses that we sometimes forget

how houses underwent seasonal transformations, being "disrobed" in the summer, and "dressed" in the autumn. This was by no means a southern custom alone, although in the semitropical southern regions people were necessarily more radical with the summer treatment than were, say, New Englanders.

Basically, summerizing involved removing rugs, curtains, and objects that tarnished, and the slipcovering (or "casing" or "sheeting") of upholstered furniture. This was common in the eighteenth century and familiar to some Americans at least until World War II. The custom can be fascinating when restored to the historic house.

Straw matting, though also used year-round, seems to have had its greatest use in the summer, sometimes as a protective cover for carpeting, but usually as a seasonal replacement. Floors were also left bare. Cotton screening was hung ungathered in openings and served as mosquito netting on beds, for protection against insects. It was also wrapped over gilt and glass surfaces—lamps, pictures, mirrors— for protection against fly-specking and dust. In the eighteenth and nineteenth centuries, chandeliers were likewise wrapped up (or as the Bostonians said, "bagged") in the summer, a practice that can be considered universal before about 1875, when dependence upon overhead lighting began to overwhelm the wish to protect the gilded surfaces of the fixtures. Metal "rolling screens" and other sorts of window and door screens could be bought in the 1780s from "wire weavers" in the more populous cities. But after window-screening became widely available during the 1870s, the custom of disrobing and bagging survived in some places until well into the twentieth century, particularly in hot climates and in affluent households, where the family might depart for the entire summer and close the house.

Slipcovers of chintz, linen, or heavy muslin were, after about 1890, much as they are today. Before that, they were much more loose, might or might not have been equipped with flounces, and were usually fastened in back with tied tabs, somewhat like a modern hospital gown—which is a good analogy to the way they fit.

Ornaments were removed to a storage area along with the rugs and curtains. Sometimes they were protected by being wrapped in screening, sometimes paper was used. Textiles were usually laid out flat, often in a large chest, where they were stored with camphor, prior to mothballs—and tobacco leaves, prior to camphor. Yet another means of protection was to keep a lighted candle in a sandbox to attract any hungry moths.

Imagine, for example, the impact on modern eyes of a historic house, say an eight-room Greek-Revival dwelling of the 1830s, disrobed for summer. Slipcovers enshroud the furniture, screening bags the fixtures, pictures, and mirrors; the rooms are shadowy with the external blinds closed, and they smell sweet from spring cleaning. The ornaments, removed, are seen in a storage area, where the curtains are stored also, laid out in boxes. Beds pulled out from the walls stripped of all but sheets; matting, cotton, glass—the household textures of summers gone by. And when the house is furnished for winter, it speaks visually of winter: the interpreter and visitors open and close doors as they move from room to room; the most frequented rooms reflect the comforts and occupations of indoor living, while the parlor, used only on formal occasions, actually seems closed-up and set aside.

In reviving old customs and staging rooms to evoke past events, you can rightly be accused of showmanship. As long as you are acting within the limitations of documented history, this is not an unfavorable criticism. Indeed the theatrical is often the magic ingredient in the successful historic house museum. A good interpreter is a good performer. Why then should the house itself not perform when it can? The active and apparently functioning

102   interior strengthens interpretation by limiting its verbal requirements.

Rooms should tell visually as much of the everyday story as they can. Though the room and the visitor may be two hundred years apart in time, the visitor himself lives in a house, an apartment, a room; he knows more about his own manner of living in rooms than he knows about anything else, though he may never have considered the matter before. Contrast and identity confront him in the historical interior on a more personal basis than would be the case on a preserved battlefield, in a ship, before the facade of a building, or in a museum gallery. His own experience becomes the seed of a historical imagination. The nourishment of that seed is the primary function of the historical interior.

Plates and Figures

James Witherspoon brought his family from Ireland to Kingstree, in the upriver area in South Carolina, in 1734, and in 1749 built this wooden house on his plantation. The family lived there until 1826; by the late 1960s, the house had spent most of its two hundred years as a tenant house virtually unchanged, hidden away in remote fields. Relocated in a park, it was restored in 1970 as a historic house museum. The "great hall" or "hall" is an amazing survivor. Originally, it was the center of family life. Cooking was not performed here, for the kitchen was in a separate structure, but there was little else that did not take place in the great hall. A bright, sunny room, this was where the Witherspoons ate meals and sat and talked. During the day, Mrs. Witherspoon would have presided here, doing whatever tasks she personally attended to, and directing the rest. For all its years, the great hall has never been repainted. The restorers cleaned the surfaces and in-painted where the original was worn away or stained. Local and regional inventories were sought out and analyzed to develop a furnishings plan, and a thorough search was made for objects in the county. The furnishings of the great hall are for the most part either of local origin or are known to have been used locally before the mid-1820s. Most of the furnishings date from the eighteenth century.—*Nolan Ninabuck Photo (Associated Creative Talents), for the Williamsburg County Historical Society*

Plate 2. Parlor, Paca House, Annapolis, Maryland, 1977   107

William Paca built his brick mansion in 1765 and with its magnificent terraced garden, the Paca house enjoyed the reputation of being one of the finest houses in Maryland. During the early 1970s, the house underwent extensive research for restoration. One aspect of that was a paint study, which turned up the bright colors seen here. It was decided not to rush into completing the interiors, but instead to suggest with a few objects how the furnishings of the whole might have been. Instead of a parlor full of furniture, behold a single table and a chair; at the windows are split festoons of the sort the English called "reefed" curtains. (However, in the eighteenth century, almost without exception, the curtains extended to the outer edge of the architrave.) That is the extent of the furnishings. The result is very interesting, and although the house is considered "empty," something rings very true about the barren rooms. They would have had many more furnishings, yet they would also have had a touch of the emptiness they have now. This quality of vacancy is usually lost in restored eighteenth-century interiors.— *M. E. Warren Photo for the Historic Annapolis Foundation and the Maryland Center for Public Broadcasting*

Plate 3. Parlor, Mount Vernon, Fairfax County, Virginia, 1971

Called in its day the "front parlor," this was the supreme sitting room in George Washington's house. He added it when he expanded Mount Vernon prior to his marriage in the 1750s, and we see the room here much as it must have been in the late 1790s. Washington memorabilia has not been as likely to fall into obscurity as most relics, as his objects were collectibles, even in his lifetime. The Washington coat of arms adorns the overmantel; in the eighteenth century it surveyed walls filled with portraits of Washington family members and friends. Although most of the portraits are elsewhere today, the majority of this furniture is original to the room. The card table and side table were here; the glass lustres and shelves were probably Washington's, as probably was the mirror. The two silver lamps with Argand burners are Neo-classical variations on the solar form. The 1800 inventory, made soon after the general's death, describes this parlor as having "1 elegant looking glass, 1 sopha, 11 mahogany chairs, 3 lamps . . . 5 china flower pots . . . 2 window curtains, 1 carpet, And Irons, Shovel, Tongs & c."—*Mount Vernon Ladies' Association of the Union*

Plate 4. Withdrawing Room, Harrison Gray Otis House, Boston, Massachusetts, 1975

The neo-classical houses of post-Revolutionary Boston reminded some visitors of London. Among the finest of these—and the only free-standing one remaining—was the house begun by the young lawyer Harrison Gray Otis and occupied in 1797. It was designed by Charles Bulfinch. The withdrawing room upstairs was to be the grandest room in the house and may have been decorated with Otis's Flemish paintings. Being in national politics, Otis was seldom at home; he sold in 1801 and built another house. In 1970 restoration work was begun by the Society for the Preservation of New England Antiquities. Documentary written and graphic sources were painfully lacking for the Otis period, though a full inventory of 1819 for a subsequent owner was used. But the idea was to restore the building itself and in the rooms to recreate from a general historical premise the elegant Boston of Otis and Bulfinch. Samples of the original wallpaper, found under many layers, had been catalogued in 1916, so the documents were copied. Color research called up muddy tones at first, then yielded a rainbow when it was realized that dead varnish had to be cut through to get to the actual colors. "Composition" ornaments are fixed to the wooden architraves, while the doors themselves are mahogany. The handsome painted and glazed fancy chairs and settee belonged to Otis. Arrangement, the hanging of pictures, and countless other details make this a setting of great historical sensitivity.—*Richard Cheek Photo for the magazine* Antiques *and for the Society for the Preservation of New England Antiquities*

Plate 5. Bedroom, The Hermitage, Nashville, Tennessee, ca. 1960   113

This was Andrew Jackson's bedroom, and it is believed to be as it was the day he died. The house was rebuilt and enlarged by Jackson in 1835 after the earlier house, completed in 1819, was largely destroyed by fire. President Jackson purchased the Grecian style bedroom furniture for the Hermitage at the time he was buying furnishings for the White House. The chintz winter hangings on the bed and windows were undoubtedly purchased ready-made with the furniture in Philadelphia. Those pictured here are copies of the originals that remain in the Hermitage collection, but are too fragile to be on exhibit. The chintz has a rust-colored ground and is glazed; the form of the curtains shows the "Masonic temple" flair for the theatrical that characterized some Grecian interiors. Wallpaper of the 1840s, greatly faded, still clings to the plaster walls. Some of the portraits hang on their original hooks: hardly a detail of the dying man's room escaped being recorded, but one can imagine that many more transient objects were present the day of his death, in June 1845.—*Ladies' Hermitage Association*

Plate 6. Bedroom, Bulloch Hall, Roswell, Georgia, 1973

This upstairs bedroom is furnished with an American cottage bedroom set of about 1850. The set, consisting of "French bed," wardrobe, washstand, night stand, bureau, towel rack, and a pair of cane-bottom chairs, is made of pine and painted a pale gray or cold, marble color. Cottage furniture was cheap and light-weight and, after its appearance in the 1840s, could be found nearly anywhere, both as sets and as odd pieces. It was extremely popular and belongs on the family tree of the fancy chair in the genealogy of furniture. Here a set is seen in a whitewashed room in a backwoods Greek-Revival mansion in Georgia. The woodwork of the room is painted according to colors that turned up in a color survey. At the windows hang festoons of the commonest kind, made according to directions in Thomas Webster's *Household Encyclopedia* (1835). By the 1830s and 1840s, festoons were largely out of style and had been replaced by the external "Venetian blind" (outside shutters with adjustable slats) and the window shade. Webster comments that they were still used in secondary rooms.—*Nolan Ninabuck (Associated Creative Talents) for the magazine* Antiques

Plate 7. Bedroom, John Jay French House, Beaumont, Texas, 1978

The Connecticut-born merchant and tanner John French moved to the Republic of Texas in the mid-1830s and built this wooden house on the Gulf Coast prairies, about 1844. A house of small—indeed, tiny—rooms, it was brightly painted and varnished inside. The second floor is one long room and was probably a bedroom. In 1969, when the house was restored, layers of dry-wall and wallpaper were peeled away to reveal some 80 percent of the original paint. Simulated baseboards or "wash" boards, blue ceilings, milk-white walls, and grained doors were in some cases reproduced, in others restored, but in most instances merely cleaned and preserved. The French house has been recreated on the interior to show the life of a Connecticut family transplanted to the Texas wilderness, 1844-1860. The industrial age, just beginning, has not reached Texas; yet, in the possessions of the Frenches we see evidence of it, not least of all in the spinning wheel, one of a type manufactured on a large scale, which shows the mark of machine construction and the telltale presence of component parts. On the right is a home-made quilting frame, which hangs from the ceiling.—*Roy Bray Photo for the Beaumont Heritage Society*

Containing most of its original furniture, the Ramsey house is an outstanding representative of the continuity of one family's life in the Midwest from 1872 through the first half of the twentieth century. The Ramsey house has proven to be a gold mine of information on nineteenth-century life, making possible such recreations as this bedroom of about 1885, with its furnishings of about a decade earlier. An interpreter is costumed as a maid. There were servants' quarters on the third floor; the two bell-cords shown activated a call box in the kitchen below, which communicated with the third floor by means of a speaking tube. The bedroom represents upper-middle-class luxury of the sort Americans relished in the nineteenth century. "Renaissance" revival would have been the "style" given for the bedroom suite; it was Renaissance, of course, only to the eye of the time, which was highly creative in its interpretation of historical revivals. The suite is doubtless the product of one of the burgeoning steam-powered furniture factories of the Midwest, only then beginning to claim dominance in the field of mass furniture manufacture. The gas fixtures, though now much brightened with electric bulbs, are original to the room. The wallpaper with its quaint "bedroom" pattern, the heavily varnished walnut woodwork, the railroad-car siding trim in the bathroom through the door, and the polished floor are in the popular taste of the era. On the table in the foreground the "export" tea pieces may represent the family's passing fancy for "antiques."—*Jerry Stransky Photo for the Minnesota Historical Society*

Plate 9. Parlor, Henry Ford Boyhood Home, Greenfield Village Museum, Dearborn, Michigan, 1978

Henry Ford restored his birthplace in 1919 with meticulous attention to details as he remembered them. Plain and of white clapboard, the house is Greek-Revival in its form; but it has little formal Grecian ornament, being largely in the vernacular of earlier farmhouses of the region. The house was built by Henry Ford's father in 1860, and Ford was born there in 1863. What Henry Ford was recreating at the age of fifty-six was probably an amalgamation of all his family's years in the house, with a certain emphasis upon the late 1870s and early 1880s, which this room seems to represent best. Most of the furniture was acquired by the father in the 1860s. It is simple cottage furniture, of walnut, in the Grecian mode, upholstered in horsehair. This is a grade better than painted cottage furniture, but still it was not expensive. The kerosene lamp of the late 1870s gives overhead light where gas is absent; the rolled-iron stove gives fairly general heat to this room and an adjoining sitting room. Pictures hang from a gilt picture moulding, which must have been added in the seventies. The dark-green window shades operate on cord-activated spring rollers of the 1860s, but they must be from the 1890s, as probably are the lace curtains that hang over them. Henry Ford's parlor demonstrates preciseness in the area of generalities but a deceptive variance in details. This is usually characteristic of recreations made from memory.—*Henry Ford Museum*

Plate 10. Library, John Ballantine House, Newark, New Jersey, 1976

Prior to its recreation as a historical interior in 1976, this room was a nondescript museum reception room, painted mostly white, with fluorescent lights and racks of brochures. Documentation for the way it looked in its heyday, as the library of John Ballantine, heir to the Ballantine beer fortune, was abundant and included the decorator's estimate, which is reproduced in Figure 13 of this book. Written documentation was further enhanced by a photograph taken in 1885, just after the library was completed. Combining such sources with a paint analysis, the Newark Museum was able to recreate this library, from its Queen Anne-style shell to the personal way in which its objects are placed, with rare accuracy. The primary function of the Ballantine house is to exhibit Victorian decorative arts. In the quest for the proper *context* for these objects, the restorers have achieved a historical point of view outstanding for its comprehensiveness. *—The Newark Museum*

124

Plate 11. Dining Room, Ruthmere, Elkhart, Indiana, 1978   125

This room is recreated to appear as it did when the house was completed in 1908 by Andrew Hubble Beardsley. Its contents sold at auction in 1945, the room had sources for recreation that varied from documents to recollections. And of course there was the room itself, which, though run-down, did survive. It is well to compare this room with the Mount Vernon parlor (Color Plate 3) and the Harrison Gray Otis house withdrawing room (Color Plate 4). The contents of the Mount Vernon parlor were acquired by Washington, object by object, from many sources; the Otis room is recreated to appear as having been furnished somewhat the same, only the market for household goods has clearly advanced, as symbolized in the set of matching fancy furniture, purchased from a budding manufactory. A century later this midwestern dining room shows a total change in the ways of furnishing houses both great and small. The trend already evident in the Otis withdrawing room has gone all the way: this room is a mirror of the current market of expensive manufactures as they apply to furniture. The "Della Robia" plaster ceiling was the sort one found in numerous "art decorating" catalogues. The "golden poppy" shade was manufactured by L. C. Tiffany for a popular market and was the sort of decoration seen in many a bungalow of the time. The wall covering, reproduced from the blackened original, is painted velvet, which was one of many types of decoration for walls provided by art-decoration companies. The "Colonial" furniture, which originated in a Grand Rapids, Michigan, factory (almost certainly Berkey & Gay) shows the most popular furniture mode of the day. It features mixtures of readily recognizable "period" touchstones—"Chippendale" claw-and-ball feet, "Sheraton" twisted columns and carved flower-baskets, "Empire" mantel mirrors, etc. The rug is a copy of the original Wilton.—*Robert Perron Photo for the Andrew Hubble Beardsley Foundation*

Plate 12. Salon, Parlange Plantation, Pointe Coupée Parish, Louisiana,
1957

The house at Parlange Plantation was built sometime after 1750 by the
Marquis de Ternant, who moved to America and established a large indigo
plantation on this site. Nearly a hundred years later, Virginie Trahan, the
widow of his son, married Captain Charles Parlange in France. Their
descendants occupy the steep-roofed, whitewashed house, which all these
years has overlooked Louisiana's romantic False River and still commands
several thousand acres of sugar cane fields. The salon—which the parlor
has always been called—is raised a full story above the ground; it richly
recalls the years of Virginie Trahan Parlange in the nineteenth century.
Virginie maintained the Ternant house in Paris at 24 rue du Luxembourg until
the outbreak of the American Civil War, when she moved permanently to
Parlange, bringing with her this Louis Philippe furniture of the "French
Antique" (Louis XIV revival) type of the 1830s and 1840s. Other objects in the
room—the chandelier, for example—appear in Claude Ternant's inventory of
1842. The salon is one of a series of rooms in this house that has survived
through the generations more or less intact. None of them is "pure" to any
period. Because there have always been little changes, the rooms must be
considered as interiors of the present—in this instance, the date the picture
was taken, 1957. Family life goes on in the salon at Parlange as it always has;
the house is not treated as a museum. There is an individuality to this room
that would be extremely difficult to recreate in a house museum. Yet it is this
sensitive element that makes the difference between an interior that has an
ability to respond to the viewer and one that is simply something to look at.
The particular quality is never absent from the successful historical
room.—*Photo by Willard R. Culver,* © *National Geographic Society*

Figure 1. Common Room, Pliny Freeman Farm, Old Sturbridge Village, Massachusetts, 1978

Derived from meticulous research in local and regional history, this common room of a New England yeoman's house (ca. 1801) defines the word *recreate* in its adherence to documentation. The room reflects the life of a "comfortable," though not rich, farmer at about the time of the War of 1812. Sparse, with few furnishings, the room's manufactured items subtly illustrate the effects of the dawning cash economy on the average home. Twenty-five years earlier, nearly all the furnishings would have been made locally, if not homemade. The desk and table are of the sort produced by local cabinetmakers, often (but not always) on special order. Such painted Windsor chairs as these were made in large numbers from standardized parts and transported everywhere to be sold cheaply. The Windsors, the wallpaper, and the tableware were things bought with cash, not got by barter, and they may have traveled greater distances to Pliny Freeman's world than he would travel from it in his whole lifetime.—*Old Sturbridge Village, photo by Donald F. Eaton*

Figure 2. Hall, Bulloch Hall, Roswell, Georgia, 1971   131

Bulloch Hall, a temple-style house of wood, was completed in 1839 on an estate, not a farm, adjacent to a small textile-making community. The builder was Theodore Roosevelt's grandfather. In 1971 it stood abandoned and neglected; the white paint that was scaling from every surface had robbed the interiors of their Greek-Revival monumentality.—*Photo Richard S. Myrick*

Figure 3. Hall, Bulloch Hall, Roswell, Georgia, 1973   133

The hall is seen from the opposite direction after restoration. Bulloch Hall has undergone a transformation. The written record revealed very little about the interiors of the house, but a microscopic analysis of paint chips taken from every surface revealed a rich palette of "Grecian" colors popular in the 1830s and 1840s, ranging from Pompeiian red to a brilliant blue, grass-green, and pale violet. There had been a uniform color of golden straw on all the architraves. It was crudely applied, as was the mahogany "graining" on the doors. The house having been otherwise unchanged, the interior was *restored* when the old colors were reproduced. Beyond that, the rooms are entirely *recreated*. Inventories of similar Georgia houses of the late 1830s through the late 1850s described central hallways furnished as is shown here, the sideboard largely for looks and for storage.—*Photo, Nolan Ninabuck for Richard S. Myrick*

Figure 4. Small Dining Room, Governor's Palace, Williamsburg, Virginia, 1935–1975

This room appears much as it did when the palace reconstruction was completed in the 1930s. The eighteenth-century inventories of the palace were found and used for inspiration. Yet the motivation of the restorers was not to *illustrate*, but to *symbolize* the past of colonial Virginia. The palace interiors were thus filled with English furnishings in settings of tasteful repose. During an era of depression, between two world wars, the result confirmed the popular image of an unwaveringly stable English heritage.—*The Colonial Williamsburg Foundation*

Figure 5. Housekeeper's Room, Governor's Palace, Williamsburg, Virginia, 1976

The small dining room (Figure 4) has become the housekeeper's room. In recent years, the inventories of the old palace have undergone the closest scrutiny. They have been analyzed in terms of more general documentary sources of the time, the contemporary rooms illustrated in prints and paintings and written descriptions. The inventories make it clear that what had been open to the public as the small dining room actually had been a housekeeper's room, the nerve center of the day-to-day- operation of the palace, up until the royal governors fled the house at the time of the Revolution. Today the room is recreated to reflect its original purpose. Besides having a bed on which to wait out the governor's late parties, the housekeeper had his desk slanted to gain a sentry's view of the service entrance to the kitchen court. The housekeeper's room is a classic example of the historical approach to recreating interiors.—*The Colonial Williamsburg Foundation*

This "Adamesque" room, considered to be Colonial, was built from the walls out prior to 1914. It is a high-style example of a sort of room that, though without much factual claim to colonial American precedent, characterized the Colonial Revival after that movement became academic. This room was not built and furnished to deceive anyone as to its authenticity. It was frankly "modern," comfortable in modern terms, its arrangement determined by such noncolonial conveniences as central heating and electric lights. It is a vignette from a dominant taste in household decoration that still exists and preceded the wide spread of historical restoration in America. Preconceived images from the Colonial Revival, as a mode of household decoration, became—and have remained—an enormous influence upon the furnishing of historic houses.—Miller, Meigs & Howe *(Philadelphia: 1914)*

Figure 7. Library, Kenmore, Fredericksburg, Virginia, ca. 1955

In the ornateness and delicacy of their eighteenth-century plaster work, the interiors of Kenmore are among the finest in the country. This ceiling is decorated to symbolize the four seasons. From a historical point of view, the library, though furnished to represent the eighteenth century, borrows heavily from the Colonial Revival: its furnishings are uniform in quality, and are "arranged" in static groupings for general effect. Highly polished pine floors gleam around the edges of Oriental rugs. Except for books (not in the picture), playing cards, and chips for the game of loo, there is not much about this room to suggest the function of family leisure that libraries served.—*The Kenmore Association*

Figure 8. Library, "The Angus Nickelson Family," Oil on Canvas by Ralph Earl the Elder, ca. 1790

Paintings and prints showing interiors are endlessly useful in recreating the historical room. Sometimes they actually document, like a photograph; other times they are imaginary. In any case, they were usually intended to be believable, so their details on objects and arrangements can illuminate the written record. The interior shutters here are closed perhaps against the night drafts. Mr. Nickelson is a man of means, and his collection of books appears to be large for an eighteenth-century library. They fill plain wooden bookcases, before which is a desk with fringed cover, probably of baize, for a blotter. The wall-to-wall floor covering might be ingrain carpeting, though in a family chamber such as this it could as easily be a painted floorcloth. The window hangings are festoons, each drawn up by two sets of cords, which are wound around pins at each side. The curtains are in a strange form, as though the tails hanging down may be made separately from the part of the curtain that rises. Though not an especially informal room, it reflects family use. The Nickelsons have pulled their sofa and chairs out from the wall and into a temporary grouping for the moment, perhaps before a fire. —*The Museum of Fine Arts, Springfield, Massachusetts*

144

Figure 9. Front Chamber, J. S. Russell's House, Philadelphia, Pennsylvania, 1835

This is the principal room in a row house, obviously on the second floor, and probably extending the full width of the house. It is strangely barren. The bureau, washstands, and wardrobe would ordinarily designate this a bedroom, with the bed removed for purposes of better showing the room. However, in 1835, this could well be a sitting room. Before the complete "suite" or "set" that became an institution through mass production, furnishings in a house were likely to be mixed rather freely. It is not surprising to find household inventories that list sofas in dining rooms, washstands in halls and sitting rooms, and beds in parlors, indicating the multiple functions of rooms. This room is arranged according to the age-old custom that was eventually to change as a result of innovations in lighting and heating. The heavy pieces of furniture are spaced around the wall, the chairs placed neatly between them. There is a subtle tone to this room as a whole that is far greater than any of its parts. The big furniture is in the Grecian style then so popular and probably cost no small amount from a local manufacturer. The fancy chairs were cheap. What appears to be a Brussels carpeting covers the floor and if it is Brussels, it represents another sizable cost. There are no lighting devices, but—since it is daytime—they may be in a central place, awaiting the night. The only features for comfort are the fireplace and the external blinds, which are doubtless adjusted several times a day.—*Nina Fletcher Little*

Figure 10. Living Room, New York City, March 1929 147

A documentary photograph showing the "living room" of the fashionable Manhattan residence of Mrs. Edgar Leonard, now no longer in existence. Furnished as a Louis XV *salon* of the mid-eighteenth century, this room—as its name implies—is not the stiff parlor it would have been two decades before, but comfortable and inviting. The "reproductions" of eighteenth-century French furniture vary in accuracy, but are generally close to the models. These pieces could have been made in any number of New York cabinet shops, which had been turning out such furniture in quantities since the early 1890s, or they could be French. Comfort is expressed visually in the downy cushions, the convenient tables. One may suppose that bold colors in the satin, velvet, and needlepoint upholstery were good company for pastels in the Aubusson rug and the painted *boiserie*, with its inset murals on canvas. The six flower arrangements, the small glass containing cigarettes, the shaded lamps and sconces, the cozy screen around the table, are personal touches to make this "period" setting not only luxurious but inviting.—*Museum of the City of New York*

Though somewhat earlier than the Leonard living room, the *salon* of Edith Wetmore at Newport also imitates eighteenth-century French interior decorating. It was added about 1908 by remodeling a room and is today part of the Chateau-sur-mer Historic House Museum. Compare this photograph to the one of Mrs. Edgar Leonard's living room taken while she occupied it. Miss Wetmore's drawing room is adjacent to a ballroom (which is in the French Revival mode of a half-century before), and while it may have served more limited purposes than Mrs. Leonard's, it was nevertheless Miss Wetmore's favorite room, and she used it as a living room. Absent in the museum setting are personal touches. The room is quite well furnished, but since the setting is largely composed of furniture alone, does it have the power to evoke Miss Wetmore's world? In 1973, before it was reconsidered by the historical society and refurbished, the room was quite clearly unoccupied. There were no books, no family pictures, no vases, papers, none of the things that make one feel that the historical occupants just stepped out between the *portieres* and might soon return.—*The Preservation Society of Newport County*

Figure 12. Broadside, Joseph Meeks & Sons, 1833   151

Documenting styles of furnishings is fairly well restricted to pattern books and surviving examples before the coming of illustrated advertisements in the late nineteenth century. This celebrated broadside, from which one ordered by number, is a rare exception. Meeks's products could be shipped anywhere. There were Meeks "warehouses" or stores in New York and New Orleans. The Meeks broadside is near to being a comprehensive catalogue of furniture in the Grecian style, the mode that coincided with the beginnings of the large-scale manufacture of furniture. Mahogany was the principal material, usually applied as veneer over pine, and the firm used some rosewood. The designs all follow English prototypes. American home furnishings underwent a sort of democratization with the Grecian style. The objects shown here have the look of fine things once available only from the cabinetmaker to the few who could afford them. Because these were manufactured in considerable quantity, the price was less; and, quite as significantly, if one had the money, one did not have to wait to possess a handsome sideboard or sofa. The designs are the epitome of "Grecian" monumentality. Heavily varnished, their plain forms blazed with crotch-graining, and they seemed immovable (though most could be dismantled and stacked). The prices tell us a great deal about this sort of furniture and its appointments. A "high post bed," number 15, was $50, and could be bought with curtains; the "canopy bed," number 1, was $90, and the crown and curtains cost $250 to $500 extra; the "window curtains" were each $200 to $300. Yet the sofa, number 23, upholstered in hair cloth (horsehair) was only $90!—*Metropolitan Museum of Art*

152

ESTIMATE.
Copy of Order
Placed With **D. S. HESS & CO.,**

New York, *June 17 1885*

Warerooms, 876 & 878 Broadway, bet. 18th & 19th Streets,
Factory, 145, 147, 149 & 151 Eleventh Avenue, cor. 21st Street.

Artistic Furniture, Interior Wood-work & Decorations.

For *J. H. Ballantine Esq*

Decorations

Library — Ceiling & Walls modelled and colored in a highly artistic manner appropriate to the shape and style of room the tone of room to be a soft Old Red. the frieze a hanging fringe as below. with a fine low relief design below in Conventional pattern over the Wainscoting. there is to be modelled a suitable border in keeping with the Wall the entire color tone of Ceiling and Walls to be a quiet harmony of blended Old Red and old Metals Picture mouldings to match — 422 —

Music Room — Ceiling to be richly decorated in Old Blue with Chaste illumination in quiet harmony with wall. the ornamentation to be in relief

Sidewalls hung in finest Moire Antique Stock (imported) and properly prepared and lined One quiet and elegant Frieze to be hand painted and modelled upon the sidewall to match Picture mouldings to match — 360 —

Forward $782 —

Figure 13. Decorator's Estimate, Ballantine Mansion, Newark, New Jersey, 1885

But a leaf from the rich documentation of the Ballantine Mansion, the decorator's estimate for the library (see Color Plate 10) gives not only details of the room but a glimpse of attitudes toward this particular decoration. That the "highly artistic" coloring of the ceiling and walls is appropriate to the size and shape of the room is not made much clearer when we learn that the tone will be "old red." A paint survey reveals exactly what they meant by that color and what they saw in it that was highly artistic. Documents as rich as this do not turn up frequently, and their value reaches far beyond their immediate relevance to one house.—*The Newark Museum*

Figure 14. Study With Chaise Longue, Anonymous Wash Drawing, England, 1840s

Interior views like this are much more abundant in Europe than in the United States. Still, foreign ones have a distinct value in recreating the historic house interior, in what they say to us about the age they came from. This study, obviously not in use at the moment, is neatly arranged. Letter boxes—objects of use ever so common but too trifling to list in an inventory—are placed symmetrically on the table against the wall. A second table is serving as a sofa table, which was a familiar convenience as late as the 1860s. It is about ten years early for wastebaskets, but one is tempted to give these the name, even though the flood of paper products had only begun to create the need. A cord to the service bell hangs down the wall. The staggered row of pictures, each held by two pins stuck through a pair of rings screwed to the top of the frame, represents an effort to be decorative. None of these details is uncharacteristic of American interiors of the time, yet this interior, partially because of the character of its furniture, is unmistakably English.—*Ashmolean Museum*

Figure 15. "The Quilting Frolic," *Oil on Canvas by John Lewis Krimmel, 1813*

This glimpse into the interior of a yeoman's farmhouse during the War of 1812 yields a rich general impression and abundant detail. Consider the great number of transient objects. Most are objects of use, such as the array of things piled on top of the cupboard, but the mantel is decorated with a vase of flowers, above which rises a symmetrical arrangement of pictures hung from rings. All are objects of ornament. An inventory of this room in 1813 would probably have omitted most of what you see. Around very little actual furniture are crowded the objects associated with daily life. Krimmel has used them, much as we do in recreating rooms, to represent human activity.—*Courtesy of the Henry Francis du Pont Winterthur Museum*

Figure 16. "The Dinner Party," *Oil on Canvas by Henry Sargent, ca. 1821–1825*

A volume could be written about this picture, which, as a domestic scene, symbolizes better than any other the prosperity in America that followed the War of 1812. It shows a Boston dinner party in an elegant neo-classical house designed by Charles Bulfinch. You look through double doors from one "parlor" to the second—in this case, a dining room. The hour is still early for dinner, to our way of thinking, but the tablecloth has already been taken away and dessert is being eaten. Dark will likely not have fallen by the time the guests depart. Present in this room there are already innovations in lighting that have begun influencing customs to change, as they brighten the night with a brilliance no candle could produce. Hanging over the table is an Argand chandelier. The cut-glass bowl beneath it catches drippings and magnifies the light from the four burners. It is possible that the magnifying power of these bowls was increased by putting water in them. The chandelier hangs on a self-contained counterweight device, by which it can be raised and lowered at a touch. This served both convenience and safety. On the table, some distance from the windows, a lone candleholder with candle supplements the natural light. Both interior and exterior blinds are adjusted to make the most of this natural light. The decorations of the room are neo-classical, which should not be confused with the Grecian that followed it in the middle 1820s, beginning about the time this picture was painted. Apparently, the table is the kind that folds into two smaller sections, so it is readily moveable to allow greater diversity in the use of the rooms. It might normally be kept in the hall, or against the walls here. The carpet, with its border, would appear to be Brussels, but the ripples around its edges suggest the thinner ingrain, which men's shoe-soles were not then so tough as to damage. It is protected from crumbs and spillage by a dropcloth laid under the table. At the window are the most Classical aspect of the room, the swags. They are probably silk, clearly unlined. They have been handsomely cut to appear "cast" or "thrown" over the gilded rods as a toga might be. Most of this effect is in the way the tails fall, their irregular hems emphasized by a darker border.—*Courtesy of the Museum of Fine Arts, Boston, Massachusetts*

Figure 17. "Friends and Amateurs at Musik," *Wash Drawing by Thomas Middleton, ca. 1825*

Not so fashionable as "The Dinner Party," and not nearly so urbane, is this musical evening in Charleston, South Carolina. It is being held in a room that shows hard day-to-day use; it is not a complete "modern" ensemble, like the Boston room, but is, rather, a mixture of furniture. The pictures are placed somewhat similarly to those in Boston, except that here the effect is not so sophisticated. These pictures comprise the only "decoration" the room has; leaning them on the mantel this way seems to have been very common. Inventories show that people were fond of pictures, whether paintings or prints, and there was no stigma at all against copies of well-known paintings. Illustrative documents of rooms show that great care was taken to arrange them, so it is hard to think of this Charleston mantel arrangement as an afterthought. In the reveal beside the fireplace, a sideboard has been placed out of the way, reflecting its then-principal function, storage. This great ark and the dining table in the center may be recent purchases, either at a manufactory in Charleston or quite possibly shipped in from Baltimore, Philadelphia, New York, or Boston. Two parts of a second table are against the wall. The dining chairs are cheap, painted fancy-chairs from a chair factory. Rush-seated and practical, they were probably painted bright yellow. No floor covering is distinguishable, though there could have been matting. This room is probably typical of the houses of well-to-do southerners. Used still more as a "great hall" than such rooms would be one day, this room might undergo several transformations in a single day, by the moving about and rearrangement of furniture. Seasonally, its entire function might be changed, say, to that of a bedroom for an overflow of guests. —*Carolina Art Association, Gibbes Art Gallery, Charleston, South Carolina*

Figure 18. "Bishop White's Study," Oil on Canvas, by His Daughter, 1836

The chaplain of the Continental Congress had his study on the second floor of his Philadelphia home. Through the doorway was his bedroom, overlooking the street. This picture was painted as a record after he died, at an advanced age, and before the division of his possessions. It is very important for a particular warning it gives us in recreating rooms: one must not be led by the apparent excellence of the architecture into a richer and more decorated interior than might have actually existed. The bishop's was a large and handsome building, as can be gathered from the fine architectural detailing in this room. But look at the complete interior! Plain bookcases have been built along the walls, with no apparent concern for their appearance. The bedroom door is flanked by clumsy cupboards or presses, probably the work of a carpenter summoned to prepare some storage in a hurry. Three Chippendale-type side chairs are mixed about with two fancy chairs, a Windsor, and an easy chair. Straw matting covers the floor. This room pretends to be nothing other than a place of work for the aged bishop, whose quantities of papers and books are supplied with shelving, to achieve some order. The room has been restored today by the National Park Service to mirror this painting.—*Independence National Historical Park Collection, National Park Service*

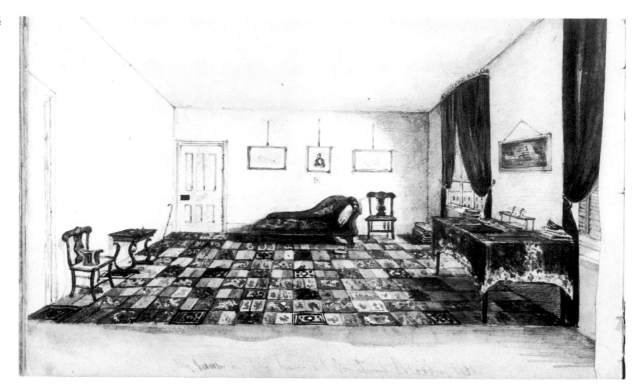

Figure 19. "My Room," Watercolor in the Sketchbook of H. G. Cantzler, 1851

  Cantzler apparently rented this room in a home in Brooklyn, New York. Compare this picture to that of the English interior—"Study with Chaise Longue" (Figure 14). The row of pictures, the lounge, the covered table with writing materials, and the fancy chairs combine to make a similar image. The floor here is probably covered by ingrain carpeting. The furniture could all be new, of the cottage type, which was inexpensive and manufactured in great quantity. All of it would have been called Grecian, which still dominated the popular current in household furniture style. The curtains are in a very ordinary form—two panels tacked or run on a rod behind pressed-metal cornices and held back to each side by bands.—*New York Public Library*

Figure 20. "Miss Firmak's," Watercolor in the Sketchbook of
H. G. Cantzler, 1851

Again in Brooklyn, Cantzler recorded a middle-class interior on the eve of the age of mass-manufacture. There is not nearly the quantity of furniture here that would be present in such a room twenty-five years hence. Now personal things dominate. Something about this interior gives the impression that it is an apartment or room divided off in a once-grand house. In any case, the occupant is clearly a musician. The upright piano is fronted by a sunburst of red fabric that matches the curtains. The piano is perhaps twenty or so years old and could be a Chickering. Music stand and another instrument stand by. Books are shelved in pyramidlike cases made from drapery cords and boards. There is the covered table, with the letterboxes and books, and a comfortable chair nearby. Except for the rocker—more than a decade before Lincoln gave it his name—that is moved about, the furniture is lined around the walls. The room is heated by the coal grate, and insulated insofar as possible by closing the curtains. —*New York Public Library*

Figure 21. William H. Prescott's Study, Boston, 1859

This study, on the top floor of Prescott's home at 55 Beacon Street, is where the great historian wrote *The Conquest of Peru*, and his histories of Philip II and Charles V. He had only partial vision in one eye and was blind in the other. The advantage of this study was that it was flooded with sunlight—so much so, in fact, that window shades are fitted to the bookcases to protect his books from the damaging effects of the light. These and the shades on the windows are the kind with spring-rollers, the spring being released by a cord hanging to the side of the window. The covering of bookcases was very common but was usually accomplished by means of curtains.—*George Ticnor,* William H. Prescott *(Boston: 1864)*

Figure 22. Parlors, Photograph by Joseph Henry, Taken in His Apartment, Smithsonian Institution, Washington D.C., ca. 1860

Joseph Henry, secretary of the Smithsonian, was an amateur photographer who left a full visual record of the way his living quarters looked before, during, and after the Civil War. This candid view of the parlors shows some of the furniture in baggy slipcovers. Florid Brussels carpeting covers the floor. The three dominant chairs are in the French Antique mode and would probably have been called *Louis Quatorze*. The little cottage table in the corner is in the Elizabethan or Swiss style. Louvred blinds are closed against the sun, making this a cool, white cave.—*Smithsonian Institution*

Figure 23. Dining Room and Bedroom, Both Photographed by Titian R. Peale in His Washington, D.C., Residence, Summer 1862

Joseph Henry's close friend Titian Peale was an amateur photographer of no small importance. Neither of these pictures would win prizes as good photographs, but they are good documents. The one on this page was taken in the rear parlor on the second floor of Peale's row-house. It is a library, but is also used for dining. The simple cottage extension table is spread for breakfast. There is an oilcloth drop over the Brussels carpeting. Potted vines

"curtain" the windows this summer day. Objects of use are everywhere. The second photograph was taken in the downstairs rear bedroom that overlooked the back yard. A pier table has become a dressing table, equipped with a looking glass that the gas bracket lights. A statue is tucked away beneath the pier table, as was often done in parlors. There are shades on the windows. A mosquito bar is draped on a frame over the low-post bed.—*Smithsonian Institution*

Figure 24. Parlor, Lockwood-Mathews House, Norwalk, Connecticut, 1868

High style was not characteristic even of the houses of wealthy Americans. The dominant ideal in the United States has always been essentially middle-class. One of the exceptions, and an outstanding one, was the mansion built by Legrand Lockwood during the Civil War and furnished sumptuously in the later sixties. This parlor, one of several, is in the Louis XVI revival style current in Paris at that time both at court and among the rich bourgeoisie. In its day, the mode appeared distinctly French and historical; to our eyes, it could not be mistaken for anything but a product of the 1860s. Gaslight overhead draws the furniture into "French" groupings, scattered over the great room-size rug, which is either an English Axminster or a French Savonnerie. The room is a completely planned and decorated ensemble, its artwork "commercial" art ordered from France. In the 1870s, the builder Lockwood lost his money and died and his widow could not meet the last payment, so lost the house. The Mathewses had it until the 1930s, when it went to the city of Norwalk, and at the time a local group decided to save it, it was being used as a city garage. So the parlor pictured here has not existed this way for over a hundred years. One chair survives of the Louis XVI suite, and the architectural elements of the room remain. Should the room be recreated, using furnishings "of the period?" Or should the documentary photograph be followed to the line, and the furniture reproduced?—*Lockwood-Mathews House Restoration*

Figure 25. Bedroom, Photographed by Joseph Henry in His Apartment, Smithsonian Institution, Washington, D.C., 1870

Elsewhere in the Joseph Henry apartment, a decade later, we have entered modern times in the area of comfort. Gaslight falls from the ceiling and a gas-bracket even permits reading in bed. Steam heat radiates from the corner beside the bed. It is a creature comfort not known for long in the world, and not yet known to many people. Nothing seen in this interior is homemade. Everything comes from the machines of manufacture, only now developing into mass-production. Brussels carpeting, the "French bed," sofa, rockers, bureau, could be selected at furniture warehouses in any city. Such things were advertised in California at the time, and appear in documentary photographs throughout the country. The whimsical lambrequin on the window and the snowy lace beneath it are classic window hangings for the 1860s and 1870s.—*Smithsonian Institution*

Figure 26. Upstairs Parlor, Massachusetts, ca. 1875   179

Disrobed and slip-covered for summer, this New England parlor takes exception to the usual rule by not having matting on the floor. The Venetian blinds are probably raised for the photographer's convenience. They are of a kind made all through the nineteenth century, though they did not enjoy the popularity of window shades or curtains. Notice the presence of increasing numbers of objects of the sort one bought at the store, as well as flower arrangements and other hand-made things that counterbalance the "store-bought" look. The room must be lighted by kerosene lamps, which are brought in as night falls. They would give only limited light, so there would probably be several. The furniture arrangement is interesting and seen in a transitional time. While the furniture is not against the wall, as in earlier years, the arrangement is decidedly traditional, with the objects pushed back from the center of the room. There are no fashionable groupings here, and that may have something to do with there being no overhead light. In 1875 it is still a bit early for the new approach to furniture arrangement to be considered universal. The innovations of gaslight and central heating are still the determining factor in making static "artistic" arrangements.—*Holman's Print Shop, Boston*

Figure 27. Sitting Room, New Bedford, Massachusetts, ca. 1885   181

Daniel Ricketson's sitting room demonstrates the personal look so avidly sought in the late nineteenth-century interior on nearly every level of society. Here we have a room furnished with middle-class furniture that was available anywhere in the country. We actually notice the furniture very little. Its presence is deliberately minimized by a conscious scattering about of personal objects that once would have been considered improper exhibits. Besides the shawl and hat, however, there are homely creations. The corner shelves with stuffed birds are personal expressions, as are the other "artistic" creations. Objects are grouped significantly into units, a custom that developed from the scattered arrangements. One decade later, the units in this room would be split up and the objects spread out to flow with the lines of the room. Much of the cluttering of rooms such as this seems to have come from nostalgia for the homelike interiors of the preindustrial age. It had nothing much to do with collecting antiques. Compare the Ricketson interior with the yeoman's house of 1813, pictured earlier in "The Quilting Frolic" (Figure 15). Both rooms are filled with objects. The earlier nineteenth-century room is crowded with objects of use, placed where they are for convenience and on "stand by" for when they are needed. In the late nineteenth-century room, which is comparable in quality and class, there is little that could be categorized as objects of use, for even where there *is* an object of use, such as the hat on the chair, it is performing as an ornament.—*The Whaling Museum, New Bedford, Mass.*

182

Figure 28. Throne Room, Iolani Palace, Honolulu, Hawaii, ca. 1884

Among American rooms, the Throne Room of the Iolani Palace is certainly the most unusual. Restored in the 1920s, it was originally completed in 1883 and occupied as a palace for only ten years. After the queen was deposed, the legislature met there, and between sessions the public found great fascination in the throne room. This is a rare example of a state room in an American house; even our governors' mansions seldom have what could be called "rooms of state," and they are usually decorated to play down the appearance of pomp and pageantry. State rooms in houses in Europe provide the premier examples of decorative styles before the early 1870s. There is no analogy at all between great houses of Europe and American houses; but, alas, palatial decoration is too often taken as inspiration in furnishing historic houses in America. There is much to be learned from the stately houses. But it must be remembered that state rooms were symbolic and served public functions. They were grand for a reason; and for the same reason, they were often flawless expressions of the high taste of the time. The Iolani Palace throne room was built after the age of building state rooms was over. Furnished by the Davenport Company of Boston, the throne room's inspiration seems to have come from hotel lobbies of the day, with royal thrones in the place usually occupied by a grand stair.—*Iolani Palace Restoration Project and State Archives of Hawaii*

Figure 29. "Oatlands Hall Drawn by a Child of 12, 1889," *Watercolor,* *Anonymous*

The child artist presumably sat in the hall of the Oatlands house near Leesburg, Virginia, and drew what she saw. The early nineteenth-century house contained an accumulation of furnishings, little, if any, of it coinciding with the dates of the house. While the Oatlands house today is preserved as occupied in the early twentieth century, this picture would raise an interesting question, if a decision were made to recreate the hall as it might have been in an earlier time: should this document be followed because it is the best and earliest documentation extant on this house? Or should a date of, say, 1835 be selected and a recreation based upon a massive research project of similar houses, even though little evidence survives that pertains directly to the house? Or should one take a cue from the hall's surviving architectural elements and simply furnish it "of the period" to conjure up an image of "pure" style?—*National Trust for Historic Preservation*

Figure 30. Dining Room, Michigan, 1909

This "Sheraton" dining room was executed by an interior decorator using furniture readily available on the market. One might think of it as manufactured high style, because it is current with Edwardian fashion in England and with the "French," "Georgian," and "Colonial" production of leading designers and manufacturers in America. It is a room that is rather in step with today. Created wholly for modern use, it forces a dominant theme based on a style associated with the late eighteenth century. This sort of "period" room was espoused by critics as timeless good taste, in contrast to the object-filled, "cozy" or "artistic" rooms most Americans lived in. It is an assertion of one idea, instead of a complexity of ideas. The decorator's objective here, supported by the manufacturer's complete "set" of matching furniture, is to capture a literal sort of reflection of a historical epoch, based on decorative arts. This idea is likewise the basis of the period museum interior, which began to appear about a decade and a half after this picture was made. Not at all antiquarian, as were earlier attempts to recreate historical rooms, the period interior reflects the academic vein of the era of its birth. It was a result of a sifting of "good" from "bad." In its separate *parts*, it was often historical, making use of actual documentary objects and modes, but as a whole room setting, they were—as most of them are still—quite as modern as the standards of selection that created them. Such rooms, while often suitable and instructive in museums of the gallery type, limit the interpretive possibilities of the historic house to the subject of design. Its roots are never deep in the particulars of history.—*The Victorian Society in America*

Figure 31. Parlor, Grant-Kohrs Ranch House, Deer Lodge, Montana, 1891

This documentary photograph is difficult to distinguish as "old," for the room remains almost the same today. The ranch house was built by a butcher whose wealth grew to immense proportions when he entered the ranching business. His parlor is a substantial middle-class interior, with its plush "Turkish chairs" and the mahogany chairs and center table that suggest the late English Georgian taste and were probably called "quaint" furnishings. While these do not imitate the originals, they are similar enough to be recognizable; they are thus *historical* revivals, as opposed to the *creative* revivals so heavily adapted that the sources, at least to our modern eyes, are sometimes obscured. The parlor is an uncluttered room, and that was not the norm for 1891; but by the later nineties, the objects were fewer and not clustered into art units. Originally illumined by gaslight, the rooms have been electrified. Bulbs hang in globes from fixtures in the ceiling. Conduit with wires has been run up the wall to the gas bracket. But on the center table the vase lamp stands by, doubtless filled with kerosene, awaiting the failure of the electricity.—*National Park Service*

The same room, July 23, 1978.—*Photo by Rodd L. Wheaton, National Park Service*

Figure 32. Bedroom and Upstairs Hall, Wetherburn's Tavern, Williamsburg, Virginia, 1976

Though in a tavern, this transverse view from bedroom through hall to a second bedroom is not so different from the same view in a private house of the Revolutionary War period. It is neat, indeed; and if it were a house, it might be more cluttered with transient objects, both in use and stored in view. Here are textures familiar to most eighteenth-century Americans—the unpainted plaster walls, the unfinished floors, the list carpeting, which was sometimes laid wall-to-wall. Other textures are those known mainly in houses of the well-to-do, such as the printed-linen bedhangings from England and the smooth-painted woodwork, which has been either rubbed with pumice or laid on in three or four coats. The form, if not the detailing, of the fine mahogany bureau has been borrowed by the cabinetmaker from a model pictured in an English pattern-book. The towering clothes press has in its lower section only a faint echo of the sort of "style" one got from books. The dominant character of this piece is not so easy to trace to a particular source, for it comes from the mainstream—the vernacular of colonial American cabinetmaking. By studying many examples, the scholar divides the general vernacular into regional groups, then local ones. Vernacular objects are important in all American interiors prior to mass-manufacture, and the study of these is the most complicated, the least documented in writing, and the most time-consuming of all.—*The Colonial Williamsburg Foundation*

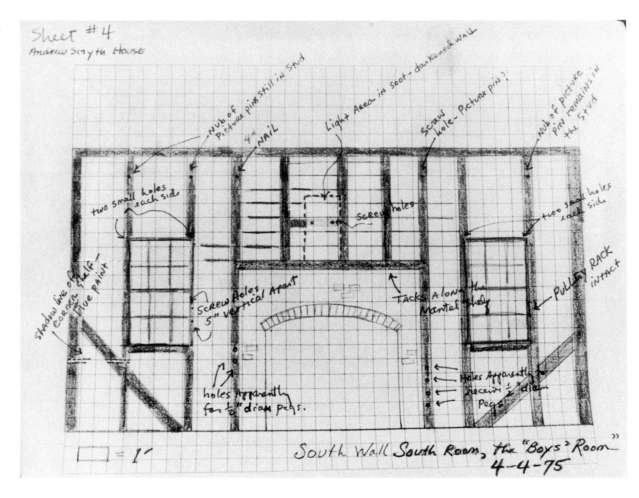

Sheet #4
Andrew Smyth House

Nub of picture pins still in stud
4" NAIL
Light Area in soot-darkened wall
Screw hole - Picture pin?
Nub of picture pins remains in the stud

two small holes each side
Shadow line of corner shelf - drive paint
screw holes
two small holes each side

Screw holes 5" vertical Apart
Tacks Along the Mantel shelf
PULLEY RACK intact

holes Apparently for ½" diam pegs.
Holes Apparently receiving ½" diam Pegs

☐ = 1'

South Wall South Room, the "Boys' Room"
4-4-75

Figure 33. Work Sheet, Andrew F. Smyth House, Jasper County, Texas 193

One of the first steps in research toward recreating an interior is to survey the interior. What this amounts to is collecting clues. Some of these may be lost during structural restoration, so they must be recorded. The main purpose, however, is to get all available information on paper, so that it can be considered as a body of facts. The house of Captain Smyth was begun in 1849 and added to in 1859. According to the usual custom in East Texas, it was central to a complex of buildings. The house was sitting and sleeping quarters only; kitchen, dining room, workrooms, slave quarters, and so on, were in separate wooden structures near the main house. The house was never ceiled inside; and, except for repairs in 1961, it has remained much as it was when first completed in 1859. Without complicating matters by taking into consideration the ages of the tacks, etc., found in the walls, let us "read" this work sheet. The wall framework is fully exposed, and the walls have never been painted, though the window sash is white. An orderly row of five holes, one a nail hole and the others containing the nubs of picture pins, suggests a row of pictures, which hung, obviously, above the height of the windows. A clock was screwed to a crosspiece fixed between two studs over the fireplace. There was a curtain or valance of some kind tacked along the mantel shelf. Window shades were on the windows, as can be seen by the pulley racks. There was a corner shelf painted bright blue. And the holes beside the fireplace? Who knows? Perhaps to attach a mantel that was never installed? But the information may yet illuminate some obscure reference to be found later in Captain Smyth's papers, and thus be of the greatest value in recreating the room. Work sheets like this are done on graph paper or on prints of finished architectural elevations for every wall in the house, as well as ceilings and floors.—*Haworth P. Bromley Photo*

Figure 34. Parlor, Kanawha Hall, Louisville, Kentucky, 1890 195

This documentary photograph shows an ordinary middle-class parlor of the nineties. The poppy wallpaper is hung to minimize the height of the room by being stopped a distance below the ceiling and being banded with bordering. There are lace curtains, Brussels carpeting and border, a Colonial Revival rocking chair, a ruffle-shaded kerosene lamp, which is on a lamp table in the *néo grec* style, somewhat earlier. The total setting is so complete and so characteristically middle-class for its era, that one is likely to miss the desk on the left. It belonged to George Washington, and was bequeathed to his old friend Dr. James Craik. Now that one knows that, does the room change? Does the overwhelming tone of the whole melt away in the dominant presence of a single object—dominant because of its historical associations?—*The Filson Club*

Figure 35. Study, Mount Vernon, Virginia, 1978   197

Until we knew the desk (Figure 34) was Washington's, it blended quite well into an actual domestic setting that existed and was photographed "live" one hundred years after General Washington had purchased the desk in Philadelphia. Sold back to Mount Vernon by Dr. Craik's descendants in 1905, it stands today in the recreated eighteenth-century study here. Many of the other objects are original to this room, and what is not has been approximated, using the inventory made immediately after Washington's death. There is more to recreating a room, however, than gathering up original objects. Even if all the original materials happen to be found and brought together, they must be combined in the room in a valid way, and supporting objects are likely to be needed, for both interest and emphasis. This requires intense historical investigation into details of the way the room was used, contemporary practices in furniture arrangement, means of heating and lighting, types of floor covering, and window hangings. To misstate any one of these can throw your principal documented objects out of focus and often rob them of the authority of their presence. Consider Washington's desk in the two different settings. There is a glaring contrast. The danger deepens when the contrast is not so glaring. Developing the correct historical tone for a historical interior is a highly sensitive matter. Nothing can ruin the process more quickly than the intrusion of personal preferences.—*Mount Vernon Ladies Association of the Union*

Figure 36. Parlor, McLean House, Appomattox, Virginia, 1977   199

In this parlor of a private home, General Robert E. Lee surrendered to General Ulysses S. Grant on April 9, 1865. The National Park Service has recreated the interior to look as it did that day. However, from the moment the event took place, the house has glowed from the magic of its great hour, and consequently it has had a bizarre history since then. It was dismanteled and transported to Chicago, lock, stock, and barrel, at one time. Plans to reconstruct it there failed, and meanwhile the furniture was scattered to various museums. At last the bricks, timbers, windows, and doors were returned to Appomattox and there rebuilt on the original site. Unable to secure the original furniture, the Park Service elected to copy it, rather than obtaining objects "of the period." The overriding purpose of this museum was to illustrate its one historical moment of grandeur, and anything but exact copies of what had been there would dilute the impact. What you see here is a room recreated through faithful reproductions of objects known to have been there. Since they are reproductions, the opportunity was taken to make them appear relatively new, as they would have been at the time of the surrender.—*National Park Service*

Figure 37. Grecian Center Table, ca. 1845–1850

   Made of mahogany veneered over a pine structure, this ordinary marble-topped center table represents very well the middle-class version of one of the most long-lived furniture styles of the nineteenth century. As the name implies, this kind of table was ordinarily used in the center of the room. An oil lamp could be placed in the middle of it to serve the whole family circle gathered there at various pursuits before bedtime. In the winter, a cover was usually thrown over the center table. This kept the family's legs warm when they sat around the table; sometimes warmers were placed beneath the table. The center table was also an altar of sorts. Long before people began to think of entire interiors as places for artistic expression, the center table held little baskets of waxed fruit, a Bible, and several awesome books, such as *Pilgrim's Progress*. The tabletop could be a powerful show of talent and taste. That is true of center tables in general, and it is true of this one. But this table also has another dimension that makes it one of a kind: it is the actual table that once stood in the McLean parlor (Figure 36) and the one Lee used while the terms of surrender were being negotiated.—*Chicago Historical Society*

Figure 38. Parlor and Dining Room, James K. Polk Memorial, Columbia, Tennessee, 1978

This remarkable collection of furniture belonged to James Knox Polk and his wife Sarah. The sofa and chairs were purchased at the close of the Polks' White House years, as were the chandeliers. They are in the French Antique mode, which was in its heyday in the East during Polk's presidency. Everything else is Grecian and may have been owned by the Polks for some years. It was Sarah Polk's wish that their retirement residence in Nashville, Polk Place, become a museum. The wish has been fulfilled only in part. After her death in the 1890s, Polk Place was demolished and the Polk tomb moved. The collection of furniture and memorabilia was, however, kept together and eventually moved forty miles from Nashville to the present house in Columbia, Tennessee. That house had been the home of Polk's parents. Though the objects are all original to the president, there is small chance that they were ever in this house before; so neither of these interiors can be considered recreations. They are part of a museum of the gallery type, containing Polk memorabilia, which happens to have part of the collection exhibited in this way.—*James K. Polk Memorial Association*

Figure 39. Library, Wheatland, Lancaster County, Pennsylvania, 1976   205

James Buchanan's furnishings and his country home remain virtually intact. Recreation here has nearly reached total restoration, for when Buchanan ran for president in 1856, the room was accurately drawn for popular publication. These illustrations, inventories, physical remains (traces, as of wallpaper), and people's recollections combined to produce rooms such as this—near duplicates of what they were when Buchanan and his niece Harriet Lane lived there.—*The James Buchanan Foundation for the Preservation of Wheatland*

Figure 40. Mary Hampton in her Drawing Room, Columbia, South Carolina, ca. 1860

That a house is large and the owner is known to have been very rich can be misleading in recreating the rooms. The fact that a family was wealthy seems somehow a temptation to restorationists to glamorize historical interiors. This picture is central to a classic instance, if not of glamorizing, certainly of misinterpretation. Mary Cantey Hampton was immensely rich, the widow of General Wade Hampton. While most of what she owned had, by 1860, been transferred to her daughter Mrs. Preston, she still maintained an extensive house and garden, manned by some thirty slaves. There was a chef, a butler, numbers of housemaids, coachmen, grooms, and gardeners. On paper, Mary Hampton's setting seemed much more fashionable than this photograph shows that it actually was. Taken in her drawing room, the view shows an unsophisticated interior that is far more middle class than her fortune and the inventory of the room would imply. The walls are papered in an ordinary floral pattern. Most of the furniture visible is quite out-of-date "fancy" furniture, plain and painted. A solar lamp on the table sheds its light on cheap statuettes and homemade odds and ends. The daylilies date the moment as early summer. Twisted in gilded bands, the curtains show that they are functional, as curtains were, and not the static "draperies" familiar in restored houses today.—*Caroliniana Collection, University of South Carolina*

208

Figure 41. Drawing Room, Hampton-Preston House, Columbia, South Carolina, 1970

Mary Hampton's house, having survived with very few changes but considerable deterioration, for a century after her death, underwent a restoration program in 1969 and 1970. The drawing room was furnished without benefit of the 1860 photograph (Figure 40), which had not yet turned up. There were other documents, not the least in significance being Mary Boykin Chesnut's *Diary from Dixie,* portions of which were written in the house. Most of the objects shown here actually belonged to Hamptons or Prestons in pre-Civil War times, though it is doubtful whether anything but the daughter's Bible on the center table was ever in Mary Hampton's house. Each object was nevertheless rich in family associations. The red silk taffeta curtains of about 1840, for example, escaped General Sherman's torches, because the "aunties," in fleeing the plantation Millwood just ahead of invading Union troops, took the curtains along as packing for fragile china. Most of the objects are of the decade or two before the Civil War, and the historical potency of this memorabilia is very strong. But the room, in an over-all sense, has none of the completeness, and little of the believability, that comes from the dim old photograph. The photograph reveals the *tone* of the original drawing room; if that single thing were all that could be gleaned from it, then the document would still be the most valuable of any associated with the Hampton-Preston House.—*South Carolina Tricentennial Commission*

Figures 42 and 43. Parlor, Ebenezer Maxwell Mansion, Germantown, Pennsylvania, 1977

Two views of the recreated parlor of Ebenezer Maxwell are shown here, with north and south perspectives, taken soon after its completion. Maxwell's suburban villa was built and occupied in 1859. A rambling stone house in the Gothic mode, it was not palatial, but it was showy, an architectural skin for the comfortable and modern residence of a city businessman. The parlor is not a room created by people of leisure, or particularly sophisticated taste. The sensitivity in its recreation is remarkable; when you stand in the room, you almost know the Maxwells: one is certain that it has taken money for the Maxwells to put the place together, but except for the antimacassars, everything here could have been rounded up in Philadelphia and bought (on credit, if necessary) in a single day. In spite of the Gothic shell of the house, the room is fitted out in the French Antique style. The furniture is designed to evoke old historical styles; but being broad-shouldered and springy, it also fully answers the comfort standards of the 1850s and 1860s. The parlor, luxurious with soft cushions, is warmed by an explosion of patterns and colors. It is a cozy room—not seedy, of course, for it clearly has the lingering

scent of varnish, and the carpeting smells new. An 1867 inventory was the guide to furnishing this businessman's parlor. The Brussels carpeting is a copy of a nineteenth-century pattern that would have been available to Maxwell; various objects in the room were actually used in other houses in the neighborhood. The form of the window hangings—lambrequins, side curtains, and lace curtains—was copied from an illustration in *Gleason's Magazine* in 1859. Barely visible is a small grille in the fireplace opening. The house was centrally heated, with a hot-air system, and, as was customary, the ducts were in the chimneys, the registers in the fireplaces. Artificial lighting's great influence upon change in furniture arrangement is illustrated here, where part of the furniture is placed as though timidly marching out from the walls, to take advantage of overhead gaslight. At that time, the stronger custom was still to line furniture up along the walls. In a more sophisticated interior, the furniture might be flamboyantly grouped in conversation circles, with many lamps and many more objects of ornament and of "refined" use than are seen here. We see the Maxwell parlor here decorated for the Christmas season 1977, precisely following instructions in an 1850s issue of *Godey's Lady Book.*—*Photos, Claire Kofsky for the Maxwell Mansion*

Figure 44. Ladies' Drawing Room, Raleigh Tavern, Williamsburg, Virginia, 1932–1976

Meant to represent the parlor of an eighteenth-century tavern, this room bears close resemblance to expensive suburban living rooms of the 1920s in Grosse Point, Michigan, and Larchmont, New York. It was used symbolically in its interpretation; its objects were all authentic to the eighteenth century.—*The Colonial Williamsburg Foundation*

The former Ladies' Drawing Room (Figure 44) of the Raleigh Tavern has been entirely revised to show a more clearly documented sort of tavern room. Eighteenth-century Americans loved to gamble, and tavern life was seldom as sedate as this room formerly implied. Here, costumed interpreters in the Raleigh's Billiard Hall recall a drawing by Benjamin Henry Latrobe of men at billiards in a Virginia tavern. The room, though bare and simple, is striking as a stage for the historical imagination. Previously a decorated scene, it now reflects human habitation and use.—*The Colonial Williamsburg Foundation*

Figure 46. Common Room, the Gomez House, Saint Augustine, Florida, 1977

Reconstructed some twenty years ago, the Gomez House is based upon a legend written in a 1764 Spanish map of the city. The "house of boards" was owned by Lorenzo Gomez and his wife Catarina Perdomo, and consisted of two tiny rooms. While nothing of the house remained, Saint Augustine has abundant inventories and descriptions from which to document interiors. From all accounts, the Spanish lived in a degree of barrenness that the English found difficult to believe, even in a poor little military outpost like Saint Augustine. All the furnishings here are reproduced from Spanish models found in Spain and Latin America. The Spanish colonials had very little seat furniture, but possessed chests for textiles and small things, perhaps a custom developed from constant moving about in Spain's vast colonial empire. The interior of Señor Gomez's house is whitewashed (though the exterior was left unpainted) and there is neither glass in the windows nor a fireplace in the room. Winter cooking was done in braziers, and summer cooking outside.—*Historic Saint Augustine Preservation Board*

Figure 47. Kitchen, Gallegos House, Saint Augustine, Florida, 1977   219

The Gallegos house is a reconstruction of a house built on the same site in 1720. Though small, it is a better sort of house than that of Lorenzo Gomez, being built of the local shellstone (*coquina*) and plastered inside and out with "tabby" (*tapia*), which was customarily kept whitewashed. There are two rooms, this kitchen and a common room, and both give on to a deep, arcaded loggia that faces the *patio*. Man and beast entered the little complex through the same gate in the *patio* wall. The kitchen recreates such a room in the dwelling of a man of some means—a tradesman, perhaps, or the owner of a store—and one whose livelihood depends upon the business he gets from the soldiers at the Castillo de San Marcos. His kitchen has very little furniture, but, like most kitchens, is filled with transient objects. The baskets and pottery are types made locally in the seventeenth and eighteenth centuries, and the iron cooking implements could have come from a blacksmith in town or at the Castillo. The latticed cupboard (left) and the hanging shelf kept foods dry and protected from the animals and fowl that wander in from the *patio*. The "Spanish stove," which is not unlike stoves found at Pompeii, is made of stone. The smoke passes up through two holes in the flat roof. Fired from the front, it has several cooking grills, as well as deep vessels sunk into it for warming liquids. These "stew holes" were not unfamiliar everywhere, before the kitchen range came into its own. They were not necessarily for soup, as the name implies, but were the forerunners of the hot-water heater. The walls of the kitchen were whitewashed from time to time, and there is a bright "washboard" simulated in paint around the base of the room to conceal the dirt and splatters that come from constantly scrubbing the *coquina* floor. This kitchen is used every day for cooking, in the course of its interpretation.—*Historic Saint Augustine Preservation Board*

Figure 48. Kitchen, White Face Camp, U Lazy S Ranch, Lubbock, Texas, 1978

This room and also the bedroom (Figure 49) at the White Face Camp are the interiors of a "dug-out" house moved to the Ranching Museum from the original location. The house was provided by a big ranching enterprise for one of its range foremen, who supervised the range crew, which spent long hours with the cattle herds on the vast, unfenced ranges far from ranch headquarters. The date is between 1890 and 1900. The "chuck room," or kitchen, is in the dug-out part of the house, like a partial cellar, with the floor joists of the second floor forming its ceiling. This is not the rustic abode of the Log Cabin Myth, in which everyone sits around on split logs and drinks from gourds. The range foreman's house is the product of civilization, or, more precisely, mass-manufacture. The joists are not logs, but milled lumber from a sawmill, and even the packed-earth walls and floor have a machine-like precision. With the possible exception of the table, the type of which is in an ancient vernacular, nothing in the room is homemade. Everything is from the rather general market of mass-production—the cast-and-rolled-iron cookstove, the hide-bottom chairs that imitate earlier vernacular modes, the tin cans, the pots and pans, and the shipping crates, which were built as objects of use, and here, as shelving, have become objects of use of another kind.—*Ranching Museum, Texas Tech University*

Figure 49. Bedroom, White Face Camp, U Lazy S Ranch, Lubbock, Texas, 1978

Upstairs, the bedroom is a shell of milled lumber, the walls painted white, the floors naked boards. By the height of the walls from the floor, one can gain some idea of the external appearance of this dug-out house. The range foreman and his family would live here for about eleven months of the year, while he managed a "line camp" for the ranch. The sense of being temporary is one of the finest qualities of this recreation. The bedroom, like the kitchen below, was recreated using contemporary accounts and ranch records. Some of the furniture is "standing furniture" provided by the ranch. Other objects are the foreman's own, for he had a good salary and ordered from the mail-order catalogue just as the ranch managers did. It can be supposed, however, that in such a mobile life—not unlike Lorenzo Gomez's, 150 years earlier (see Figure 46)—the range foreman's possessions will all pack away into the trunk, when it is time for him to move on.—*Ranching Museum, Texas Tech University*

224

Figure 50. Common Room, Settler's Cabin, Lancaster, Pennsylvania, 1978

The settler's cabin at Landis Valley is a hypothetical building, its interiors executed with great care for detail on the basis of research in eighteenth-century inventories and other local sources of the Pennsylvania Germans. Both this room and the kitchen of the Settler's Cabin (Figure 51), shown in recent views, recreate German farm life in the area ca. 1780. The common room was called the *stube*. Furnished with furniture of regional origin, it is filled with transient objects that tell of busy hands in a farmer's family. The log walls are chinked with clay mortar, and the entire interior is whitewashed, which was not only clean but made the room—which was likely to get sooty—brighter. There is substantial evidence for such crowded conditions in small eighteenth-century houses, and contemporary views inside yeomen's houses in Europe draw interesting parallels. There is indication that a new tendency toward starkness in interiors appeared at about the time of the upsurge of the Protestant religious revival movement at the beginning of the nineteenth century, somewhat in advance of the classical movement in high style—*Pennsylvania Farm Museum of Landis Valley*

Figure 51. Kitchen, Settler's Cabin, Lancaster, Pennsylvania, 1978

This kitchen adjoins the *stube* (Figure 50) in the cabin at the Landis Valley Museum. It is as simple and functional as historical records indicate that it would have been. The great fireplace of stone, whitewashed, is the place where the cooking was done. Coals were raked out onto the hearth, beneath a "dog" or grill, or a footed pot. This kitchen tells of the "one-pot" meals that were the principal diet of a Pennsylvania German. Happily, objects have not been arranged here in "artistic" units. Note how the mantel is crowded with kitchen implements. The dresser, too, holds objects as it actually may have done, in no special order.—*Pennsylvania Farm Museum of Landis Valley*

Figure 52. Parlor, McFaddin House, Beaumont, Texas, 1974   229

Completed in 1906, the McFaddin House was first occupied by W. P. H. McFaddin and remains in his family. The parlor is furnished in a version of the on-going French Antique mode; known first in the 1890s in this form, it is heavier than the earlier revivals, and while a similar style was popular in France, neither bore much resemblance to eighteenth-century furniture. But neither were there record-players in the eighteenth century. This gilded one, painted with cherubs and roses, goes well with the other furniture, though it is not original to the room. A slightly redder pink than "ashes of roses" is the dominant color, with ivory-colored woodwork highly glossed with varnish. The walls and ceiling are canvased and painted with garlands of flowers. *Boiserie* is simulated in plaster panels. Originally, the polished floor was partially covered by a Savonnerie rug. The window hangings, original to the room, consist of lambrequins, side panels (which will tie back), and lace curtains. The glass chandelier replaces an earlier "electrolier," which was a glass bowl ringed by deep fringe. Without the cuts and bruises of radical change, the McFaddin parlor, like most of the rest of the house, has changed subtly over the years. It is not nearly so austere as it started out being. If this house were turned into a museum house, it should be frozen as it is. Any alteration would constitute a risk with the special flavor the rooms now have. Would the risk be worth the effort? For all the detailed documentation of this parlor, it is doubtful that total recall of 1906 would be a wise objective.—*Theodore B. Powers Photo*

Figure 53. Library, Ruthmere, Elkhart, Indiana, 1974   231

Unlike its contemporary, the McFaddin house, the A. H. Beardsley house was sold by the descendants of the builders, and its contents auctioned off soon after World War II. In the early 1970s, it was restored by the Beardsley family foundation as a museum. The interiors were recreated on the basis of family recollections, an inventory of 1924, and various family papers. (See also Plate 11.) Built in 1910 and restored to that date, Ruthmere is one of those big, solid houses one finds all over the United States, built during the two decades before World War I. Deep porches, wide windows, large but not foreboding interior spaces characterize these modern "family" houses that seemed to purr with creature comforts. They were considered practical, and were largely without pretensions to visual grandeur. Theirs was an aura of convenience— steam heat, electric lights, fans, irons, toasters, gas ranges, refrigerators, foot-warmers, bell-call systems, telephones, and those gleaming caves of white tile that encased bathtubs, flush toilets, and heated towel-racks. The McFaddin house (Figure 52) was built to be this sort of house, too, but the ideas of intervening generations have come to bear, so the image is not so bold as in recreated Ruthmere. The Ruthmere library was the family retreat. Sofa, carpeting, shaded electric bulbs make human comfort a theme; luxury enters to enhance the theme through damask-covered walls, which rise above rich mahogany wainscoting, and the gilt decoration on the ceiling above the chandelier combines the ciphers of the Beardsleys. The bookcases contain red leather-bound editions of the classics, another attention to creature enjoyment. Books were obvious symbols of culture in a day when people read and re-read. By the twentieth century, multivolume sets were available on the market to nearly any level of society, to satisfy a popular need. By the time Ruthmere and the McFaddin house were built, the mass-manufacture of household furnishings was a full generation removed from its first frightening impact after the Civil War. It had come to be acceptable to own objects that were "machine made" (in spite of the term's inaccuracy). There was no longer a compulsion to warm the chill of manufactured furnishings with handmade objects.—*Andrew Hubble Beardsley Foundation. Robert Perron Photo*

Figure 54. Parlor, Lansdowne, Natchez, Mississippi, 1958   233

A Greek-Revival house on a plantation, Lansdowne is another rare survivor, having undergone only the normal changes brought by family living since it was completed in 1853. This gas-lit parlor opens off a long, gallery-like hall; the principal features of the parlor have remained the same since the 1850s. At the windows, damask lambrequins in the French Antique taste hang from Louis XV revival cornices. Faded to a pinkish orange, the lambrequins were originally brilliant red-orange. The "parlor set" is an example of the florid, carved mode of the French Antique in the 1850s. Appliquéd wallpaper roses and leaves are cut out and pasted into borders, thus giving the parlor walls the effect of being paneled in rich, painted silk, in the eighteenth-century French mode. The *néo grec* mantel mirror is late 1860s, at the very earliest. And the Aubusson rug surely replaces all-over Brussels or Wilton carpeting, or perhaps straw matting.—*Natchez Garden Club. Woody Ogden Photo*

Figure 55. Manderfield Parlor Furniture, Museum of New Mexico, 1966

Except for the center table, the Bible, and the Aubusson rug, the furnishings in this picture were transported overland on the Santa Fe Trail by the Manderfield family, about 1849. Many unlikely stories are told of fine furnishings going west in that way. This one is thoroughly documented. The furniture must have been packed in straw, and the fragile alabaster pitchers and the mirrors in bran or cotton. Today the furniture is placed in a domestic setting in a room of the ancient Palace of the Governors, now the state museum. The rich furniture, the mirrors, the marble mantel, are a curious contrast to the adobe walls and log beams of the ceiling. This is used as a period room setting, which features the furniture in a visual context it may have known in early Santa Fe. The purpose here is to exhibit the furniture for its historical associations, not its design.—*Museum of New Mexico*

Figure 56. Bedroom, Fountain Elms, Utica, New York, 1977 237

The Gothic-style house Fountain Elms was furnished to reflect not the history of the house but the taste of the 1850s. A bold ambition at best, the result is usually to create a very up-to-date version of the time one wishes to represent. This is the result here: a room not footed in anything very precise; a room reflecting a selective eye of the 1950s. The details are generally true of the 1850s, but the general effect is much later, the 1870s or 1880s. The impression is more of a parlor than a bedroom. Modern responses to aspects of the taste of the 1850s are evident in the extravagant use of lambrequins on the bed, the immense patterns of the wallpaper and carpeting. There are side tables with lamps, and for all the objects present, most of the table tops are as bare as those in a hotel suite. This bedroom represents a point of view, as did the little dining room at the Governor's Palace in Williamsburg. What is central is the furniture and its presentation in a way that makes it appealing to those who see it.—*Munson Williams Proctor Institute*

Figure 57. Parlor, Hunter House, Newport, Rhode Island, 1975   239

Although it may be in part as early as 1719, the Hunter House took its present form soon after 1758. The paneling of this room is another of those exceptional products of American colonial craftsmen, who, in certain localities, achieved personal styles that showed considerable refinement. This can be appreciated better at hindsight, of course, as the quality that sets their work apart lies in their departures from established norms. The Hunter House paneling is a virtuoso performance, featuring Corinthian pilasters, arched and shell-backed closets, and curious little carved angels. Some years ago the original colors were restored, the greens, the black-marbled pilasters. Most of the furniture here was made by eighteenth-century Newport cabinetmakers, but as a complete interior, this room has little to do with ways of living in the eighteenth century. In combination the furnishings follow the Colonial Revival taste of the twentieth century. The Oriental rug surrounded by highly polished flooring and the swags at the windows strengthen the Colonial Revival impression. Overelaboration is not the problem here; what is lacking is a feeling for the late eighteenth century as a historical period. The 1756 inventory of this house may not be relevant, because the house probably reached its present state no earlier than 1758. The inventory, however, calls for numerous pieces of furniture and surprisingly fine appointments. Going by that, one can imagine rather full rooms, but also the very different look of furniture lined along the walls, transient objects all around, interior blinds adjusted for daily use—in short, rather an alienation from a setting such as this one, so familiar to our eyes today.—*The Preservation Society of Newport County*

A Shaker community was divided into "families," among which the center family was composed of members of good standing and seniority within the community. They occupied the center house, both men and women, somewhat as a rigidly segregated boardinghouse. The Pleasant Hill settlement of Shakertown was commenced just prior to the War of 1812, and the big limestone center house was occupied before 1820. What one sees is part recreation and part preservation; the community was dissolved in September 1910, and while the architectural restoration emphasizes the early nineteenth century, the collections include objects from all the years the Shakers lived here. Since, in the objects they created, the Shakers perpetuated a great number of vernacular designs, the strict cut-off date on architecture and the long continuity of objects is not confusing, except to one very familiar with Shaker history. This kitchen has its original cooking fireplace, with early implements. The room served the center family, and also their household business of producing preserves (sweetmeats). The board with pegs for hanging things is immediately associated with Shaker interiors, but also appears in many other vernacular houses of the eighteenth and much of the nineteenth century. Such boards were sometimes hidden in the plaster and served for hanging pictures. The kitchen has its original "workshop-red" paint.—*Shakertown at Pleasant Hill*

Figure 59. Double Parlor, Whittlesey House, Rochester, New York, 1968   243

Located in the old third ward of Rochester, the modified temple-style house was built in 1835 and 1836 by a rich grain merchant who was soon ruined after the market crashed in the Panic of 1837. The Whittlesey family bought the house in 1841, and it remained with them until 1937, when it was acquired for use as a historic house museum. It was not restored to reflect the family's occupancy, but to symbolize the first decades of Rochester's prosperity on the Erie Canal. The Greek Revival enjoyed great popularity in the rich trading towns that flourished along the canal after its opening in 1825. These parlors are furnished primarily in the Grecian style, and also with some pieces—the armchair and table in the foreground—which, though neo-classical, are earlier than the popular sort of Grecian we see elsewhere. A color survey was done of the interior in the 1930s, and the results caused a sensation. The straw yellows, stone color, terra cotta, the grays, the lavish wood-graining and bronze effects seemed extraordinary to people who thought only white was appropriate to old houses (Williamsburg, in the same decade, was finding many exceptions to "colonial white"). The parlors approximate the sort of rooms a wealthy businessman might have had, selecting his furniture from the small-scale manufactories that were blooming in the 1830s. Manufacturing of all kinds was encouraged by the convenience of the canal. The parlors are believable and not unlike what one sees in the backgrounds of portraits of the 1830s. Astral lamps are on the center tables, while candles serve elsewhere. There are no curtains. The Brussels carpeting is from the 1840s. Tacked down in strips, it is designed to appear to be one great rug, with center medallion and a pattern that moves in ripplelike garlands to the edges.—*Landmark Society of Western New York. Stans Padelt Photo*

Rosedown was sold intact by descendants of the builders in 1956. The interiors and romantic thirty-five-acre garden remained, though shabby, indeed, virtually as they had been when the complex was completed in about 1855. Work had commenced in 1835, and the house had grown with the family and with its prosperity in the "flush times." In the course of restoration, much of the rich historical tone of the interiors as they had survived was lost. That is, the rooms, like the gardens, were a combination of plain and fancy put together by amateur hands anxious to live in surroundings of elegance. Today they show the assuredness and modern viewpoint of professional decorators. The library, in a wing added in 1845, is the exception, but it is also a case in point. The rug and the Argand chandelier are added to an interior otherwise very much restored to what it was. The furniture is almost all original; the crimson window hangings are copies of those that were still there and near collapse in 1956; the wallpaper and border are also copied from the original; objects on the "Louis Quatorze" library table are personal things that belonged to the nineteenth-century occupants of the house. Envision this same room with all-over carpeting, ingrain or Brussels, or straw matting; imagine the library table piled with folio volumes, as it was, and with many more books and letterboxes; try to see straight chairs lined up close together around the walls. Creating the right historical tone in an interior involves far more than the use of furnishings that we naturally find appropriate in our lives today.—*Rosedown Plantation*

Figure 61. Study, Sunnyside, Tarrytown, New York, 1970   247

Washington Irving's study was well documented by the author himself in a series of descriptions and sketches. It is a very personal room, first occupied by Irving when he bought the house in 1836. Then he slept behind the curtains in the book-alcove. Later the house was expanded, and he moved to a separate bedroom, retaining this as his study. Sunnyside is restored to the way it was in 1859, when Irving died. Nearly everything in this picture belonged to Irving—even the Oriental rug, which is here an exception to nearly all rules. Candles in prismed girandoles are on the mantel, while on the desk is a moderator lamp, a very costly variation on the Argand, employing a strong spring to force a fast and even flow of oil. Books written by Irving and those that he owned complete a setting that is less a recreation than an actual restoration that has emerged with distinction from documentary evidence.—*Sleepy Hollow Restorations*

Figure 62. Kitchen, Sunnyside, Tarrytown, New York, 1970   249

Irving's kitchen was up to date and built for domestic convenience. The woodwork is natural, under heavy varnish. Abundant cabinets show the early stages of having to house and wishing to conceal the increasing numbers of objects one seemed to accumulate. A fine old kitchen range (earlier called a "ranger") is set, as they usually were, in a fireplace made to hold a range. Often such fireplaces are restored as cooking fireplaces, where, by the height of the opening (and often the presence of worn or round-edged bricks knee-high at each side), it is evident that there was a range. Objects of daily culinary use lie on the table, and a grandly brimming woodbox stands by. Dishes are stacked about; the whole effect of this room—which seems to be between meals—is particularly successful. —*Sleepy Hollow Restorations*

Figure 63. Dining Room, Sarah Jordan's Boarding House, Greenfield Village, Michigan, 1972

Mrs. Jordan's was the first house in the world to be lighted with electricity, which brightened this dining room for the first time on New Year's Eve 1879. She lived near Thomas A. Edison's laboratory in Menlo Park, New Jersey. Edison's unmarried assistants roomed there, and the whole staff ate lunch in this room. So when it came time to put on a demonstration of his electric bulb, Edison wanted to apply his invention to domestic circumstances. Mrs. Jordan agreed to let him wire her house. Like practically everyone else, she used kerosene lamps. Edison installed his wiring as you see here. In 1929 Henry Ford bought the house and moved it to Greenfield Village, along with Edison's lab, as a feature of the fifty-year anniversary of the invention of the incandescent lamp. Ford's interest was in a total recall of the scene of a great event. Thus there were interviews with people who remembered the night, and considerable effort was expended to make this room accurate to the time when it was wired by Edison. This particular approach to furnishing a historic interior, highly unusual for 1929, is rather closely akin at least in its results to the present-day objective of illustrative realism.—*Collections of Greenfield Village and the Henry Ford Museum*

252

Figure 64. Library, Bulloch Hall, Roswell, Georgia, 1973

The recreation of a room of the mid-1840s, Bulloch Hall's library is based upon local and regional inventories, but little that actually pertains to this house. The furniture is pulled out from the walls in a temporary configuration around the center table. Practically every piece of furniture has casters (which are seldom used on furniture today), because furniture was moved around frequently for convenience, taking advantage of heat, light, and cool. The room is whitewashed, its seat furniture loosely "cased" or slip-covered, according to the custom of the day. The flat, woven carpeting, laid down in strips, is made of coarse woolen threads and is "natural" in color, with stripes of brilliant red, yellow, and green. Scattered over the room, as though actually in use, are various objects of use that reflect a rural family's early-evening amusements.—*Richard S. Myrick*

Chronology of Interiors Illustrated

1. Documentary views with their dates and page numbers:

2. Historical recreated interiors illustrated with the dates or approximate dates they are intended to represent and page numbers:

For Further Reading

The following list is composed not only of useful books that are current, but also of books that have been, for the most part, laid aside—old volumes opened today largely for their illustrations. This list is deliberately a mixed bag. The old books are often still valuable in parts. They also tell us much about attitudes in the times in which they were written. This is true of the romantic patriotism of the "antiques" books of the late nineteenth and early twentieth centuries. The old books on decorating can be very revealing in the way they endorse or react against popular customs. Examples of the latter are Downing's *Country Houses* (1850) and Wharton and Codman's *The Decoration of Houses* (1897), which tell us as much about how things *were* as how they ought to be. While you will find many such titles in this list, they are mingled with a majority of books and articles that correspond to our present standards of scholarship. You will further find several entries on European subjects. These are recommended as good sources for comparison.

Interiors

Alpern, Andrew. *Apartments for the Affluent*. New York, 1975.

Ames, Winslow. "Inside Victorian Walls." *Victorian Studies* 5, no. 2 (1961): 151–162.

Artistic Houses. New York,1883; reprint, 1971.

Church, Ella Rodman. *How to Furnish a Home*. New York, 1883.

Cleveland, Rose, E., editor. *Social Mirror: A Complete Treatise On the Laws, Rules, and Usages That Govern Our most Refined Homes and Social Circles*. St. Louis, 1888.

Clifford, Chandler Robbins. *Period Decoration*. New York, 1901.

Cook, Clarence. *The House Beautiful: Essays on Beds, Tables, Stools, and Candlesticks*. New York, 1878.

Cummings, Abbott Lowell. "Notes on Furnishing the 17th-Century New England House." *Old Time New England* 46, no. 3 (January–March 1956): 57–67.

DeWolfe, Elsie. *The House in Good Taste*. New York, 1913.

Downing, Andrew Jackson. *The Architecture of Country Houses*. Boston,1850; reprint, 1969.

Downs, Joseph. "Three Early New England Rooms." *The New-York Historical Society Quarterly*, April 1951, pp. 143–155.

Eastlake, Charles Locke. *Hints On Household Taste*. London,1868; reprint, 1969.

Eberlin, Harold D. *The Practical Book of Interior Decoration*. Philadelphia and London, 1919.

Elwell, Newton W. *Colonial Furniture and Interiors*. Boston, 1896.

Faude, Wilson H. "Associated Artists and the American Renaissance in the Decorative Arts." *Winterthur Portfolio* 10 (1975.)

———. *The Renaissance of Mark Twain's House*. Larchmont, 1978.

Fowler, John, and John Cornforth. *English Decoration in the 18th Century*. London, 1974.

French, Lillie H. *Homes and Their Decoration*. New York, 1903.

Garrett, Wendell D. "The Furnishings of Newport Houses, 1780–1800." *Rhode Island History* 18 (January 1959): 1–19.

Giedon, Siegfried. *Mechanization Takes Command*. New York, 1948.

Gowans, Allan. *Images of American Living*. Philadelphia, 1964.

Grant, Ian, editor. *Great Interiors*. New York, 1967.

Halsey, R. T. H. *The Homes of Our Ancestors, As Shown in the American Wing of the Metropolitan Museum of Art*. New York, 1925.

Hunt–Jones, Conover. *Dolley and the Great Little Madison*. Washington, D.C., 1977.

Jones, Mrs. C. S. *Household Elegancies: Suggestions in Household Art and Tasteful Home Decoration*. New York, 1875.

Kettell, Russell Hawes. *Early American Rooms: A Consideration of the Changes in Style Between the Arrival of the Mayflower and the Civil War in the Regions Originally Settled by the English and the Dutch*. Portland, Maine, 1936.

Lancaster, Clay. *New York Interiors at the Turn of the Century*. New York, 1977.

Bibliography

256

Lichten, Frances. *The Decorative Art of Victoria's Era.* New York, 1951; reprint, 1968.

Little, Nina Fletcher. "An Approach to Furnishing." *History News* 9, no. 4 (February 1964): 59–64. American Association for State and Local History *Technical Leaflet 17.*

Lynes, Russell. *The Tastemakers.* New York, 1954.

Maass, John. *The Victorian Home in America.* New York, 1972.

McClelland, Nancy V. *Furnishing the Colonial and Federal House.* Philadelphia, 1947.

Morningstar, Connie. *Flapper Furniture and Interiors of the 1920s.* Des Moines, Iowa, 1971.

Parsons, Frank Alvah. *Interior Decoration: Its Principles and Practice.* New York, 1918.

Peterson, Harold. *Americans at Home.* New York, 1970.

Praz, Mario. *An Illustrated History of Furnishing.* Milan, 1964; New York, 1966.

Roth, Rodris. "Interior Decoration in City Houses in Baltimore in the Federal Period." *Winterthur Portfolio 5* (1970).

Schwartz, Marvin D. *American Interiors, 1675–1885: A Guide to the American Period Rooms in the Brooklyn Museum.* Brooklyn, 1968.

Seale, William. *The Tasteful Interlude: American Interiors Through the Camera's Eye, 1860–1917.* New York, 1975.

Sexton, Randolph Williams. *Spanish Influences on American Architecture and Decoration.* New York, 1927.

Varney, Almon C. *Our Homes and Their Adornments: Or, How to Build, Finish, Furnish, and Adorn a Home.* Detroit, 1881.

Rogers, Meyric R. *American Interior Design.* New York, 1967.

Wallick, Elkin. *The Small House for a Moderate Income.* New York, 1915.

Waugh, Alice. *Interior Design: A Laboratory Manual for House Furnishing.* Minneapolis, 1945.

Wharton, Edith, and Ogden Codman, Jr. *The Decoration of Houses.* New York, 1897.

Wheeler, Candace. *Principles of Home Decoration.* New York, 1908.

Wright, Richardson L. *House and Garden's Book of Interiors.* New York, 1920.

Wyllys, Charles. *The Book of American Interiors.* Boston, 1876.

Furniture

Albers, Marjorie. *Old Amana Furniture.* Shenandoah, Iowa, 1970.

Ames, Kenneth L. "Grand Rapids Furniture at the Time of the Centennial." *Winterthur Portfolio 10* (1975).

———. "What is the Neo-Grec?" *Nineteenth Century* 2, no. 2 (Summer 1976): 12–21.

———. "Renaissance Revival Furniture in America." Ph.D. Thesis, University of Pennsylvania, 1970 [University Microfilms, Ann Arbor, Michigan].

Arts Council of Great Britain. *French 18th-Century Furniture.* London, 1960.

Aslin, Elizabeth. *The Aesthetic Movement: Prelude to the Art Nouveau.* New York and Washington, 1969.

———. *Nineteenth-Century English Furniture.* New York, 1962.

Baker, Muriel. "Decorated Furniture and Furnishings." *The Connecticut Historical Society Bulletin* 25, no. 3 (July 1960).

Barfield, Rodney. *Thomas Day, Cabinetmaker.* Raleigh, 1975.

Bishop, Robert. *Guide to American Furniture.* New York, n.d. [1973?].

———. *How to Know American Antique Furniture.* New York, 1973.

Bjerkoe, Ethel Hall. *The Cabinetmakers of America.* Garden City, 1957.

Brown, Mills. *Cabinetmaking in 18th-Century Williamsburg.* Williamsburg, 1959.

Brunhammer, Yvonne. *Meubles usuels: Restauration, Louis Philippe.* Paris, 1953.

Burton, E. Milby. *Charleston Furniture, 1700–1825.* Charleston, 1955.

Butler, Joseph T. *American Furniture from the First Colonies to World War I.* London, 1973.

———. *American Antiques, 1800–1900.* New York, 1965.

Carpenter, Ralph, Jr. *The Arts and Crafts of Newport, Rhode Island, 1640–1820.* Newport, 1954.

Colonial Society of Massachusetts. *Boston Furniture of the Eighteenth Century.* Charlottesville, 1974.

Cornelius, Charles O. *Furniture Masterpieces of Duncan Phyfe.* Garden City, 1922.

Cornu, Paul. *Meubles et Objects de goût, 1796–1830.* Paris, 1914.

Covell, Alwyn T. "The Real Place of Mission Furniture." *Good Furniture* 4, no. 6 (March 1915): 358–365.

Davidson, Marshall B. *American Heritage History of American Antiques from the Revolution to the Civil War.* New York, 1968.

———. *American Heritage History of American Antiques from the Civil War to World War I.* New York, 1969.

Donaldson, Harold, and Albert McClure. "Architects' Furniture." *Good Furniture,* August 1915, pp. 84–94.

———. *The Practical Book of Period Furniture.* Philadelphia and London, 1914.

Dorman, Charles. *Delaware Cabinetmakers and Allied Artisans, 1655–1855.* Wilmington, 1960.

Downs, Joseph. *American Chippendale Furniture, a Picture Book.* New York, 1949.

Elwell, Newton W. *The Architecture, Furniture, and Interiors of Maryland and Virginia During the 18th Century.* Boston, 1897.

Fales, Dean A. *American Painted Furniture, 1660–1880.* New York, 1972.

Flayderman, Philip. *Colonial Furniture, Silver, and Decoration.* New York, 1930.

Foss, Charles H. *Cabinetmakers of the Eastern Seaboard: A Study of Early Canadian Furniture.* Toronto, 1977.

Freeman, John. *Wallace Nutting's Colonial Revival.* Watkins Glen, N.Y., 1969.

———. *Furniture for the Victorian House from the Works of Andrew Jackson Downing and J. C. Doudon.* Watkins Glen, N.Y., 1968.

Gloag, John. *A Social History of Furniture Design from 1300 B.C. to A.D. 1960.* London, 1966.

Greenlaw, Barry A. *New England Furniture at Williamsburg.* Charlottesville, 1974.

Hanks, David, editor. *Victorian, Gothic, and Renaissance Revival Furniture: Two Victorian Pattern Books Published by Henry Carey Baird, 1868.* Philadelphia, 1977.

Hendrick, Robert E. P. "New York High Style Furniture." *Brooklyn Museum Annual Number Eight,* pp. 103–111.

Hill, Amelia L. "American French-Colonial Furniture." *Old Furniture* 8, no. 28 (September 1929): 33–38.

Holloway, Edward Stratton. *American Furniture and Decoration, Colonial and Federal.* Philadelphia and London, 1928.

Hopkins, Thomas Smith, and Walter Scott Cox. *Colonial Furniture of West New Jersey.* Haddonfield, 1936.

Iverson, Marion Day. *The American Chair, 1630–1890.* New York, 1957.

Kane, Patricia E. *Furniture of the New Haven Colony.* New Haven, 1973.

Kirk, John T. *American Chairs: Queen Anne and Chippendale.* New York, 1972.

———. *Early American Furniture: How to Recognize, Evaluate, Buy and Care for the Most Beautiful Pieces—High Style, Country, Primitive, and Rustic.* New York, 1970.

Kovel, Ralph, and Terry Kovel. *American Country Furniture 1780–1875.* New York, 1965.

Lazeare, James. *Primitive Pine Furniture.* Watkins Glen, N.Y., 1951.

Lockwood, Luke Vincent. *Colonial Furniture in America.* New York, 1901, and many subsequent editions.

McClelland, Nancy V. *Duncan Phyfe and the English Regency, 1795–1830.* New York, 1939.

———. *Furnishing the Colonial and Federal House.* Philadelphia, 1947.

Mackson, I. *American Architecture, Interiors, and Furniture During the Latter Part of the 19th Century.* Boston, 1900.

Madigan, Mary Jean. "The Influence of Charles Locke Eastlake on American Furniture Manufacture, 1870–1890." *Winterthur Portfolio 10* (1975).

———. *Eastlake-Influenced American Furniture, 1870–1890.* Yonkers, N.Y., 1974.

Madden, Betty I. *Arts, Crafts, and Architecture in Early Illinois.* Urbana, 1974.

Montgomery, Charles F. *American Furniture: The Federal Period.* New York, 1966.

Morningstar, Connie. "The Fortunes of Berkey & Gay." *The Antiques Journal* 27, no. 2 (February 1972): 10–12.

———. *Early Utah Furniture.* Logan, 1976.

Morse, John D., editor. *Country Cabinetwork and Simple City Furniture.* Winterthur Museum Conference Report, 1969.

Morse, Frances C. *Furniture of the Olden Time.* New York and London, 1910.

Nutting, Wallace. *Furniture Treasury.* New York, 1948.

Bibliography

258   Oliver, John L. *The Development and Structure of the Furniture Industry*. New York, 1966.

Otto, Celia Jackson. *American Furniture of the 19th Century*. New York, 1965.

Ott, Joseph K. "Rhode Island Furniture Exports 1783–1800." *Rhode Island History* 36, no. 1 (Feburary 1977): 2–13.

Pennsylvania Museum of Art. *A Picture Book of Philadelphia Chippendale: Chippendale Furniture, 1750–1780*. Philadelphia, 1931.

Poeche, Jessie J. *Early Furniture of Louisiana*. New Orleans, 1972.

Ransom, Frank Edward. *The City Built on Wood: A History of the Furniture Industry in Grand Rapids, Michigan, 1850–1950*. Ann Arbor, 1965.

Ray, Mary Lyn. "A Reappraisal of Shaker Furniture and Society." *Winterthur Portfolio* 8 (1973).

Sack, Albert. *Fine Points of Furniture: Early American*. New York, 1950.

Saunders, Richard. *Collecting and Restoring Wicker Furniture*. New York, 1976.

Schild, Joan Lynn. "Furniture Makers of Rochester, New York." *New York History* 37, no. 1 (1956): 97–106.

Seidler, Jan. "The Furniture Industry in 19th-Century Boston." *Nineteenth Century* 3, no. 2 (Summer 1977): 64–69.

Shea, John Gerald. *Antique Country Furniture of North America*. New York, 1975.

Sikes, Jane E. *The Furniture Makers of Cincinnati, 1790–1849*. Cincinnati, 1976.

Singleton, Esther. *The Furniture of Our Forefathers*. New York, 1913.

Speed Art Museum. *Kentucky Furniture*. Louisville, 1974.

Steinfeld, Celia, and Donald Stover. *Early Texas Furniture and Decorative Arts*. San Antonio, 1973.

Stoneman, Vernon C. *John and Thomas Seymour, Cabinetmakers in Boston, 1794–1816*. Boston, 1959.

Swan, Mabel M. *Samuel McIntire, Carver, and the Sandersons, Early Salem Cabinetmakers*. Salem, 1934.

Sweeney, John A. H. *The Treasure House of Early American Rooms* [at the Henry Francis du Pont Winterthur Museum]. New York, 1963.

Taylor, Lonn, and David Warren. *Texas Furniture: The Cabinetmakers and Their Work, 1840–1880*. Austin, 1975.

Theus, Mrs. C. M. *Furniture and Cabinetmakers of Early Coastal Georgia*. Savannah, 1952.

Tracy, Berry B. *Classical America: 1815–1845*. Newark, 1963.

Tracy, Berry B., et al. *Nineteenth-Century America: Furniture and Other Decorative Arts*. New York, 1970.

Van Ravensway, Charles. "The Anglo-American Cabinetmakers of Missouri, 1800-1850." *Missouri Historical Society Bulletin*, April 1958, pp. 231–257.

Wallace-Homestead Book Company. *Oak Furniture Styles and Prices*. Des Moines, n.d. [1976?].

Walters, Betty Lawson. *Furniture Makers of Indiana: 1793–1850*. Indianapolis, 1972.

Watson, A. A. *Country Furniture*. New York, 1974.

Wenham, Edward. *The Collector's Guide to Furniture Design*. New York, 1928.

Wemyss, Robert, and B. B. Whineray. *Victorian Furniture*. London, 1962.

Winchester, Alice, editor. *Living With Antiques*. New York, 1941.

Winters, Robert E., Jr., editor. *North Carolina Furniture, 1700–1900*. Raleigh, 1977.

Inventory Studies

Cummings, Abbott Lowell. *Rural Household Inventories Establishing the Names, Uses, and Furnishings of Rooms in the Colonial New England Home*. Boston, 1964.

Daniels, Bruce C. "Probate Inventories as a Source for Economic History in 18th-Century Connecticut." *The Connecticut Historical Society Bulletin* 37, no. 1 (January 1972): 1–9.

Dow, George Francis. "House Furnishings in Salem [Massachusetts] in 1685." *Old-Time New England* 13, no. 3 (January 1923): 143–145.

Fabian, Monroe H. "An Immigrant's Inventory." *Pennsylvania Folklife* 25, no. 4 (Summer 1976): 47–48.

Ford, W. Chauncey. *Inventory of the Contents of Mount Vernon, 1810*. Cambridge, 1909.

Giffen, Jane C. "A Selection of New Hampshire Inventories." *Historical New Hampshire* 24, nos. 1 & 2 (1969): 3–78.

Given, Lois V. "The Great Stately Palace." *The Pennsylvania Magazine* 83, no. 3 (July 1959): 265–270.

Grimes, J. Bryan, Secretary of State. *North Carolina Inventories*. Raleigh, 1912.

Hood, Graham, editor. *Inventories of Four Eighteenth-Century Houses in the Historic Area of Williamsburg*. Williamsburg, n.d. [1971?].

New-York Historical Society. "The Furnishings of Richmond Hill in 1797, the Home of Aaron Burr in New York City." *New-York Historical Society Quarterly Bulletin* 11, no. 1 (April 1927): 17–23.

Schiffer, Margaret B. *Chester County, Pennsylvania, Inventories, 1684–1850*. Exton, Pa., 1974.

Tolles, Frederick B. "Town House and Country House, Inventories From the Estate of William Logan, 1776." *The Pennsylvania Magazine* 82, no. 4 (October 1958): 397–410.

Wainwright, Nicholas B. *Colonial Grandeur in Philadelphia: The House and Furniture of General John Cadwalader*. Philadelphia, 1964.

Watkins, C. Malcolm. "The Cultural History of Marlborough, Virginia." *United States National Museum Bulletin 253*. Washington, D.C., 1968.

Textiles

Beer, Alice Baldwin. *Trade Goods: A Study of Indian Chintz*. Washington, D.C., 1970.

Brightman, Anna B. "Fabrics and Styles of Colonial Window Hangings as Revealed through Boston and Salem, Massachusetts, Records, 1700–1760." Thesis, Florida State University, 1966 [University Microfilms, Ann Arbor, Michigan].

Cole, George S. *A Complete Dictionary of Dry Goods and a History of Silk, linen, wool, and Other Fibrous Substances . . . Various Useful Tables*. Chicago, 1892.

Cox, Ruth Y. *Copperplate Textiles in the Williamsburg Collection*. Williamsburg, 1964.

Cummings, Abbott Lowell. *Bed Hangings: A Treatise On Fabrics and Styles in the Curtaining of Beds, 1650–1850*. Boston, 1961.

Fikioris, Margaret A. "Textile Cleaning and Storage." *Museum News* 55, no. 1 (September-October 1976): 13–18.

Halsey, R. T. H. "Textiles as Furnishings in Early American Homes." *Metropolitan Museum of Art Bulletin* 29, no. 6 (June 1924): 148–151.

Hunter, George Leland. *Decorative Textiles: An Illustrated Book on Coverings for Furniture, Walls, and Floors, Including Damasks, brocades, and velvets, tapestries, laces, embroideries, chintzes, cretones, drapery and furniture trimmings, wallpaper, carpets and rugs, tooled and illuminated leather*. Philadelphia and London, 1918.

———. "Modern Fabrics: A Study of Chintzes and Cretones." *Good Furniture* 7, no. 6 (December 1916): 334–350.

Lanier, Mildred B. *English and Oriental Carpets at Williamsburg*. Charlottesville, 1975.

Montgomery, Florence M. *Printed Textiles: English and American Cottons and Linens, 1700–1750*. New York, 1970.

Nylander, Jane C. *Fabrics for Historic Buildings*. Washington, D.C., 1977.

Pettit, Florence H. *America's Indigo Blues: Resist-Printed and Dyed Textiles of the 18th Century*. New York, 1974.

———. *America's Printed and Painted Fabrics, 1600–1900*. New York, 1970.

Taylor, Lucy D. *Know Your Fabrics: Standard Decorative Textiles and Their Uses*. New York, 1951.

Victoria and Albert Museum. *English Chintz* [small picture book no. 22]. London, 1955.

Wingate, Isabel B. *Fairchild's Dictionary of Textiles*. New York, 1967.

Curtains

Brightman, Anna B. "Fabrics and Styles of Colonial Window Hangings as Revealed Through Boston and Salem, Massachusetts, Records, 1700–1760." Thesis, Florida State University, 1966 [University Microfilms, Ann Arbor, Michigan.]

———. *Window Treatments for Historic Houses, 1700–1850*. Washington, D.C., 1966.

Candee, Helen C. *Weaves and Draperies, Classic and Modern*. New York, 1930.

Dornsife, Samuel J. "Design Sources for Nineteenth-Century Window Hangings." *Winterthur Portfolio 10*, 1975.

Montgomery, Florence M. *Printed Textiles: English and American Cottons and Linens, 1700–1750*. New York, 1970.

Moreland, Frank A. *Practical Decorative Upholstery: Containing Full Instructions for Cutting, Making,*

260   *and Hanging All Kinds Of Interior Upholstery Decoration.* Boston and New York, 1890.

Heating

Bankart, George P. "Old Fire Grates." *Old Furniture* 3, no. 11 (April 1928): 211–219.

Curtis, Will, and Jane Curtis. *Antique Wood Stoves, Artistry in Iron.* Ashville, Md., 1974.

Edgerton, Samuel Y. "Heat and Style: Eighteenth-Century House-Warming by Stoves." *Journal of the Society of Architectural Historians* 20, no. 1 (March 1961): 20–26.

————. "Heating Stoves in Eighteenth-Century Philadelphia." *Bulletin of the Association for Preservation Technology* 3, nos. 2-3 (1971): 15–104.

Ferguson, Eugene S. "An Historical Sketch of Central Heating, 1800–1860." Charles E. Peterson, editor, *Building Early America.* Radnor, Pa., 1976, pp. 165–185.

Gould, Mary Earle. *The Early American House: Household Life in America, 1620–1850, with Special Chapters on the Construction and Evolution of Old American Homes, Fireplaces, and Iron Utensils.* Rutland, Vt., 1949; reprint, 1965.

Hosler, Connie. "Unique Designs in Stoves." *The Antiques Journal* 30, no. 10 (October 1975): 19–21.

Hough, Walter. *Collection of Heating and Lighting Utensils in the United States National Museum.* Washington, D.C., 1928.

Hummel, Charles F. "The Fireplace." *The Delaware Antiques Show Catalog 1967.* Wilmington, 1967.

Kauffman, Henry J. *The American Fireplace: Chimneys, Mantelpieces, Fireplaces, and Accessories.* Nashville, 1972.

Ladd, Paul R. *Early American Fireplaces.* New York, 1977.

Peterson, Charles E. "Early House-Warming by Coal Fires." *Journal of the Society of Architectural Historians* 9, no. 4:21–26.

Pierce, Josephine Halvorson. *Fire on the Hearth: The Evolution and Romance of the Heating Stove.* Springfield, Mass., 1951.

Putnam, John Pickering. *The Open Fireplace In All Ages.* Boston, 1881.

Vanderweil, Gary. "Draft Heating and Ventilating Systems of the Victorian Era." *Nineteenth Century* 2, no. 1 (Spring 1976): 14–18.

Yule, Don. "Cooking and Heating in the 19th-Century Way." *Old House Journal* 4, nos. 9 and 10 (September 1976): 1–4, 5–7.

Wright, Lawrence. *Home Fires Burning: A History of Domestic Heating and Cooking.* London, 1964.

Lighting

Butler, Joseph. *Candleholders in America, 1650–1900.* N.p., 1967.

Cooke, Lawrence S., editor. *Lighting in America: From Colonial Rushlights to Victorian Chandeliers.* New York, 1976.

Cox, Warren Earle. *Lighting and Lamp Design.* New York, 1952.

Darbee, Herbert C. *A Glossary of Old Lamps and Lighting Devices.* Nashville, 1965.

Davidson, Marshall B. "Early American Lighting." *Metropolitan Museum of Art, Bulletin* 3, no. 4 (July 1944): 30–40.

Hayward, Arthur H. *Colonial Lighting.* Boston, 1923; reprint, 1968.

Hebard, Helen Brigham. *Early Lighting in New England, 1620–1861.* Rutland, Vt., 1964.

Kalin, Nancy. "History of the Rushlight." *Early American Life* 5, no. 1 (February 1974): 36–39.

King, James W. "The Development of Electrical Technology in the 19th Century." *Museum of History and Technology Technical Papers* 28–30, 3 vols.

Myers, Denys Peter. *American Gas Lighting: A Survey for Historic Preservationists.* Washington, 1978.

Russell, Loris S. *A Heritage of Light.* Toronto, 1968.

————. "Early Nineteenth-Century Lighting." Charles E. Peterson, editor. *Building Early America.* Radnor, Pa., 1976, pp. 186–201.

Watkins, Malcolm C. "Artificial Lighting in America, 1830–1860." *Smithsonian Institution Annual Report, 1951.*

Paint and Color

Allen, Edward B. *Early American Wall Paintings.* Cambridge, 1926.

Baird, H. C. *The Painter, Gilder, and Varnisher's Companion.* Philadelphia, 1854.

Candee, Richard M. "Preparing and Mixing Colors in 1812." *Antiques* CXIII, no. 4: 849–853.

Claiborne, Herbert A. *Some Paint Colors From Four 18th-Century Virginia Houses.* Portland, Me.: Walpole Society, 1949.

Davidson, E. A. *A Practical Manual of House-Painting, Graining, Marbling and Sign Writing, Containing Full Information On the Processes of House Painting in Oil and Distemper* . . . London, 1900.

Downs, Arthur Channing, Jr. "Zinc for Paint and Architectural Use in the 19th Century." *Bulletin of the Association for Preservation Technologists* 8, no. 4 (1976): 80–97.

Flaherty, Carolyn. "19th-Century House Colors." *Old House Journal* 4, no. 8 (August 1976): 4–6.

Frohne, Henry W. *Color Schemes for Home and Model Interior.* Grand Rapids, 1919.

Gardner, Franklin B. *Everybody's Paint Book.* New York, 1884.

Hartshorne, Penelope. "Paint Color Research and Restoration." *History News* 19, no. 2 (December 1963): 25–28. See also American Association for State and Local History *Technical Leaflet 15.*

Holmes, John M. *Colour in Interior Decoration.* New York, 1931.

Jennings, Arthur Seymour. *Paint and Color Mixing.* New York and London, 1926.

Little, Nina Fletcher. *American Decorative Wall Painting, 1700–1850.* New York, 1952.

Loth, Calder. "A Mid-19th-Century Color Scheme." *Bulletin of the Association for Preservation Technology* 9, no. 2 (1977): 82–88.

Seldon, Marjorie Ward. *The Interior Paint of the Campbell-Whittlesey House, 1835–1836.* Rochester, 1949.

Tingry, P. F. *The Painter and Varnisher's Guide* . . . *The Art of Making and Applying Varnishes.* London, 1804.

Wallpaper

Clark, Fiona, editor. *William Morris: Wallpaper and Chintzes.* New York, 1973.

Cook, Clarence. *What Shall We Do With Our Walls?* New York, 1880.

Frangiamore, Catherine Lynn. *Patterns, Stripes, Flowers, and Gold: A Brief History of the American Taste in Wallpaper, Its Technology and Preservation.* Washington, D.C., 1977.

————. "Rescuing Historic Wallpapers, Identification, Preservation, and Restoration." *History News* 29, no. 7 (July 1974): 157–164. See also American Association for State And Local History *Technical Leaflet 76.*

Greysmith, Brenda. *Wallpaper.* London, 1976.

McClelland, Nancy V. *Historic Wallpapers from Their Inception to the Introduction of Machinery.* Philadelphia and London, 1924.

Petit, Eugene Claudius. *Trois siècles de papiers peints.* Paris, 1967.

Sugden, Alan Victor. *A History of English Wallpaper, 1509–1914.* London, 1926.

Floorcoverings

Beaumont, Roberts. *Carpets and Rugs.* London, 1924.

Belcher, M. *Floorcoverings.* London, 1973.

Landreau, Anthony N. "America Underfoot: A History of floor coverings from Colonial Times to the Present." *American Antiques* 5, no. 4 (April 1977): 28–34.

Little, Nina Fletcher. *Floor Coverings in New England before 1850.* Sturbridge, Mass., 1967.

Page, Ruth. "English Carpets and Their Use in America." *The Connecticut Antiquarian* 19, no. 1: 16–25.

Roth, Rodris. *Floorcoverings in 18th-Century America.* Washington, D.C., 1967.

Sanford, Bigelow Carpet Company. *A Century of Carpet- and Rug-Making In America.* New York, 1925.

Tattersall, C. E. C. *A History of British Carpets.* Leigh-on-Sea, 1966.

Whittlesay, T. "American-Made Rugs in Oriental Patterns." *House and Garden,* October 1910, pp. 216–217.

Hardware and Fixtures

Blackall, Clarence Howard. *Builders' Hardware: A Manual for Architects, Builders, and House Finishers.* Boston, 1890.

William H. Carr & Co. *Catalog* for 1838; reprint, Hagley Museum, 1972.

Goodison, Nicholas. "The Victoria and Albert Museum's Collection of Metal-Work Pattern

262   Books." *Furniture History* 11 (1975): 1–30 and
         appendix 1–59.
      Hummel, Charles F. "Samuel Rowland Fisher's
         Catalogue of English Hardware." *Winterthur
         Portfolio 1*, 1964.
      Kauffman, Henry J., and Quentin H. Bowers. *Early
         American Andirons and Other Fireplace Acces-
         sories.* Nashville and New York, 1974.
      Rubenstein, Lewis C. *American Hardware: Architec-
         tural Hardware Typical of New York State.*
         Katonah, N.Y., 1964.
      Schiffer, Herbert. *Early Pennsylvania Hardware.*
         Whitford, Pa., 1966.
      Streeter, Donald. "Early American Wrought-Iron
         Hardware, English Iron Rim-Locks: Late 18th-
         and Early 19th-Century Forms." *Bulletin of the
         Association for Preservation Technology* 6, no. 1
         (1974): 41–67.
      Woolsey, Theodore S. "Notes on House Hardware,
         1790–1810." *Old-Time New England*, January
         1922, pp. 127–129.

Kitchens

Broome County [N.Y.] Historical Society. *The
   American Hearth: Colonial and Post-Colonial
   Cooking Tools.* Binghamton, N.Y., 1976.
Franklin, Linda Campbell. *From Hearth to Cookstove:
   An American Domestic History of Gadgets and
   Utensils Made or Used in America from 1700 to
   1900.* Florence, Ala., 1976.
Harrison, Molly. *The Kitchen in History.* New York,
   1972.
Lifshey, Earl. *The Housewares Story: A History of the
   American Housewares Industry.* Chicago, 1973.
Norwalk, Mary. *Kitchen Antiques.* New York, 1975.
Phipps, Frances. *Colonial Kitchens, Their Furnishings
   and Their Gardens.* New York, 1972.
Shorr, Mimi. *Objecct For Preparing Food.* Washing-
   ton, D.C., 1972.
Sprackling, Helen. *Customs of the Table Top: How
   New England Housewives Set Out Their Tables.*
   Sturbridge, Mass., 1958.
Whitehill, Jane. *Food, Drink, and Recipes of Early
   New England.* Sturbridge, Mass., 1963.

Index

Page References in boldface type refer to illustrations. All other page references are to text.

Index

Index